The French at Waterloo: Eyewitness Accounts

The French at Waterloo: Eyewitness Accounts

II and VI Corps, Cavalry, Artillery, Imperial Guard and Medical Services

Andrew W. Field

Pen & Sword
MILITARY

First published in Great Britain in 2020 by
PEN & SWORD MILITARY
An imprint of Pen & Sword Books Ltd
Yorkshire – Philadelphia

ISBN 978-1-52676-850-6

Typeset by Concept, Huddersfield, West Yorkshire, HD4 5JL.
Printed and bound in England by TJ Books Limited, Padstow, Cornwall.

Pen & Sword Books Ltd incorporates the Imprints of Aviation, Atlas, Family History, Fiction, Maritime, Military, Discovery, Politics, History, Archaeology, Select, Wharncliffe Local History, Wharncliffe True Crime, Military Classics, Wharncliffe Transport, Leo Cooper, The Praetorian Press, Remember When, White Owl, Seaforth Publishing and Frontline Publishing.

For a complete list of Pen & Sword titles please contact
PEN & SWORD BOOKS LTD
47 Church Street, Barnsley, South Yorkshire, S70 2AS, England
E-mail: enquiries@pen-and-sword.co.uk
Website: www.pen-and-sword.co.uk
or
PEN & SWORD BOOKS
1950 Lawrence Rd, Havertown, PA 19083, USA
E-mail: uspen-and-sword@casematepublishers.com
Website: www.penandswordbooks.com

Contents

During the Waterloo campaign Reille commanded the II Army
Corps.

Reille's account, like that of d'Erlon, is frustratingly short on
detail on Waterloo. It was included in a book published by
Marshal Ney's son who was writing to defend the honour of his
father whose handling of aspects of the battle had been
criticised by Napoleon in his various accounts of the campaign.
It was published in 1840, but we cannot be sure exactly when it
was written. Reille criticises the repeated attacks on Hougoumont, but seems to have done nothing concrete to stop them.
He also tells us that by the time the battle started, his corps was
only half the strength of which it started the campaign due to
the loss of Girard's division and the casualties suffered at
Quatre Bras.

In 1815 Trefcon served as *adjutant-commandant* (senior staff
officer with the rank of colonel), chief-of-staff to General
Bachelu, commander of the 5th Infantry Division, part of
II Army Corps (Reille).

The main value of Trefcon's account is his description of the
infantry attack of Bachelu's division and one of Foy's brigades
onto the Allied ridge after the cavalry charges, which is rarely
mentioned by histories of the battle. This also confirms that

these formations took no part in the attack on Hougoumont as claimed by almost all British accounts of the battle.

During the Waterloo campaign Jérôme commanded the 6th Infantry Division in Reille's II Army Corps.

Jérôme claims that once his division was reduced to the strength of just two battalions in the attacks on Hougoumont that he left command of it (presumably to General Guilleminot) and joined Napoleon. He roundly blames Ney for the premature commitment of the cavalry and first mentions the Prussians at six o'clock, describing that at first they were mistaken for Grouchy's arrival. This seems to undermine Napoleon's own account that he was aware of the Prussians before the battle started.

In the Waterloo campaign, Jolyet commanded the 1st Battalion, 1st *légère* (Colonel Cubières) in the 1st Brigade (Bauduin) of Prince Jérôme's 6th Infantry Division, part of Reille's II Army Corps.

Jolyet gives so little detail on the attacks on Hougoumont that one would be forgiven for thinking that his battalion was not involved and he was just a spectator, but we know this isn't true. However, he does give a few personal vignettes which make his account interesting and he seemingly restricts himself to those things that he saw for himself.

In the 1815 campaign, Lebeau commanded the 1st *de ligne*, which was part of the 2nd Brigade (Soye) of Prince Jérôme's 6th Infantry Division, part of Reille's II Army Corps.

This account is extracted from a letter addressed to Marshal Soult, then Minister of War, dated Périgueux, 16 April 1833. The letter addressed the issue of the utility of rifled carbines, recommending their introduction into the French army. To strengthen his case, Colonel Lebeau, as he was then, drew on his experience in command of the 1st *de ligne* at Waterloo.

Lebeau rather obtusely claims to have captured Hougoumont and although not the only Frenchman present to do so, it is generally accepted that the French did not come close to occupying it. He makes an interesting reference to using units that had suffered heavy casualties and were unable to function as a formed body, as skirmishers. Allied accounts of the fighting around La Haye Sainte towards the end of the battle suggest this tactic was also used there.

Pierre Robinaux served as the company commander of the 4th Company of the 2nd Battalion of the 2nd *de ligne* (Tripe [or Trippe]), in the 2nd Brigade (Soye), 6th Infantry Division (Jérôme), part of Reille's II Army Corps.

Robinaux gives us little detail on the attacks on Hougoumont, but a rather more interesting account of the break-up of II Corps during their retreat.

At Waterloo, Foy commanded the 9th Infantry Division of Reille's II Army Corps.

Foy gives a detailed and interesting account of the actions of his division around Hougoumont and particularly the attack on the ridge conducted by Bachelu's division and a brigade of his own division.

At Waterloo Lemonnier-Delafosse served as chief-of-staff to General Foy in the 9th Infantry Division of Reille's II Army Corps.

Here we see the account of an unapologetic admirer of Napoleon who having blamed Wellington's luck for the loss of the battle, proceeds to stress the defeat of the British army and even names one of Wellington's aides-de-camp as providing evidence! He makes a number of dubious claims, not least of which was the capture of Hougoumont. Interestingly, he challenges Napoleon's assertion that a Prussian despatch was captured that betrayed the Prussian presence. He finishes his account of the battle by claiming that both the British and French were defeated and the Prussians alone were the victors! Despite all these and other rather dubious claims, it is still an account worth reading, including a number of interesting vignettes.

In 1815 Puvis served as a lieutenant in the 93rd *de ligne* which was commanded by *Chef de Bataillon* Massot, part of the 1st Brigade (Tissot) of the 9th Infantry Division (Foy), of Reille's II Army Corps.

Puvis only speaks of his own personal experiences and although there is rather thin detail on his regiment's attacks around Hougoumont, it gives a good feel for how the actions of II Corps seemed isolated from the rest of the battle until the retreat. He gives a good account of how quickly French morale collapsed at the end of the battle.

During the Waterloo campaign, Larreguy de Civrieux served as sergeant-major in the 93rd *de ligne*; the same regiment as Lieutenant Puvis. The regiment belonged to the 1st Brigade (Tissot) of Foy's 9th Infantry Division, part of Reille's II Army Corps.

Larreguy de Civrieux's account was written long after the events and he has thus included much detail that he would not have known at the time. Like the II Corps eyewitnesses we have already heard from, there is little real detail on the fighting around the château; but on the ground it must have been impossible to have an overall feel for the fighting much beyond their own location, and in the Hougoumont wood where many of them found themselves, they could probably see little more than just a few yards.

During the Waterloo campaign, Henckens served as adjutant-major in the élite company of the 6th Chasseurs à Cheval of Piré's division, under command of Colonel Faudouas.

This regiment belonged to the 1st Brigade (Huber) of the 2nd Cavalry Division (Piré), part of Reille's II Army Corps.

Henckens' regiment had fought hard at Quatre Bras and had suffered heavy casualties. At Waterloo, they fulfilled the classic light cavalry task of flank protection. After their experiences at Quatre Bras I suspect the regiment was grateful not to have been involved in heavy fighting during the battle and he describes only skirmishing.

During the Waterloo campaign, Janin served as colonel (*adjutant-commandant*), deputy chief-of-staff of VI Army Corps which was commanded by Lieutenant General Count Lobau. He claims to have been the chief-of-staff of VI Corps, but this was only after the true chief-of-staff, General Durieux [or Durrieu], was wounded quite early in the battle, as he describes himself.

This account was written in response to Gourgaud's history of the campaign which was published on his return from St Helena where he had shared Napoleon's exile. One of the key issues in French accounts of the battle is the extent to which Napoleon was surprised by the arrival of the Prussians, which Janin addresses. He clearly describes VI Corps being taken unawares by their arrival and the changing of the VI Corps' mission from supporting the attack of I Corps to countering the Prussian advance. Napoleon claims he was well aware of their impending arrival, as described elsewhere in volume one of this work, and had taken appropriate measures to counter them; including the early deployment of VI Corps. Janin's account also offers a new and credible reason why the Hougoumont wood needed to be secured; not purely as a diversionary attack as it is so often described.

Like Janin, Combes-Brassard served as a *sous-chef d'état-major* (deputy chief-of-staff) of VI Army Corps commanded by Lieutenant General Count Lobau.

This account was apparently penned on 22 June 1815 at the château of L'Échelle, or Léchelle, near Guise (this is where Combes-Brassard took refuge after the battle), thus giving it some credibility for having been written soon after the battle. However, he is clearly in error on the sequence of the battle in the centre, which he could not have observed for himself or had the time to learn after the battle; he has the French cavalry attacking before d'Erlon's I Corps. He speaks with more authority and interest on the actions of his own corps. His account is also noteworthy as it finishes with a damning indictment of Grouchy's performance which is reminiscent of much later criticism, suggesting that this may have been added after the original account.

During the Waterloo campaign, Tromelin commanded the 2nd Brigade of the 20th Infantry Division (Jeanin), part of Lobau's VI Army Corps.

Tomelin does not reflect on whether the Prussian appearance was a surprise, but restricts himself to describing the deployment of VI Corps and the fighting against the gradually overwhelming numbers of Bülow's corps.

During the Waterloo campaign Marq served as sergeant-major of voltigeurs in the 107th *de ligne* (Colonel Druot) which was part of the 2nd Brigade (Tromelin) of the 20th Division (Jeanin), part of Lobau's VI Army Corps.

Marq states that his account was written in 1817. He restricts himself to describing his own personal experiences during the battle fighting against the Prussians.

During the Waterloo campaign, Kellerman was commander of the 3rd Reserve Cavalry Corps.

Kellerman was a reluctant Bonapartist and his writing is more a critique of the battle and Napoleon than a true account of his experiences. However, it concentrates on the cavalry action that Kellerman witnessed for himself and this adds real value and interest. Unlike many other French writers, he does not claim that Wellington was saved from defeat by the appearance of the Prussians. He does, however, speak of the reluctance of the cavalry to retire from the Allied ridge in order to avoid dragging the rest of the army back. He laments the useless destruction of the carabinier brigade and praises the action of Lobau's corps and the Young Guard.

During the Waterloo campaign, Dieudonné Rigau served as *chef d'escadron* in the 2nd Dragoon Regiment (Colonel Planzeaux). This regiment was part of the 1st Brigade (Picquet) of the 11th Cavalry Division (l'Héritier), part of the 3rd Reserve Cavalry Corps (Kellerman).

Rigau suggests that the great cavalry charges were the result of other units following a charge made by his regiment against British cavalry charging some guns that were deployed just in front of them. He makes no mention of infantry action which for much of the battle he would not have been able to see.

During the Waterloo campaign, Létang served as a squadron commander in the 7th Dragoons (Colonel Léopold). This regiment was part of the 1st Brigade (Picquet) of the 11th Cavalry Division (l'Héritier), part of the 3rd Reserve Cavalry Corps (Kellerman).

Writing in the third person, Létang's account is clearly very self-serving. However, his description of the feelings of his men as they charged the British line is of particular interest.

During the Waterloo campaign, Delort commanded the 14th Cavalry Division of the 4th Reserve Cavalry Corps (Milhaud).

Unlike like Kellerman, Delort was an admirer of Napoleon and his account seems to follow those of his emperor, including Napoleon's excuses for the loss of the battle. Although written quite soon after the battle, it is riddled with facts that he could only have learnt from other histories and not directly from his own experiences. He suggests that the great cavalry charges were launched to support the counter-attack against the British Household and Union brigades by a brigade of cuirassiers. He also claims that squares made up of the British Guards were broken.

During the Waterloo campaign Michel Ordener commanded the 1st Cuirassier Regiment. This regiment was part of the 1st Brigade (Dubois) of the 13th Cavalry Division (Wathier St-Alphonse), part of the 4th Reserve Cavalry Corps (Milhaud). With Dubois wounded early in the battle, Ordener took command of the brigade, which consisted of the 1st and 7th Cuirassiers, and led it in the great cavalry charges.

Ordener gives us an interesting and detailed account of the counter-attack against Ponsonby's brigade and the great cavalry charges.

In the Waterloo campaign, Pilloy served as a cuirassier in the 9th Cuirassiers (Colonel Bigarne). The regiment was part of the 2nd Brigade (Vial) of the 14th Cavalry Division (Delort), part of the 4th Reserve Cavalry Corps (Milhaud).

One of the few French accounts from the lower ranks, Pilloy gives us a little detail on his experiences in the great cavalry charges.

During the Waterloo campaign, de Salle served as the commander of the artillery of the I Army Corps (d'Erlon).

Napoleon appointed de Salle as the commander of the grand battery, although he does not use this title to describe it until the end of his narrative. In fact, de Salle's rather muddled account, however interesting, gives little clarification on the points in dispute. Firstly, his maths in calculating the number of guns in his battery appears to be awry and while he describes a move forwards it appears never to have been completed and he is rather quick to condemn it (perhaps with the benefit of hindsight). He suggests the Imperial Guard artillery were only used to replace the losses caused by the British cavalry charge; many historians have Guard artillery in the initial battery. He seems to have made little effort to co-ordinate the withdrawal of his guns at the end of the battle. He clearly feels the advance of the battery was a mistake and worries that many have blamed him for ordering it.

During the Waterloo campaign Petit commanded the 1st Regiment of the Grenadiers à Pied of the Old Guard; the senior regiment of the Guard.

As Petit's account is such an interesting insight to the Foot Guard of 1815, I felt that it would be of interest to include the whole account, rather than restrict it to Waterloo. Most French histories of the battle base their account of the attack of the Guard on that of Petit, but the truth is, as Petit commanded the 1st Regiment of Grenadiers à Pied, he did not actually take part in the attack he describes, although he may have put himself in a position to observe it and would certainly have spoken to officers who did take part.

During the Waterloo campaign, Christiani commanded the 2nd Regiment of Grenadiers à Pied of the Imperial Guard.

Christiani's regiment sent one battalion to the fighting in Planchenoit, and the other to support the assault on the Allied ridge. As the regimental commander, he led the battalion forward to support the assault on the ridge. His order of events is a little mixed up; he describes the attack of the Guard taking place before he sent a battalion into Planchenoit. In fact, these actions took place the other way around as Napoleon attempted to secure his right flank before launching part of his Guard against the Allied ridge. For a comparatively senior regiment of the Guard, his battalion seems to have broken up rather easily at the end of the battle.

During the Waterloo campaign Pelet was Major of the 2nd Regiment of Chasseurs à Pied of the Imperial Guard.

Pelet's account of Waterloo is by far the longest and most detailed of the accounts written by officers of the Imperial Guard and therefore holds the most interest. Unfortunately, he did not take part in the attack on the Allied ridge, but fought in Planchenoit, of which he gives some fascinating detail of the fighting. However, whilst he also describes the attack on the ridge, it must be remembered that this is based on the accounts of others and is therefore not so trustworthy. He actually wrote two accounts of the Waterloo campaign; the first was his journal which he wrote during the campaign, and the second formed a part of his memoirs written later in life, but based on his journal.

During the Waterloo campaign Duuring commanded the 1st Battalion of the 1st Regiment of Chasseurs à Pied (Cambronne) of the Imperial Guard.

As Duuring makes clear, his battalion remained at le Caillou to protect the headquarters established there and Napoleon's baggage and treasury. He therefore saw nothing of the battle or the final attack of the Guard, but does describe the Prussian encroachment into the rear of the French army and his attempts to halt the increasing flood of men to the rear.

During the Waterloo campaign Prax was *adjutant-major* of the 3rd Regiment of Chasseurs à Pied (Poret de Morvan) of the Imperial Guard. This regiment took the heaviest casualties of all the Guard regiments having almost certainly faced the British Guards on the ridge. He writes that the attack was made in closed column.

Lieutenant General Guyot 131

During the Waterloo campaign, Guyot served as the commander of the Imperial Guard Heavy Cavalry Division, which
consisted of the regiments of grenadiers and dragoons, and two
batteries of Guard horse artillery (twelve guns).

Napoleon accused Guyot of engaging his division in the great
cavalry charges without orders and that because of this, he was
left without a capable reserve once the attack of the foot Guard
had been repulsed. In his account, Napoleon ascribes the attack
by British cavalry as responsible for the rout of the French in
front of the Anglo-Dutch army and that he could have repulsed
this if Guyot's division had been available. Guyot spent many
years writing to deny the charge and trying to expose the truth.
His accounts describe his contribution to the battle.

Captain de Brack 136

During the Waterloo campaign, de Brack served as a captain
in the chevaux-légers-lanciers of the Imperial Guard who were
commanded by General Édouard Colbert. The regiment was
part of the Imperial Guard Light Cavalry Division (commanded by General Lefebvre-Desnouëttes) along with the
Guard chasseurs à cheval and two batteries of Guard horse
artillery (twelve guns).

De Brack gives an unusual description of how the cavalry of
the Guard were committed and an interesting, if relatively short,
description of the charges. He reserves most space for a commentary on his division's retreat from the battlefield, including
an interesting vignette when they met Napoleon at Quatre Bras.

Maréchal des Logis-Chef **Chevalier** 143

During the Waterloo campaign Chevalier served as *maréchal des
logis-chef* (the senior sergeant or First Sergeant in American
parlance) of the 4th Company of the regiment of chasseurs à
cheval (General Lallemand) of the Light Cavalry Division of
the Imperial Guard (Lefebvre-Desnouëttes).

Chevalier's manuscript appears to have been written in 1835.
His souvenirs give a fascinating glimpse into the lives of the
light cavalry and particularly in the campaigns in which he took

part. Unfortunately, the detail he gives becomes increasingly thin as his career progresses and his personal anecdotes reduce as he spends more time on a general history of the campaigns in which he took part. Therefore, much of his account of Waterloo is general history clearly based on what he has read rather than experienced. However, there is enough of his personal experiences for it to warrant inclusion, but it will be noted that much of it closely follows Napoleon's account whose 'themes' are repeated.

During the Waterloo campaign, Pontécoulant served as a *sous-lieutenant* in the horse artillery of the Imperial Guard (Duchand); he commanded the 3rd Section of the 3rd Company which was attached to the grenadiers à cheval.

Pontécoulant is an unrepentant admirer of Napoleon and his account closely follows Napoleon's memoirs, suggesting that he did not witness much of what he describes. However, in the book he tells a couple of anecdotes of his own personal experiences and it is these that we are most interested in.

During the Waterloo campaign Fée served as *Pharmacien aide-major* to Marcognet's 3rd Infantry Division, which was part of d'Erlon's I Army Corps.

His account of Waterloo is interesting in so much as he seems to have generally neglected his medical responsibilities during the battle; his account centres on his observations of Napoleon and ignores any attempts he might have been expected to make to find his ambulance from which he was separated at the very beginning of the battle! It was only towards the end of the day that he joined Larrey's hospital and carried out his duties as a doctor.

During the Waterloo campaign Lagneau served as *surgeon-major* to the 3rd Regiment of Grenadiers à Pied of the Old

Guard. This regiment was commanded by General Poret de Morvan and with the other regiments of foot grenadiers of the Guard were under the orders of General Friant.

Lagneau kept a record of his day-to-day movements and some impressions of his campaigns throughout his career starting in 1804. He re-copied them and completed them in 1847 although they were not published until 1913. He speaks little of the battle, which he was unlikely have been a witness to, but concentrates on building a case against Grouchy for the loss of the battle, including conversations he had much later with Generals Gérard and Pajol.

List of Plates

Reille commanded the II Corps. He wrote only a brief description of the battle and seems to have used it primarily to deflect blame for the failure around Hougoumont onto his subordinates.

Trefcon served as chief of staff to General Bachelu. He gives a rather uncontroversial account of the battle but is notable for having abandoned the army after the battle.

Napoleon's brother Jérôme was a divisional commander in the II Corps and was primarily responsible for the French action around Hougoumont. He appears to have abandoned his division sometime during the battle to join the emperor.

Foy commanded a division in the II Corps. He made little contribution to the action around Hougoumont, but his description of his attack on the British ridge is interesting.

Tromelin commanded a brigade in the VI Corps. His brief account describes the fighting against the Prussians on the French right flank.

Kellerman was an unenthusiastic supporter of Napoleon but accepted the command of the 3rd Cavalry Corps. He gives us some interesting detail on the French great cavalry attacks.

Delort commanded a cuirassier division at Waterloo and gives an interesting account of the battle in general and the cavalry charges in detail.

Ordener inherited the command of a cuirassier brigade early in the battle after its original commander was wounded. His account concentrates on the great cavalry charges.

Pelet commanded the 2nd Regiment of Chasseurs à Pied of the Imperial Guard. He gives a long and detailed account of the fighting against the Prussians in Planchenoit.

Guyot commanded the heavy cavalry division of the Imperial Guard. He describes the actions of the division during the battle before he was wounded.

De Brack served as a captain in the lancers of the Imperial Guard. He gives some interesting detail of the attacks against the Allied squares.

This famous painting of the battle shows the fighting around Hougoumont. French accounts prove that far fewer troops were committed to the fighting here than is generally portrayed in Allied histories.

This rather romanticised print shows Ney leading the great French cavalry attacks against a British square. The accounts of these charges are some of the most detailed of the French participants.

This sketch was drawn by Captain de Brack to show the futile charge of the carabiniers which is described by Kellerman in his account of the battle.

This near contemporary map gives a good feel for the topography of the battlefield before it was changed by the construction of the Lion Mound.

Introduction

The French never got over Waterloo because at one stage, in spite of everything, they had won the battle.[1]

In this second volume of French eyewitness accounts of Waterloo, I cover the remaining accounts of that portion of the French army not covered in the first volume. As previously, my aim is to present the unedited and unabridged French eyewitness accounts with the aim of allowing readers to try and understand the view of the battle from 'the other side of the fence'. Presenting the full accounts will also allow readers to make their own interpretation of what happened in that momentous battle by balancing them against the more readily-available British and Allied accounts.

Unlike many British officers and soldiers, the French did not write prolifically about Waterloo. This should not be surprising given the humiliating defeat they had suffered. Whilst the victorious British army wrote home in the days following the battle to reassure family and friends that they were safe and spread the news of their great victory, the French army was in complete disarray, scattered across the countryside of southern Belgium and northern France, exhausted and demoralised. They had neither the time nor the inclination to write of their defeat and many, realising Napoleon's dream was over, returned to their homes and families. Nor when time was available after the final exile of Napoleon and the restoration of the monarchy, or in their retirement, was there the political or social appetite to re-live the nightmare. Two hundred years later, this relative paucity of French accounts is a great frustration to both the amateur enthusiast and professional historian who want to try to establish the truth of what happened that day.

Perhaps the battle of Waterloo has more controversies and myths surrounding it than any other in history. Over the years since the battle, these controversies have been debated and argued about and the myths recycled to the point that many of those who are interested in it may no longer know what to believe.

In more recent times historians have taken a much closer look at the accounts of all those (not just the British) who were actually present at Waterloo to try and get to the bottom of what really happened, feeling that those who actually took part in those momentous events were perhaps best placed to accurately describe what they witnessed with their own eyes. Whilst these accounts have indeed clarified a number of controversial points and episodes, the truth is that some have actually muddied the water still further! It is now clear that whilst many eyewitness accounts are full of fascinating detail that give us a real feel for the experience of battle in those times, others have rather wandered from the truth, for good or malicious reasons, and it is vital to understand the motivations of those who put pen to paper to describe their experiences and their perspective of what really happened if we are to finally settle on something a bit nearer to the truth.

In the first volume of this series, I wrote at length about the difficulties of using eyewitness accounts of experiences of the battlefield as a basis upon which to try and get to the truth of what really happened and in particular the many reasons why they may not have told the whole truth. Whilst I do not want to repeat everything that many of the readers of this volume may have already read in the first, I cannot assume that everyone who reads these lines has also read those of volume one. What follows is therefore a précis of what appears in the first chapter of volume one, because as I have already explained, it is vital to understand the motivations of those who experienced the battle if we are to give due credit to the detail of what they have written. For those who have read the first volume, then this introduction should be skipped or used as revision.

There are many reasons why an eyewitness may not tell the truth in their description of their experiences, either by deliberate omission or by deliberately not telling the whole truth. The first thing to be decided is whether the writer is pro- or anti-Napoleon, or whether they purely tell their own story without entering into the political aspects of the battle. Those who were pro-Napoleon generally based their own accounts on those that were written or directly influenced by Napoleon's own accounts that were covered in the first volume; these are most likely to praise his handling of the battle and place the blame of its loss on others. Those who were anti-Napoleon are clearly critical of his direction of the battle and place all the blame for the loss onto his shoulders alone. Neither of these two approaches are likely to give us a balanced and objective account and almost by definition tell lies or stretch the truth in order to prove their basic thesis. Those who are neutral in their analysis and objective in their approach are far more likely to be telling the truth; at least as they understood it. The following reasons are also likely undermine the veracity of accounts:

Their Role and Position on the Battlefield. All the younger and more junior contributors will have been concentrating hard on their particular responsibilities within the unit they were serving in and will have had little time to spend looking around them to see what was going on beyond their immediate vicinity. This, and in particular where they were located on the battlefield, often in the thick of the fight and on foot, perhaps shrouded in smoke or in dead ground, prevented them from writing of the wider battle beyond their immediate experiences. They would therefore have little or no idea of what was going on across the majority of the battlefield.

Exaggeration. Having witnessed such an intense and probably terrifying experience, possibly for the first time, it is perhaps human nature that an eyewitness exaggerates what they did and observed during the battle. Exaggeration might be used to promote their individual actions, that of their regiment and/or their own army.

The Deliberate Underplaying of an Individual's Role and Contribution. Given the fall of Napoleon after the battle and the restoration of the monarchy, senior officers in particular were prepared to underplay both their willingness to serve and their role in the battle to ensure they were not seriously penalised or punished by the new regime.

The Passage of Time. Some accounts were written in the days immediately after the battle, and others, many years later; whilst those written in the year or so after the battle, or from notes made in a journal or diary, are far more likely to be accurate than those written in people's dotage. Recollections of much later years were likely to be affected by fading memory or coloured by conversations with others and the reading of other accounts.

Whilst for even the most serious military historian there should be plenty of fascinating interest in the accounts that follow, it must always be remembered that they are quite probably some way from the absolute truth. For the full value to be drawn from these accounts and to get a little closer to what really happened at Waterloo, it is necessary to remain open-minded and to corroborate them as far as possible with the eyewitness accounts of the British and their allies.

The overwhelming majority of the translation of these accounts is my own and I accept full responsibility for any mistranslation. Whilst I have endeavoured to maintain the feel of the originals there is inevitably some interpretation required of the true meaning the author was trying to convey and it is quite possible that in some instances I may have been mistaken. I apologise for any errors and hope that despite these that my work has broadened the understanding of this great battle and people's enjoyment of studying it.

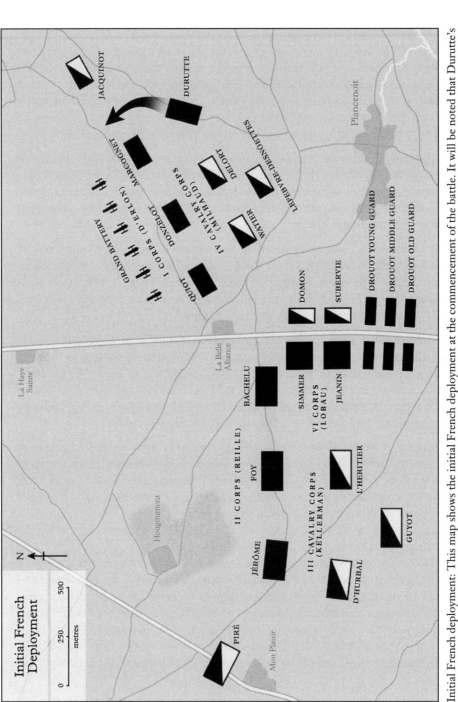

Initial French deployment: This map shows the initial French deployment at the commencement of the battle. It will be noted that Durutte's division of d'Erlon's I Corps was still moving into its allocated position when the battle started.

Chapter 1

II Army Corps

Introduction

Reille's II Corps had started the campaign with four infantry divisions and a light cavalry division. However, Girard's 7th Infantry Division had found itself forming a link between Ney's and Grouchy's wings on 15 June having followed the retreating Prussians that Reille had been in contact with for most of that day. On the morning of the 16th, Napoleon ordered Girard to Ligny where his division fought against the Prussians on the left flank of the French line. Involved in some desperate fighting, Girard was mortally wounded and his division suffered over 50 per cent casualties. Napoleon left them behind at Ligny to recuperate and they did not rejoin their parent corps for Waterloo. Reille therefore fought the battle with only three of his four infantry divisions. These three had borne the brunt of the fighting at Quatre Bras and had suffered accordingly; although official figures record just over 1,500 casualties, the official figures are not complete and Reille suggests the actual figure was closer to 3,500, although some of the more lightly wounded would not have left their units.

Deployed initially between the Charleroi to Brussels road and the Nivelles to Brussels road, most of the corps faced Hougoumont. Piré's light cavalry division was deployed to the west of the Nivelles road covering the left flank of the army and, as we shall see, took little part in the fighting. In Napoleon's preliminary orders II Corps were to advance on I Corps' (d'Erlon) left flank to support the main attack on the Allied ridge. No mention of attacking Hougoumont was made in these orders, so subsequent orders must have been sent from the emperor to do so. Napoleon claims the attack on Hougoumont was a diversionary attack to draw British troops from the centre where he planned to make his main attack, but no mention of this is made by other eyewitnesses.

Many British accounts claim that the whole of the French II Corps was committed to the attack on Hougoumont, but as the following accounts make clear, this is one of the many myths of the battle. A number of the following accounts also describe a significant infantry assault made by half the corps against the Allied line straight after the great cavalry charges. There is little to corroborate this in Allied accounts, but there is no doubt that it took place, though even French accounts describe a half-hearted attack which seems to have been easily repulsed by some unspecified Allied troops formed in square.

With most French accounts agreeing that the disintegration of the army started on the right flank, it seems that II Corps maintained their cohesion during the initial stages of their retreat, but this quickly broke down and most troops followed the general rout.

Lieutenant General *Comte* Honoré Charles Michel Reille

Joseph Napoléon Ney, *Documents inédits sur la Campagne de 1815, publiés par le Duc d'Elchingen* (Paris: Anselin, 1840), pp. 54–63.

Honoré Reille was born in 1775 and joined the Var Volunteers as a grenadier in 1791 aged just sixteen. His promotion was swift and within a year he was commissioned. In 1793 he fought at Neerwinden and the following year transferred as a lieutenant into the Army of Italy where he began a long association with Massena. He took part in the siege of Toulon where Napoleon first made his mark, and then participated in the invasion of Genoa as Massena's aide. He fought under Napoleon at Montenotte, Dego and the crossing of the Lodi in 1796, after which he was promoted to captain. Later in the same year he fought at Saint-George, Caldiero and Arcola. He fought at Rivoli as a squadron commander with the 15th Dragoons. Having been cited for bravery at the capture of Tarvis, his promotion to chef d'escadron *was confirmed by the Directory in May 1797. In 1799 he was once more back on Massena's staff in the Army of Switzerland and promoted to* adjutant général de brigade *before fighting at Massena's victory at Zurich and serving through the siege of Genoa. He filled various staff appointments during 1800 to 1805 and oddly found himself at the naval battle of Cape Finisterre, but had left the fleet before the catastrophe of Trafalgar. Having joined the army for the Austerlitz campaign, he was only given a brigade command after the famous battle. He fought under Suchet at Saalfeld, where his brigade distinguished itself, and again at Jena, deploying onto the plateau early and thus allowing the rest of the French army to establish a toehold for the following battle. Towards the end of 1806 he moved from command of an infantry brigade to one of cavalry for the pursuit of the Prussian army, but returned to his infantry brigade for the battle of Pultusk. At the end of the year he was promoted to* général de division. *Appointed chief-of-staff of V Corps early in 1807, he commanded it for a short while after his corps commander was wounded. Appointed an imperial aide, he fought again at Friedland. In this role he travelled to Spain in 1808 and spent a year there, but found himself in command of a division at the failures at the fortress of Rosas and the first siege of Gerona. He was recalled for the Wagram campaign in which he commanded the Imperial Guard tirailleurs at the battle. In 1810 he returned to Spain where he fought for the next four years during which, like many French generals, he enjoyed little success against the British army there. He started off fighting the guerrillas as governor of Navarre and then as a corps commander in Catalonia. In June 1813 he became commander of the Army of Portugal and was once more in action against guerrillas, but with Wellington's thrust north in 1813 he was forced to fall back from position to position. The retreat finished at Vitoria where Reille commanded the French right. Outmanoeuvred by General Graham, his troops fought rather better later in the day but disintegrated with the rest of the army at the end of the battle. In the rest of 1813 he fought unsuccessfully against the British at Roncesvalles, Sorauren, on the Bidassoa and Nive. Early in 1814 he resigned over an issue of command and left the army; however, he was ordered to return and his insubordination was over-looked. Back in command for the battles of Orthez, Tarbes and Toulouse, he finished his time in Spain with no notable achievements or success against the British. Employed by Louis after Napoleon's abdication, he did not commit himself on the emperor's return until summoned. He was immediately given command of II Army Corps and commanded it at Quatre Bras and Waterloo. Placed on the non-active list after the Second Restoration, he was included in the general amnesty of 1818 and became something of a committed royalist. Stripped of all his posts after the 1830 Revolution, he was only restored again by Louis-Philippe who made him Marshal of France as one of the few available possibilities. Surviving the transition to Louis Napoleon, he was elected senator and became a firm supporter of the Second Empire before his death in 1860.*

Reille's account, like that of d'Erlon, is frustratingly short on detail on Waterloo. It was included in a book published by Marshal Ney's son who was writing to defend the honour of his father whose handling of aspects of the battle had been criticised by Napoleon in his various accounts of the campaign. It was published in 1840, but we cannot be sure exactly when it was written. Reille criticises the repeated attacks on Hougoumont, but seems to have done nothing concrete to stop them. He also tells us that by the time the battle started, his corps was only half the strength of which it started the campaign due to the loss of Girard's division and the casualties suffered at Quatre Bras.

Historic notice on the movements of the 2nd Corps in the campaign of 1815, by Lieutenant General Count Reille.

The 2nd Army Corps commanded by Count Reille was composed, on its entry into campaign, of four divisions of infantry, one of cavalry and forty-six guns. That is:

> 5th Division: Lt Gen Bachelu, nine battalions, 4,103 men
> 6th Division: Prince Jérôme, thirteen battalions, 7,819 men
> 7th Division: Lt Gen Girard, eight battalions, 3,925 men
> 9th Division: Lt Gen Foy, ten battalions, 4,788 men

Total: forty battalions, 20,365 men
Artillery: 1,430 men
Cavalry: Lt Gen Piré, fifteen squadrons, 1,865 men
Engineers: 431 men
Corps total: 24,361 men
...

Count Reille began his march at day break on the 18th [having passed the night at Genappe], and towards 9am., formed his army corps to the left of the main road, opposite the farm of Caillou [actually la Belle-Alliance]. Towards eleven o'clock, Napoleon gave his instructions for the attack; it was to be made in echelons formed with the right in front. I Corps to the right of the main road and II Corps to the left; in this manner I Corps, which had not been engaged with the enemy, was to approach him first, whilst II Corps supported this movement by covering the left of the Hougoumont wood. Prince Jérôme, commander of the 9th [6th] Division, was directed on this point, having Piré's cavalry division behind his left; General Foy was placed in the centre, and General Bachelu to the right, touching the main road. Girard's division, which had suffered severe losses at Ligny, had been left to hold that battlefield, and which, combined with the losses of the 15th and 16th, reduced II Corps to around 12,000 infantry.

The troops advanced under the protection of a strong battery situated facing la Haye-Sainte, which marked the centre of the English. The 9th Division [the 6th!] descended on the Hougoumont wood. Its first brigade advanced and wanted to capture the farm of this name, which had been fortified; instead of holding in the back of the wood, it kept ahead a strong line of skirmishers. The order was given several times but other attacks were uselessly attempted by the other brigade, and this division spent the whole day involved in this operation. The divisions of Foy and Bachelu deployed on the plateau between the wood and the road. Soon after a division of infantry of I Corps was thrown into disorder by a charge of English cavalry, which was then thrown back by some of ours. But instead of reforming the troops that were broken, in order to make a new attack and support them by a good reserve of infantry, someone had all the cavalry reserve advance; these troops, after several brilliant charges against the English cavalry, which had advanced to meet them, were forced to retire behind the English infantry squares, but was not able to break this infantry that was in good order and which had not suffered up to that point. Our squadrons were long exposed to their fire and the ground was so soaked by rain, that the artillery could only advance with great difficulty to support them. The divisions of Foy and Bachelu, and those of I Corps, advanced in the middle of our cavalry to attack the English infantry. They were too weak against all the English infantry to have any chance of success and it would have only been with the aid of all the Guard that one would have had a chance of success.

When this reserve advanced, the cavalry and infantry of the first line had already suffered for so long that part of the plateau had been abandoned and they were unable to second this attack with much vigour; besides, the Prussian attack had already made good progress on our right, since we were fighting in Planchenoit; the infantry thus had to stop and the English army, seeing our right outflanked, advanced. The three divisions of II Corps retired in good order until night; but at Genappe and Quatre Bras, all mixed up, and in the darkness it was not possible to maintain any sort of order.

If the commander of II Corps had known the exact state of what passed on its right, he would have taken a line of retreat on Nivelles; but he never knew there was such a great disaster, he could have taken position there, hoping that the army would hold at Quatre Bras, and this loss of time could have compromised him and he would have inevitably lost all hope of retreat.

The loss of II Corps on the 18th was about 4,000 men killed or wounded.

Certified to conform to a note furnished at the time.

Signed, Count Reille

5th Infantry Division

Adjutant-Commandant (Colonel) Toussaint-Jean Trefcon

Carnet de Campagne du Colonel Trefcon, 1793–1815 (Paris: Edmond Dubois, 1914), pp. 184–94.

In 1815 Trefcon served as adjutant-commandant *(senior staff officer with the rank of colonel), chief-of-staff to General Bachelu, commander of the 5th Infantry Division, part of II Army Corps (Reille).*

Toussaint-Jean Trefcon was born in Saint-Quentin in 1776. Although destined for a career in the law, in a fit of popular enthusiasm under the threat of invasion he joined the local National Guard in 1792 aged just sixteen. He was soon in action at a number of sieges, but despite quick promotion to sergeant, he left the National Guard. However, soon after [Year VII], he was conscripted in to the regular army. He fought at Hohenlinden as a sergeant and became a lieutenant in 1807. He missed Friedland due to sickness, then served in Spain as a captain in the 1st de ligne. He fought at Burgos (where he received his first wound), then at the taking of Corunna and Oporto. He was seriously wounded at Astorga in 1810 at the moment he took a redoubt at the head of his grenadier company. For this he was promoted to chef de bataillon and posted to the 56th de ligne with whom he went to Russia. Wounded in the neck at Polotsk he took no further part in the campaign. He fought in 1813 as a staff colonel in Maison's division at all the major actions of that year and became Amey's divisional chief-of-staff for the 1814 campaign; he was taken prisoner at Fère Champenoise. He went onto half pay during the First Restoration, was ordered to return to the army to oppose Napoleon's march on Paris in 1815, but arrived in Paris after the emperor. For the 1815 campaign he served as the chief-of-staff to Bachelu's division and was present at Quatre Bras and Waterloo. During the retreat he made his way to Maubeuge and remained there until sending his submission to the king. However, he was not allowed to serve again, despite his appeals, until 1818. By 1828 he was the most senior colonel in the army, though he was not promoted further. He married in April 1831, demanded his retirement in August and his new wife left him the next day! He was nominated colonel of the National Guard of Saint-Quentin in 1834, forty-two years after he had first joined them. He was interned in a lunatic asylum soon after and died in 1854.

The main value of Trefcon's account is his description the infantry attack of Bachelu's division and one of Foy's brigades onto the Allied ridge after the cavalry charges, which is rarely mentioned by histories of the battle. This also confirms that these formations took no part in the attack on Hougoumont as claimed by almost all British accounts of the battle.

On the 17th June, we remained in our positions the whole day. In the evening, we received the order to go to occupy Genappe. General Count Lobau's corps was already in this town, as well as Kellerman's division.

Our division bivouacked around the outside of the town. A terrible rainstorm came in the afternoon and evening which waterlogged the roads, covering us in a thick mud which covered us from head to foot.

The ration convoy only arrived in the night when it was too late, which resulted in many soldiers laying down for the night without having eaten.

I worked late with General Bachelu in a barn. We received reports from the colonels and generals, the strength returns and took our detailed dispositions in view of the battle that would take place the next day.

After having dined in a summary fashion, the general and I shared a bundle of straw.

In the night, General Husson [commander of Bachelu's 1st Brigade], who had nowhere to lodge, came to join us; all lay where they could, most of them simply slept in the mud.

18 June 1815, the battle of Waterloo. We stood to arms at first light and were ready to move.

General Reille gave the order to depart at 5am.

En route we received an order from general headquarters to stop so that we could clean ourselves up and cook.

This news was well received, for many soldiers were dying from hunger and we did not like to fight when we were dirty.

At eight o'clock we started our march forwards again. We stopped at the farm of Caillou. The emperor was there with a numerous headquarters. He was eating there.

The emperor had General Reille called for and had a long conversation with him. From where I was I could see the emperor clearly. He had an air of calm and the look that I had always seen.

After a short stop at the farm of Caillou, we re-started our march.

We moved to the left of the main road which led to Brussels.

The emperor passed us in review. I cannot recall without great emotion this last review and I can only compare it to the feelings I had when I crossed the Niemen in 1812.

The enthusiasm of the soldiers was great, the music played, the drums beat and a shiver excited all the men for many of whom this was to be their last day. They cheered the emperor with all their might.

Close to us, the English saw us and heard all our shouts.

The review complete, our division received the order to move to the right [he must mean left] of the road to Brussels, opposite the farm of Belle-Alliance and took position there.

It was close to midday when we were in position. The most formidable battle that I had ever assisted in was about to commence.

The fighting only started towards one o'clock in the afternoon.

At the beginning of the action, General Reille gave the order to Prince Jérôme Bonaparte's infantry division to capture the Hougoumont farm. This division formed the left of the army corps and it found itself in position facing this farm.

The division launched itself on this position and did prodigies of valour. It was on the point of seizing it when the English, sending reinforcements, forced it to retire after having suffered considerable losses. *Général de Brigade* Baudouin [*sic*] was killed.

Jérôme's division reformed and, augmented by a brigade of General Foy's, it launched itself again to the assault of Hougoumont. The combat was violent and lasted until evening, the adversaries taking and re-taking their positions. It was a fight of giants!

At three o'clock, the battlefield resembled a veritable furnace. The sound of cannon, that of the fusillade, the shouts of the combatants, along with a hot sun, made it resemble hell!

The fire of the English artillery was so violent that their balls and their canister fell as far as our division, even though it was not engaged and was at long range of cannon. The general directed us to go closer to the small

Goumont [*sic*. Hougoumont] wood, where the debris of the divisions of Jérôme and Foy came to rally.

In the face of the terrible determination of our army, the English showed admirable tenacity and courage. However, without the support of the Prussians, they would have been forced to retreat.

They held well; the day advanced and our infantry had not been able to break them. The order was given to our cavalry to launch themselves on them.

Our division still occupied, with ordered arms, the same position. We had still not been committed. From the position where I found myself, at the edge of the Goumont wood, I had a good view of the battlefield. The charges of our fine cavalry were certainly the most admirable thing I have ever seen.

More than ten times they launched themselves on the English, and, despite the fire, they reached their bayonets. They came back to reform near the small wood where we were and then charged again.

I was more excited than I can express and despite the dangers that I ran myself, I had tears in my eyes and I cried out my admiration to them!

The carabiniers struck me particularly. I saw their gilded cuirasses and their helmets shining in the sun; they passed by me and I did not see them again!

During the battle, I did not see the emperor, but one of the aides-de-camp of General Foy, who at this moment returned from headquarters, told me that he looked calm and content.

Our division and a brigade of General Foy's division still occupied the same position at 6pm. We had witnessed the battle without participating in it. One would have thought that we had been forgotten!

At six o'clock, I remember looking at my watch, as it was getting late in the day, we received the order to leave the Goumont wood in order to support the efforts of our cavalry.

Hardly had we left the wood and formed ourselves in *colonne de division* than a hail of balls and grapeshot struck us. I found myself by the side of General Bachelu when several projectiles struck him and he had his horse killed under him.

The brigade commander having been struck at the same moment, I provisionally took command of the division.

Carried away by our élan and despite their fire, we went to attack the English when an important reinforcement arrived for them. There is no doubt that without this they would have been forced to fall back.

A fire of extraordinary violence welcomed us at the very moment we reached them with our bayonets. Our soldiers fell by the hundred, the others had to beat a hasty retreat: otherwise not a single one would have returned.

I received two heavy bruises to the chest and I had my horse killed under me by caseshot. In my fall I sprained my left wrist.

The violence of the fall and the pain I suffered caused me to lose consciousness.

Very happily for me, I was unconscious for only a short time and I quickly regained my wits. Sheltered behind the body of my horse, I let pass a charge of English dragoons who were pursuing my unfortunate division.

Once the English were far away, I tried to orientate myself so that I could join a French unit, before I was taken by the Allies that covered the plain in every sense.

A short distance away I saw a troop rallying in the small valley close to the Hougoumont wood. I went towards it as quickly as possible and with infinite precautions. It was the debris of the divisions of Bachelu and Foy which were reforming.

My state did not allow me to stay in the fighting. I moved to the rear.

It was close to eight o'clock in the evening. The fire was diminishing little by little and our troops had lost most of their positions. For all those who knew war, the battle was lost.

As I went towards the place where I thought I would find the ambulances, I encountered an old *chef d'escadron* of the cuirassiers that I had known in Spain. He was also wounded and looking for the ambulances. Approaching me he said,

'My dear Colonel, we have been unlucky. The battle is lost!'

I was furious and I think I was rude to him in response.

The *chef d'escadron* did not reply: he nodded his head sadly and with an air of being dazed. He pitied me. Not finding the ambulances, we continued our journey in the direction of Genappe [*sic*]. The road was already full of fugitives of all arms and all ranks, who shouted 'We are betrayed! Save yourselves!' whilst knocking down all those in their way.

The disorder was at its height. It surpassed in horror what I had seen in the return from Russia and the retreat from Leipzig.

Enveloped in this mass of men, having lost my companion in misfortune and above all weakened by my bruises, I would certainly have perished if the idea of leaving the road and moving across country had not occurred to me.

I preferred to be captured than to die so miserably.

My idea was crowned with success. I was soon able to grab a loose horse and across the fields I reached the road to Nivelles. This road was much less crowded than that to Charleroi. I joined a small group of general and superior officers who, wounded, were getting away from the battlefield and trying to get beyond the enemy pursuit.

The night was dark and we were pushed along by the irresistible flood of fugitives. It was necessary to concentrate hard to avoid being thrown from your horse and to distance yourselves from these unfortunates, pursuing our way as long as our mounts were able to carry us.

In the morning we were near Maubeuge. I had not eaten since the day before, but I had other worries in my head!

I remained at Maubeuge. The excitement of combat had exhausted me. I sensed that the defeat would have grave consequences and that, once more, the Allies would march on Paris. I was discouraged and without strength.

I lodged at the house of a brave widow named Simon who cared for me with much devotion. My sprained wrist caused me particular suffering; as for my bruises to the chest, they caused, along with my extreme fatigue, a violent lumbago.

I decided not to continue to serve and remained in Maubeuge without reporting and without presenting myself to the general who commanded there.

On the 13th July, I was completely healed. I then resolved to retire to my mother's house at Saint-Quentin. I thus left Maubeuge on the 15th and arrived in Saint-Quentin the same day.

The emperor had abdicated and King Louis XVIII had remounted the throne.

On the 18th July I wrote a letter of submission to His Excellence the Minister of War. I asked him to give me his order. I did not receive a favourable response.

6th Infantry Division

Prince Jérôme Bonaparte

Mémoires et Correspondance du Roi Jérôme et de la Reine Catherine (Paris: Dentu, 1866), Volume Seven, pp. 21–4.

During the Waterloo campaign Jérôme commanded the 6th Infantry Division in Reille's II Army Corps.

Jérôme was Napoleon's youngest brother, born in 1784. It was Napoleon's wish that Jérôme should follow a naval career and thus in 1800 he joined the French navy as a midshipman. His naval career was marked more by insubordination than military achievement and his advancement to rear admiral in 1806 was due more to his name than his competence. However, his naval career came to an end the same year when he chose to accompany Napoleon on the 1806 campaign against Prussia. Rather bizarrely, he was given command of the 2nd Bavarian Division, and after only a short time, including two sieges, he left his command to re-join Napoleon, who, judging he had now learnt his trade, put him in command of a corps! However, with Vandamme as his deputy, he completed the conquest of Silesia. After the Treaty of Tilsit in 1807, he became King of Westphalia. He was well respected by his subjects who did not generally support the nationalist attempts to overthrow him. From the time of his coronation his main responsibility was supplying troops for his brother's armies. In 1809 he successfully led 11,000 Westphalian troops into Saxony to help his ally against the Duke of Brunswick's Black Legion. In 1812 he demanded a role in the invasion of Russia and Napoleon gave him command of the right wing, consisting of nearly 80,000 men in four corps. In July 1812, after delivering several rebukes to his brother for his delays, Napoleon removed him from command and left Jérôme with only his own Westphalian corps to command. In a huff, Jérôme left the army and returned to his capital. He continued to recruit for his brother and rebuilt his army for the 1813 campaign. Hoping for a new command in the coming campaign, Jérôme was to be disappointed. As the Allies closed in, he finally fled his kingdom for France at the end of October 1813. He took no part in the 1814 campaign and fled to Switzerland on his brother's abdication. Ending up in Trieste, he left there on Napoleon's return and landed back in France in May 1815. He was warmly received by Napoleon, who gave him command of the 6th Infantry Division in II Corps, one of the strongest in the army. His division fought hard at in the Bossu wood at Quatre Bras where he was very slightly wounded. His division led the assault on Hougoumont during the battle of Waterloo. After the battle he rallied his division at Avesnes, then led them back to Laon before leaving them to join Napoleon in Paris. He fled the French capital before his brother's abdication and took refuge in his wife's homeland of Württemberg. After wandering the continent for thirty years, he finally returned to France in 1847. He was eventually named Marshal of France in 1850, after his nephew became president. Jérôme's influence waned with the birth of the Prince Imperial after Louis became Emperor and he died of a stroke in 1860.

Jérôme claims that once his division was reduced to the strength of just two battalions in the attacks on Hougoumont that he left command of it (presumably to General Guilleminot) and joined Napoleon. He roundly blames Ney for the premature commitment of the cavalry and first mentions the Prussians at six o'clock, describing that at first they were mistaken for Grouchy's arrival. This seems to undermine Napoleon's own account that he was aware of the Prussians before the battle started.

Letter written by Jérôme to his wife Catherine dated 15th July 1815.

The day of the 17th was employed in the pursuit of the enemy who, in the evening, took up a position in front of the Soignes forest at Mont Saint-Jean; the weather was terrible. The whole night of the 17th/18th was used to concentrate the army and take position for the next day.

On the morning of the 18th, whilst passing in front of the emperor's general headquarters, I stopped with him for an hour; he received me with a particular affection and tenderness. He assembled the principal generals and once the plan of battle was settled, each went to his post. At midday, the army was in line; I was on the extreme left, before a wood occupied by the English. We had 70,000 men and 280 guns; the enemy had 96,000; Marshal Grouchy, with 36,000 men, observed the Prussian army on our extreme right, but was not in communication with us.

At 12.15pm, I received the order to begin the attack; I marched on the wood of which I occupied the majority after a lively resistance, killing and losing many men. At 2pm, I was master of the entire wood and the battle was engaged along the whole line, but the enemy, who realised the importance of this point, rushed forward a reserve and took it from me. I advanced with my whole division and at 3pm, after a bloody fight, I took it again, and from then on, held it to the end of the battle. The enemy left in this wood 6,000 dead and I lost 2,000, with one of my generals [Bauduin] and almost all my senior officers; furthermore, the wounded and the losses that I had suffered at the battle on the 16th reduced me to two battalions. I received the emperor's order to move back to him; he received me again as on the day before and said to me, 'It is impossible to fight better; now that you have only two battalions left remain here and you can go wherever there is danger'. The affair was going marvellously; it was three o'clock and we had already gained a lot of ground from the enemy, who was in his last position: it was then that the emperor ordered Marshal Ney to move, with a great part of the cavalry, two infantry corps and the Guard, against the enemy's centre to deliver a hammer blow and it would certainly have done for the English army if the marshal had executed the emperor's orders. But Ney, carried away by his courage and by the hope of succeeding without the support of the Guard, did not await its arrival and attacked three quarters of an hour too early. I was close to the emperor when he saw the marshal's mistake. He said these words to me, 'The wretched man, it is the second time since the day before yesterday that he has compromised the fate of France'. The attack was failing, it had to; it was the decisive moment and it required the help of the Guard to assure success. The English, already shaken, retook their position. However, the emperor, calm and composed in the middle of all these events, repaired the faults of Marshal Ney by a movement in advance that he made himself with part of his reserve. We thus fought stubbornly without gaining or losing ground, when at 6pm, an artillery barrage, two leagues to our right, led us to believe that Marshal Grouchy had arrived. It was the Prussians; the moment was critical, it was necessary to either withdraw, or our right, outflanked by the Prussians, that

Grouchy was not strong enough to contain, would lose us the battle. Therefore it was necessary to chase the English from their positions in order to
allow us to fall on the Prussians and stop their advance. The emperor, hoping
that Grouchy would arrive, said to us, 'The battle is won, it is necessary to
occupy the enemy's positions, march'. And all, with the exception of six battalions of the Old Guard, marched with us. Ney received the four regiments
of the Guard, commanded by General Friand [*sic*: Friant] and arrived at the
English guns; we supported from the foot of the position with other troops.
All was going well, when Friand was wounded and, by what fatality I don't
know, the attack of the Guard failed!! The Guard retreated ... it was necessary to retreat, but there was no longer time; the emperor wanted to get
himself killed; we were in the middle of balls and enemies. Wellington had
fresh cavalry which he launched into the plain at eight o'clock in the evening;
at nine o'clock a panic seized the army, at ten o'clock it became a rout, our
guns had no ammunition, etc., etc. The Emperor was dragged along, no one
gave any orders; we ran to get behind the Sambre ...

Chef de Bataillon Jean-Baptiste Jolyet

Souvenirs et correspondence sur la bataille de Waterloo (Paris: Teissedre, 2000),
pp. 76–80.

*In the Waterloo campaign, Jolyet commanded the 1st Battalion, 1st légère (Colonel
Cubières) in the 1st Brigade (Bauduin) of Prince Jérôme's 6th Infantry Division,
part of Reille's II Army Corps.*

   *Jolyet was born at Vesoul in 1785. He attended the École de Fontainebleau and
in 1805 he was commissioned into the 42nd de ligne. He first served in Italy and
from 1809 to 1812 in Spain, fighting in a number of battles and sieges in Catalonia.
In the 1813 campaign in Germany he fought at Bautzen and Leipzig. Under the
First Restoration he commanded the 1st Battalion of the Régiment du Roi (infanterie
légère). His account suggests he was a reluctant adherent to Napoleon on his return,
foreseeing the catastrophe that was about to happen. He had his horse killed under
him at Quatre Bras and at Waterloo he fought around Hougoumont through the
whole day. Wounded in the lower body towards the end of the action, he was carried by
some of his men to Genappe where he remained until made prisoner by the Prussians.
He was transported to Brussels and then into captivity in England. He returned
to France at the end of December 1815. He continued to serve after the Second
Restoration and served in Spain and then Morea in Greece. He retired just before the
1830 Revolution as a lieutenant colonel in the 35th de ligne and died in 1863.*

   *Jolyet gives so little detail on the attacks on Hougoumont that one would be
forgiven for thinking that his battalion was not involved and he was just a spectator,*

but we know this isn't true. However, he does give a few personal vignettes which make his account interesting and he seemingly restricts himself to those things that he saw for himself.

We bivouacked in the area of Genappe. The rain that had started on the 17th lasted the whole night.

The next day, the 18th June, we set off at 5am, and made a halt close to a farm where the emperor was. Towards 11am, our regiment resumed its march and arrived on a large plateau, to the left, where there was already a large number of troops drawn up in column. From there we could see the masses of English infantry drawn up on the heights in front of the Soignes forest.

Hardly had we arrived on this plateau, than we received the order to move forward and we deployed to the left of the 5th Division (the first division of our corps). Before we arrived on our designated ground, my company of skirmishers was sent to search the small Hougoumont wood on which the left of our army was anchored. I deployed the rest of my battalion to the left of the 69th [this is a mistake. 61st?] which formed the left of the 5th Division. A fold in the ground hid this battalion from the view of the English and also my battalion. A sunken lane which cut through this fold seemed to serve as shelter for our second battalion; but as in establishing itself there it made a small kink in the line, our *général du brigade* [Bauduin] (who was killed a short time later) ordered the second battalion to establish itself in front of the sunken lane. This put it in view of the enemy: hardly had the 1st Division got into position than the English batteries, established in front of their line, opened a lively fire which knocked down twenty men of the second battalion and more balls followed so rapidly that it was obliged to drop back down into the shelter of the lane. This cannon fire seemed to give the signal for the principal action and fire opened along the whole line.

After various manoeuvres, about one o'clock, I sent support to the skirmishers in the Hougoumont wood. At the exit of this wood there was a house that the English had fortified. Several times our skirmishers, despite the orders that limited them to prevent the enemy from manoeuvring against our left, wanted to seize the house that was in their way. Each time they were repulsed and retired to our side of the wood; then I tried hard to support them and put them back in their positions; for I had been informed that we were to become the pivot of the army and consequently it was vital to maintain our position at all costs. Thus I passed part of the day, often having men wounded by English balls or by their howitzer shells.

Whilst I was sitting at the bottom of an embankment, on the edge of the wood, I heard something rolling behind me. I turned round and saw a shell which was coming down the slope on my right. I had time to lie flat and it exploded without doing me the least harm.

Towards five o'clock a small retrograde movement could be noticed in our line. This movement was, I believe, occasioned by the return of our cavalry which had not had the hoped-for effect. This appeared to us a bad omen, but did not stop us presenting a bold front to the English.

It was getting late and, despite all our efforts, we had not been able to capture the château of Hougoumont; we had lost more than two-thirds of our strength, our colonel, the brave Cubières, was grievously wounded. General of Brigade Bauduin had been killed. All that remained of our regiment rallied in the sunken lane to reform. Next to us was General Guilleminot, who sent his aide-de-camp to Prince Jérôme for some news. It was about 7pm when the aide-de-camp came to tell us, from the Prince, that Grouchy had debouched onto the left of the English and that consequently the battle was won. Mistaken joy! Then the general had what remained of us march ahead placed in line, in front of the sunken lane, next to a squadron of Red Lancers of the Guard.

Soon the enemy batteries, which had retired at first, re-took their first positions and showered us with balls; then, suddenly, we saw a battalion of the Old Guard retreating on the road!

Seeing that the battle was no longer looking like a victory, I decided to form into column what remained of my battalion and of the 3rd (whose commander had prudently disappeared). The commander of the 2nd followed my example. A moment after I made these arrangements, a ball, coming from a nearby small wood, wounded me in the lower body and I fell from my horse.

Two chasseurs of my battalion took me under the arms and dragged me a little to the rear of the battlefield. I regained consciousness and, despite the pain I suffered, I forced myself to march. The balls and shells fell in abundance. A shell broke the musket of one of my chasseurs without doing him any harm. Arriving close to the road, I saw that our troops were fleeing in all directions; but I continued to march despite my wound, hoping that all this disorder would cease at the first favourable position. Alas! The more I marched, the more I saw the disorder get worse.

Major Lebeau

The original of the following letter is held in the archives de l'Armée de Terre at Vincennes and was reproduced in *Les Carnets de la Campagne, Number 1, Hougoumont* (Brussels: Éditions de la Belle Alliance, 1999), pp. 44–5.

In the 1815 campaign, Lebeau commanded the 1st de ligne, which was part of the 2nd Brigade (Soye) of Prince Jérôme's 6th Infantry Division, part of Reille's II Army Corps. The regiment had twenty-seven officers killed or wounded at Quatre Bras and a further eighteen, including Lebeau himself, at Waterloo.

On its entry on campaign, the 1st de ligne numbered 1,736 men in three battalions. It fought at Quatre Bras where it suffered considerable casualties, including two of its three battalion commanders. It had been commanded by Colonel Cornebize since September 1814, but as he was a royal appointment, and thus politically unreliable, he was forced to hand command over to the regimental major, Lebeau. After Waterloo, Lebeau went on to become colonel of the 57th de ligne.

The following account is extracted from a letter addressed to Marshal Soult, then Minister of War, dated Périgueux, 16 April 1833. The letter addressed the issue of the utility of rifled carbines, recommending their introduction into the French army. To strengthen his case, Colonel Lebeau, as he was then, drew on his experience in command of the 1st de ligne at Waterloo. It is this portion of the letter that is translated here. Lebeau rather obtusely claims to have captured Hougoumont and, although not the only one to do so, it is generally accepted that the French did not come close to occupying it. He makes an interesting reference to using as skirmishers units that had suffered heavy casualties and were unable to function as a formed body. Allied accounts of the fighting around La Haye Sainte towards the end of the battle suggest this tactic was also used there.

I commanded the 1st Line Regiment at Waterloo. While approaching the enemy I received the order to take the farm of la Belle-Alliance [he means Hougoumont!], known in the history of this battle. It was unwise to risk the three battalions that made up my regiment, in view of the resistance it had put up against the previous failed assaults (it was fortified); I ordered the 2nd and 3rd Battalions to remain in reserve, and by a normal movement, forgetting that I was closed up, I marched at the head of the first battalion to attack the farm from which I was repulsed with heavy losses, and those mostly among the officers. I returned to the charge with the second battalion, combined with the debris of the first; with the same result as the first, despite supernatural efforts; but, being calmer in my second assault I observed and recognised the cause of the prompt destruction of my officers [Note of Lebeau: I have observed in twenty battles that the number of officers killed or wounded in our army was comparatively larger than those of the soldiers. I have acquired the proof, and notably at Waterloo, that the enemy had specially trained soldiers ordered to shoot at officers; I had taken prisoners, I questioned them, I have taken their arms, their cartridges that are clean and all their ancillaries necessary for their weapons and their equipment.] Breaking down as skirmishers the remains of these two battalions onto the two flanks of this farm, from where the murderous lead came specifically at my officers, I marched on it with the third battalion, my last resource, and by the extraordinary efforts this position was able to produce, I took it by escalade, and the enemy was hunted down; but how could I hold it? I had no more officers; more than sixty had fallen; it was necessary to create them. The non-commissioned officers took the place of the captains and in a necessity determined by circumstances, when I was ordered to leave the farm to advance, I was in the middle of the enemy's rolling crossfire. Obliged to create *peloton* leaders from amongst the corporals, how was it possible to maintain good order in such a state of things? How can you resist a well-organised cavalry and other masses that presented themselves before me? It was very difficult; I even dare to suggest the word 'impossible'. I fell in my turn; the ball that struck me had been aimed specifically at me.

Captain Pierre Robinaux

Journal de Route du Capitaine Robinaux (Paris: Gustave Schlumberger, 1908), pp. 207–11.

Pierre Robinaux served as the company commander of the 4th Company of the 2nd Battalion of the 2nd de ligne (Tripe (or Trippe)), in the 2nd Brigade (Soye), 6th Infantry Division (Jérôme), part of Reille's II Army Corps.

Robinaux was born into a farming family in 1783 and was taken by the conscription in 1803. Corporal in 1807 and sergeant in 1810, he was commissioned in 1812 and became lieutenant the following year. It seems that he did not enjoy his early service in Holland and in February 1804 he deserted with four of his friends. His freedom did not last long before he was arrested, but was soon released back to his regiment having promised not to desert again. In 1805 he was part of the invasion of Austria and was present at Ulm, though he missed the great victory of Austerlitz. He spent the years 1806 to 1808 in garrison in Illyria and northern Italy. In 1809 he took part in the campaign in north Italy against the Austrian forces of Archduke Charles and fought at Sacile, the passage of the Piave and the many minor actions of this campaign. After six months with his family over the winter of 1810 to 1811, he passed the next two years in garrison in the French Alps. After commissioning early in 1813, he was sent to the army that was being re-built after the disastrous retreat from Russia. He fought at Lützen, Bautzen, Leipzig and Hanau before retreating back into France. His battalion reduced to the strength of a company, he went back to Paris as a cadre and although eventually brought up to strength with conscripts he somehow contrived to miss all the battles of the campaign in 1814. He writes that he had no enthusiasm for the return of Napoleon and planned to stay loyal to the king. However, on Louis' flight he accepted service under the emperor and fought at Quatre

Bras and Waterloo; at the latter he was struck twice by spent balls, but only bruised. He was able to gather a small group of men after the battle and led them to Laon where they joined the rallying army and he rejoined the sad remains of his regiment. They eventually got back to Paris and skirmished with the Prussians around the capital until Napoleon's abdication. There is then a ten-year gap in his journal, but as he was still serving in 1834 when his journal ends, we can be sure that he continued to serve after the Second Restoration.

Robinaux gives us little detail on the attacks on Hougoumont, but a rather more interesting account of the break-up of II Corps during their retreat.

On the 18th June, the farm of Hougoumont, fortified and defended by the English, was attacked by II Corps commanded by Count Reille who captured it as well as La Haye Sainte; Planchenoit and the farm of la Belle-Alliance were occupied by the French; it was towards this direction that Bülow came. On the night of the 17th/18th, Napoleon slept at Planchenoit [Caillou] and on the 18th, he stayed on the mound of la Belle-Alliance during the battle. Vandamme commanded the Army of the Ardennes [III Corps], established at Fumay. The Army of the Moselle [IV Corps], commanded by General Gérard, came from Philippeville and came into line. The armée du Nord was commanded by Lieutenant Generals Derlon [*sic*], Reille, Vandamme, Gérard and Count Lobau; the cavalry, commanded by Grouchy, was divided into four corps under the orders of Generals Pajol, Exelmans, Milhaud and Kellerman.

At 10am, on the 18th, the whole French army was put in motion and advanced onto the plain; the army was echeloned in close columns, by the foot of the mound where the emperor was and they each went to where they were assigned. The corps of which I was a part was directed on the farm of Hougoumont, fortified and defended by the English; it was situated on a small height which dominates the plain at all points and at the foot of this farm there is a big wood irregularly planted, below which we were in closed columns; we formed the extreme left of the army. Count Reille, who commanded II Corps, came to give us the order to take the position held by the English and to take the farm as a strong point and to maintain ourselves in this position during the battle without losing or seizing terrain. Immediately the charge was sounded and we set off en masse, bayonets lowered on the enemy who put up a stiff resistance. The fighting, which was stubborn on both sides and the musketry was murderous, continued with equal determination; half an hour sufficed for the French to take this formidable position; if we had had two regiments of cavalry, we would have made a great number of prisoners, while in the centre and on the right of the army, the cannonade was very lively and the musketry the best sustained that had been heard; we always held firm in this important position.

At six o'clock in the evening, Marshal Ney came to our position and shouted to us in a strong voice, 'Courage, the French army is victorious, the enemy is beaten everywhere!' The emperor, seeing a body of troops deploying onto the plain, immediately announced the arrival of Grouchy, commander-in-chief of the cavalry. Immediately, he ordered the attack on the plateau called Mont-Saint-Jean, occupied by the English under the orders of the commander-in-chief of the combined armies Lord Wellington. There he met a firm resistance; a numerous artillery, well positioned, vomited fire and flame on all parts; the Imperial Guard immediately advanced and took the position in an instant, but it was immediately re-taken: the Guard immediately formed square and beat a retreat with an unequalled determination; summoned several times to surrender, it preferred death to dishonour, and we heard those words so worthy of the character and fine name of France; 'The Guard dies, but does not surrender!' The so-called corps of Grouchy was none other than a Prussian corps, 15,000 men strong commanded by Blücher, who came to cut up our army and take it in flank; the confusion became general; throughout the whole army. Perhaps one day, posterity will inform us of the reasons why Grouchy did not receive the emperor's orders to advance into the plain at the indicated hour; I refuse to be drawn on this subject.

In the position in which we found ourselves, we were not able to easily see the movements of our army; concerned by no longer hearing the cannonade, except in the distance, with one of my friends named Wanroo, a captain like me, I left the position for an instant and we advanced from two to three hundred paces into the plain to see where our army was, for we had received no orders. What did we see? Our troops were clearly in retreat; we immediately warned the general who commanded, 'Columns of retreat', as soon as he was convinced and recommended us to keep the closest silence and to stay in good order; this did not last long; we received several balls from behind us, and the frightened soldiers, looking behind them, saw our Polish Lancers and took them for English cavalry; 'We are lost!' The shout was repeated throughout the column and soon we were in complete disorder: each thought only of his own salvation; it was impossible to rally such distracted soldiers. The cavalry followed the impulsion of the infantry; I saw dragoons in retreat, galloping, knocking over the unfortunate infantrymen and riding over their bodies with their horses; this happened to me once; irritated by such disorder, exhausted and without the strength to run, for we had already run for half an hour in the plain without being pursued, which I had noticed several times and I did not cease to shout as loudly as possible, 'Halt, rally, no one is pursuing us!' Seeing that my efforts were useless, I found myself a musket and faced up to two or three dragoons, raising my bayonet and aiming my musket at them, and calling on them in a loud voice and in a firm tone that nothing pursued us, and that I would shoot the first man that passed me. I finally imposed upon them to stop and I managed to gather together about twelve cavalrymen and sixty infantry. I said to them, 'Follow me, I will lead you and get you across the Sambre without trouble'. They put their confidence in me and I did my utmost not to mislead them. I led them to a point I knew, named Pont-sur-Sambre; we marched all through the night and arrived there at 6am in the morning of the 19th.

After the battle Robinaux gathered up a small force of a dozen cavalrymen and about sixty infantrymen and led them back towards France. On the 19th they passed through Charleroi and Beaumont. He used his own money to feed his men. He eventually met some senior officers who were attempting to rally the army; a force of about 600 were formed although most were without arms. At Avesnes they met some of the Imperial Guard who were in good order. After a short rest they moved to Laon (which had been designated as the rallying point for the army) where they arrived on the 21st. Here attempts were being made to reorganise the debris of the army and they learnt that Napoleon had abdicated in favour of his son. On the 25th they left Laon to retreat on Paris, arriving at St-Denis the next day. Here the regiment was reinforced by its 4th Battalion, whose men were distributed amongst the first three.

9th Infantry Division

Lieutenant General *Comte* Maximilien Sebastien Foy

Girod de l'Ain, *Vie Militaire du Général Foy* (Paris: Plon, 1900), pp. 277–82.

At Waterloo, Foy commanded the 9th Infantry Division of Reille's II Army Corps.
  Maximilien Foy was born in 1775 and entered the artillery school at la Fère in 1790. He was commissioned into the artillery and fought through the Revolutionary Wars. Promotion came quickly and by the following year he was capitaine-commandant, *but he fell foul of dabbling in politics and ended up in jail, stripped of his rank. He was reinstated in 1795 and commanded a foot battery in the Army of the Rhine-Moselle. He was severely wounded at Diersheim in 1797 and although he took no further part in the campaign, he was promoted to* chef d'escadron *for his conduct. In 1797 he fought in the Army of Switzerland and again distinguished himself, becoming* adjutant général de brigade. *He took a key part in the battle of Zurich against the Russians. He commanded the 5th Horse Artillery Regiment in 1800 during the campaign in Germany and the following year became chief-of-staff to General Lorge. He missed Marengo but fought in the remainder of the campaign. A firm supporter of Moreau, his future looked bleak when that general was brought to trial for treason. He took little active part in operations again until he joined Junot's*

Army of Portugal in 1807. He fought at Vimeiro and was wounded in the leg. Shipped back to France after the Convention of Cintra, he was one of the few officers who came out of the campaign with any credit and was promoted to général de brigade. In the second invasion of Portugal in 1809 he commanded an infantry brigade for the first time. He inevitably performed well against Portuguese forces, but fell short against the British at Oporto. He accompanied Massena into Portugal in 1810 and his brigade was initially successful at Busaco where he was wounded. He was twice sent back to Paris by Massena where he impressed Napoleon and was promoted to général de division. He was present at Salamanca, providing Marmont a defiant rearguard, but suffered a mauling at Garcia Hernandez. He fought with credit against the British during 1812, but failed to support King Joseph at Vitoria. However, he gave support to the French retreat and subsequently fought at Sorauren, on the Bidassoa, on the Nive and at Orthez where he was badly wounded. He remained in service after the First Restoration and was initially cautious in committing himself on Napoleon's return. In April 1815 he was given command of the 9th Infantry Division which he led in heavy fighting at both Quatre Bras and Waterloo. Wounded at Waterloo, he led the remains of his division back to France and across the Loire. Put on the inactive list, he re-started his service in 1818, but quickly turned to politics in which he soon established a fine reputation. He started writing a history of the Peninsular War, but his work was never completed as he died of a heart attack in 1825.

Foy gives a detailed and interesting account of the actions of his division around Hougoumont and particularly the attack on the ridge conducted by Bachelu's division and a brigade of his own division.

Ham, 23rd June.
On campaign, it is easy to out-manoeuvre the English, to outflank them, to stop them, interfere with them. In battle, using the ground and in line, there is not a more redoubtable enemy. Their infantry is steady under fire, well trained, and fire perfectly; their officers are the bravest and most patriotic in Europe. Lord Wellington is not a remarkable genius, and it is the same in his intellect, a mediocre man; he is a good general, he knows his business perfectly; he is loved and respected by his troops; he does not expose them to useless dangers, but he does not spare them at critical moments. Since the 18th June his head must be in the clouds. How were we so humiliated by the proud English? Rule Britannia!
. . .
On the night of the 17th/18th, we ate with Prince Jérôme at the King of Spain Inn. A waiter, who served at table, said that Lord Wellington had eaten at the inn the day before, and that one of his aides-de-camp had announced at table that the English army was awaiting the French at the entrance to the

Forest of Soignes and that it would be joined there by the Prussian army, which was moving on Wavre. This report was vital intelligence for Guille-minot [Jérôme's second-in-command] and I. On the morning of the 18th, Jérôme being with his brother at the Caillou far on the main road, reported this story of the waiter in Genappe. The emperor replied; 'The junction of the Prussians with the English is impossible for two days after a battle such as Fleurus [Ligny], and being followed, as it is, by a considerable body of troops'. His Majesty added, 'We should be very happy that the English want to hold. The battle will save France and be celebrated in the annals of the world. I will play on them with my numerous artillery, I will charge them with my cavalry to force them to show themselves, and, when I am sure of the point occupied by the English troops, I shall march directly on them with my Old Guard.'

Between 11am and midday, the army calmly deployed itself in the order indicated in the *Moniteur*; the infantry divisions formed for battle in two lines; the artillery took position in front of the infantry. We deployed more than 200 guns in front of the enemy; he did not have that many. His guns were in position before ours; one could see only a few skirmishers. Following the excellent custom of the English, the main body of their infantry and cavalry was hidden by the contours of the ground; they only showed themselves when they were to be employed. The enemy's right rested on a stream, below Braine-l'Alleud, his centre crossed the main road towards Mont-Saint-Jean; I could not see his left. Seeing such an extended line, I presumed there was on this ground more than just Wellington's army. In the distance, we could see the Soignes forest; it was probable that the English had identified a position on the edge of the wood to occupy in case they were forced to leave their principal position.

At first the emperor occupied a low height behind la Belle Alliance; I saw him with my telescope, walking to and fro, dressed in his grey riding coat, and often resting his elbows on the small table on which he had his map. After the charge of the French cavalry, he moved to La Haye Sainte; at the end of the day, he charged with his Guard. I waited for him to travel along the lines to inflame the morale of the soldiers. In the evening, when I saw the Old Guard charge along the main road, and when I was told that the emperor was at their head, I thought he wanted to die. Fate spared him. A terrible destiny for someone who had once been the master of the world!

The battle started with the attack on the Hougoumont wood. Jérôme's division took it straight away, but it was not able to take the houses that were beyond it. During the whole day, we never ceased to attack it; the enemy maintained himself there and we suffered considerable losses to Jérôme and to me that supported him. My division operated on the edge of the wood and the hedges of Hougoumont; it advanced and withdrew, and did not leave the field of battle until after the centre had given way. Now and again I supplied battalions into the wood to support or replace those of Jérôme. Bachelu was to my right and a little in front of me. The infantry and cavalry of the Imperial Guard were formed on the main road. We had behind us Kellerman's cavalry corps and to our extreme left, the light cavalry division of Piré which skirmished on the road which ran from Brussels to Namur. The lay of the ground hid the deployment of the right.

The affair of the Hougoumont wood had drawn towards the left the attention and fire of the enemy. It was evidently a secondary attack; it had lasted on its own, without slackening, close to two hours. Then, the right attacked the hamlet of Mont-Saint-Jean. I did not see its advance, nor the check that it suffered. On our line, the artillery had maintained a lively fire. The gunners of the Imperial Guard are the bravest soldiers in the army. The large consumption of ammunition, from the start of the action, meant that there was a shortage towards the end.

At 3pm, the cavalry in the centre marched against the enemy. Our corps of cavalry on the right and left had rushed to join and support their comrades. In a few minutes, the plateau between Hougoumont and the roads to Charleroi and Nivelles were covered, inundated by the *procella equestris* ['storm of horses']. Also there was the cavalry of the Imperial Guard, the carabiniers, the cuirassiers, all the best that France possessed. Our cavalry met the English cavalry and broke it. Thirty to forty guns were momentarily in our possession. Then, for the first time, I saw the English squares scattered on the rear slope of the plateau. I do not know if our cavalry sabred any of them; it returned to the charge several times; they fought hand to hand for an hour. I have seen nothing like it in my life. The squadrons had broken through the centre of the English army and come to reform behind my division, after having turned the Hougoumont wood.

When the French cavalry made this long and terrible charge, the fire of our artillery had already begun to slacken and our infantry did not move. When the cavalry had come back, the English artillery, which had ceased fire for half an hour, recommenced its fire. The divisions of Bachelu and Foy were ordered to climb the plateau, right to the squares which had advanced during the cavalry charge and which had not retired. The attack was made in column by echelons of regiment; Bachelu forming the most advanced echelons. I held my left on the hedge; I had on my front a battalion deployed as skirmishers. As we got close to the English we received a very heavy fire of grapeshot and musketry. It was a hail of death. The enemy squares had the front rank kneeling and presented a hedge of bayonets. The columns of the 1st Division took flight first: their movement swept away my own columns. At this moment

I was wounded; the top of my right *humerus* was shot through from the top down; the bone was not touched. Having received the blow, I thought I was only bruised; I remained on the battlefield. Everyone was fleeing: I rallied the debris of my division in the valley next to the Hougoumont wood. We were not followed; even our cavalry continued to hold onto the plateau; that of the enemy did not dare to move.

The enemy's fire was so lively and so heavy that it reached our soldiers even in the valley. The Hougoumont wood was deadly for us. Towards seven o'clock in the evening, we heard a heavy cannonade towards Planchenoit; it was the Prussians who had arrived on our right and rear. Our cannon deployed on the main road replied to their attacks. It was necessary to either retire without waiting for their attack, or to attempt a last effort against the English. The Imperial Guard marched; it was repulsed. The enemy army took the offensive along the main road. In a few instants our magnificent army was nothing more than a mass of fugitives. The cannon were unlimbered, the traces of the horses cut. All the army's materiel, equipages and artillery, were lost. No one remained with the colours; everyone had fled to save himself across the Sambre. The enemy charged our left weakly, level with the Maison de Roi. They pursued the large column of the centre, where the emperor was, as far as Genappe.

Chef d'Escadron Marie-Jean-Baptiste Lemonnier-Delafosse

Campagnes de 1810, 11, 12, 13, 14, 1815, en Portugal. Espagne, France, Belgique, ou Souvenirs Militaires (Havre: Imprimerie du Commerce, 1850), pp. 350–1, 370–96 and 406–7.

His souvenirs, written in 1849, only start in the year 1810; they are widely considered to be among the best French accounts of the Napoleonic era, although there are a number of verifiable errors in his account of Waterloo.

At Waterloo Lemonnier-Delafosse served as chief-of-staff to General Foy in the 9th Infantry Division of Reille's II Army Corps.

Lemonnier-Delafosse was a captain in the engineers who served in Saint Domingue (later Haiti) from 1803 to 1809. After the capitulation of the garrison to the British, he was repatriated to France at the end of 1809. On return he wished to continue to serve in the military engineers, but was posted captain in the 31st légère, who were then serving in Spain.

After having been involved in the preparations for Napoleon's marriage to Marie-Louise, he joined his regiment. As part of the Army of Portugal he fought at the battle of Busaco, where he was wounded. He described the fire of the British infantry thus, 'I admit that in my whole life I never saw it executed with such precision and speed.

Our first company of voltigeurs was completely destroyed.' He spent time in front of the lines of Torres Vedras and took part in the increasingly ignominious retreat back into Spain. He later fought on the Coa, after which he describes how his regiment was half destroyed in seven months almost without fighting. After a short time at the regimental depot, he hoped to enter the Imperial Guard, but claims that although the order was signed by Napoleon himself, it was subsequently lost and he found himself back in Spain with his own regiment. After some fighting with Mina's guerrillas, he fought the British again at Salamanca in 1812 and the following year was attached to the headquarters of General Clausel, being present at the battle of Sorauren on 28 July 1813. Later in the same year he became aide-de-camp to General Soult, the marshal's brother, who commanded a division of light cavalry. In this appointment he fought at the battle of Orthez and in 1814 at Toulouse. He continued to serve after the First Restoration and describes the flight of Louis XVIII on Napoleon's return. Made chef d'escadron *he became chief-of-staff to General Foy in 1815 and fought with him at Quatre Bras and Waterloo.*

Before we go to his account of Waterloo, it may be of interest to read his few words on the morale of the army.

Although the entire army was superb and full of enthusiasm, it was necessary to rejuvenate its head [its leaders]; but the emperor, blinded more than can be imagined by his memories and habits, made the mistake of putting it back under the command of its old chiefs. Most of them, despite their addresses to the king, had not ceased to wish for the success of the imperial cause; however, they did not appear prepared to serve with the ardour and devotion that was demanded by circumstances. These were no longer the men who, full of youth and ambition, risked their lives or rank and fame; these were men who were tired of war and who, having reached high rank, enriched by the spoils of the enemy or the generosity of Napoleon, had no other desire than to peacefully enjoy their fortunes in the shade of their laurels.

The colonels and generals entered their careers after them, trying to find places where they could benefit from their tutelage. The soldiers themselves were discontented, but this discontent did not alter their confidence in victory: Napoleon was at their head. The effect he exercised on the morale and courage of the soldiers was truly incomprehensible; a word, a gesture, sufficed to enthuse them and to make them confront the most terrible dangers with a blind joy. If he ordered a movement that seemed risky or useless to the good sense of the soldiers, they said, 'He knows what he is doing', and they rushed to their deaths with shouts of '*Vive l'empereur!*' ...

We now jump to his account of the battle. Here we see the account of an unapologetic admirer of Napoleon, who having blamed Wellington's luck for the loss of the battle, proceeds to stress the defeat of the British army and even names one of Wellington's aides-de-camp as providing evidence! He makes a number of dubious claims, not least of which was the capture of Hougoumont. Interestingly, he challenges Napoleon's assertion that a Prussian despatch was captured that betrayed the Prussian presence. He finishes his account of the battle by claiming that both the British and French were defeated and the Prussians alone were the victors! Despite all these and other rather dubious claims, it is still an account worth reading, including a number of interesting vignettes.

This same day [the 17th], the emperor, with 65,000 men, marched towards his left to approach I and II Corps [at Quatre Bras]; in the day we saw him arrive at the head of his columns, marching like us despite the rain that lasted twenty-four hours; the road was a veritable river, the ground to right and left not being any better. Thus the army marched along the only road possible, a road already ruined by the passage of the English army which we were following, and along which for two days it had travelled. Infantry, cavalry, artillery, etc., etc., in a single column, leaving the last corps in the most terrible mud; this state of things made the night of the 17th/18th deplorable.

Without losing time, the emperor wanted, from first thing in the morning, to attack the English where they stood, whilst Marshal Grouchy pursued the Prussians; some objected that the English army was still intact and ready to give battle, while our own troops, exhausted by the fighting and fatigue of Ligny, were no longer, perhaps, in a state to fight with vigour. So many objections were put to him that finally he consented to leave the army time to rest. Misfortune makes you timid; if, as otherwise, Napoleon had only listened to his inspirations and audacity, it is probable, it is certain, that he would have led his army to Brussels. What rest; a bivouac in the mud!

That evening the emperor made a reconnaissance of the enemy's position and said, 'If the English army remains there tomorrow, it is mine'. Never, it is fair to say, has a general displayed less science in his choice of battlefield. I speak not of the disposition of his troops, the deployment of his army was good, without doubt, but placed in front of a forest, Soignes, it was unable to manoeuvre and found itself stuck there like a strongpoint holding out until capitulation. The side of Merbre-Braine [*sic*], to the hamlet of Terre-la-Haie, gave him all the space necessary to establish his troops, but none in which it was possible to manoeuvre; his army was thus forced to fight solely on the ground he occupied; it was a great and dangerous decision! The English general was obviously convinced he would not be beaten, and consequently not required to have to retreat. And what a retreat it would have been, leaving the battlefield, suffering from inevitable disorder which defeat occasions, encumbered with materiel, the embarrassment of all armies, driven back into the forest, having only a few major openings ... What would have become of it? His army would have been forced to lay down its arms before it got to Brussels.

The emperor spoke the truth, he had quickly identified his enemy's fault, and with good reason did he say the day before the battle, and repeat on the morning of the 18th: 'This army is mine!'

But good luck, the true talisman of the Duke who, so many times had been successful, had only abandoned him for half a day ... cruel moment! ... and that one of his aides de camp, M. Hamilton, that I encountered and saw in Marseille in 1826, had informed me, my having then promised to write the truth on the battle of Waterloo ...

Did he keep his promise? This is what he told me:

On the evening of the 18th June, at five thirty [presumably in the afternoon], Lord Wellington, bare-headed, leaning against a tree, seeing without moving, his army beaten ... it was fleeing all around him ... overwhelmed by his desperation ... I saw tears in his eyes ... alone, around him at this moment, all his aides de camp carrying orders or killed, I was able to examine him closely ... This poor lord was painful to see, he was no longer a man ... plunged into desperate reflections, he was a statue in his stupor ... suddenly, we heard cannon to our left, in the direction of Vavre [*sic*: Wavre], he raised his head, listened and shouted, 'They are Prussian cannon ... SAVED!' [his capitals] ... And the man, the general, re-appeared. He rallied etc, you know what followed ...

The patriotism of M. Hamilton 'will have restrained his pen', but this suffices to make known that Lord Wellington was beaten before the arrival of the Prussians.

The night of the 17th to 18th seemed to predict the misfortunes of the day. A violent and uninterrupted rain did not allow the army to savour a single moment of rest. To exacerbate this misfortune, most of the soldiers, like the officers, were without food. However, they supported this double disgrace with good spirits, and at dawn, seeing the emperor, they announced to him by their repeated exclamations, that they were ready to steal a new victory for him. Towards eight o'clock, the sky retook its serenity, but Napoleon was still not able to deploy his army; the incessant rain had so waterlogged the ground that it was impossible to put a foot on it without transforming it into liquid mud.

On what depends the fate of a battle? Here it is the storm of twenty-four hours which destroyed all the combinations of a captain. Indeed, if the emperor had been able to start the battle at five o'clock in the morning, at midday Lord Wellington would have been beaten; was it not from midday to six o'clock in the evening? ... despite the faults and despite the state of the battlefield. We cannot deny it, and even the English confessed that the Prussians saved their army.

Before daylight on the 18th, the emperor was mounted; he thought that Lord Wellington, isolated from the Prussians, would not dare to hold his position ... one can see that Lord Wellington not only had his troops concentrated, but in position from the day before, while Napoleon, although having all his troops 'to hand', was not able to deploy them earlier than he did. As to the letter [the captured letter that informed Napoleon that the Prussians were marching to Waterloo], how could it have been intercepted? Blücher's couriers had no need to travel through our army to get to Wellington. This fact, besides, had it been true, would it have changed the state of the battlefield?

[He continues here talking about the comments of Marshal Marmont; but this has no relevance to our study and is omitted.]

On the 18 June 1815, at eleven-thirty, the whole army was in line and started the attack: deployed in a concave semi-circle, from the Hougoumont farm to Frischermont, it followed the form of a plateau occupied by the English army, which held Hougoumont and La Haye Sainte in front of the farm of Mont-Saint-Jean. One can see therefore, that it is wrong that this battlefield was called Waterloo, a village in front of the Soignes forest, a league and a quarter away, on ground where not a single musket shot was fired ... But Waterloo sounded better to the ear, had something more distinguished; and besides, it had been the headquarters of Lord Wellington.

Prince Jérôme Bonaparte's division (the 6th) with General Guilleminot, was engaged first at the Hougoumont farm, which was surrounded by tall trees, hedges, crenulated around the circumference of its walls, and with fortified gates it offered a vigorous resistance; its defence lasted a long time; it was taken, but promptly re-taken. It was fought hand-to-hand and the combat was terrible to both sides. The French division remained masters.

To the right of this division was that of General Foy (the 9th) deployed in line, having already conducted a movement forward of its batteries, which replied to those of the English, under whose fire it was exposed. Further to the right, Bachelu's division (the 5th), deployed the same, touching the main road. Behind and in reserve, was the brigade of carabiniers, on which fell all the balls that passed over us. To avoid their attention, this brigade moved towards the left, which provoked the mocking response of General Foy: 'Ah! Ah! The big heels do not like "le brutal"'. We received this fire stoically; they covered us with mud, and the soaked ground, showing the mark where they struck, made it look like a field that had been ploughed up by the wheels of a vehicle. This was good for our men, because many projectiles buried themselves or lost their power striking this muddy ground.

For four hours the general attack across the whole line continued without an advantage to either side; the enemy defended admirably. Suddenly, we saw a mass of cavalry pass between the lines, advancing, climbing the height of La Haye Sainte, making head of column to the left and making an all-out charge on the enemy batteries which lined the plateau, then arriving on one of them which consisted of sixty guns; all were taken, knocked over; but our cavalry, unsupported by infantry, were thrown back! ... It made a second charge, which had the same success, but the same final result for the same reason.

During these charges, the 6th Division with Foy's division had held the Hougoumont farm; their batteries were twice moved forwards and we asked ourselves: why are we not marching on the plateau; it required an order, and the one who had to give it, Marshal Ney, was occupied ... It was him who, with a brave and fiery élan, had led off all the cavalry, thinking that with them alone he could cut the English army in two and decide the victory: he had forgotten his infantry ... This immense charge of 20,000 cavalry, under which the ground trembled, had actually achieved the success that the marshal had wanted. Only the carabiniers had remained in reserve.

The centre of the English army had been forced, and its right flank beaten, and it would certainly have routed if the infantry of the left wing had arrived on the plateau! Our cavalry, for two hours, had achieved miracles, taken sixty guns, six colours, cut up four regiments, broken all the English lines; we lost there the élite of our intrepid cuirassiers, and that of the cavalry of the Guard; at this moment the enemy thought the battle was lost. History says that terror had reached Brussels, where numbers of fugitives had already arrived.

It was five thirty in the evening, and all the advantages were with the French army, when fortune had momentarily abandoned Wellington, came to his aid. Masses of troops appeared in the direction of Saint-Lambert and Jean-Loo. The Prussians had arrived, announced by cannons. The morale of the English general, like that of his army, returned, and we saw them rally, reform in line, and defend their batteries once more! ... It was General Ziethen, who, on his arrival in line, had taken the troops of Prince Saxe-Weimar for French and had forced them, after a lively fire, to abandon a village that they were defending. At this moment the emperor shouted 'Here is Grouchy, victory is ours!' ... Labédoyère, the emperor's aide de camp, rushed along the lines at the gallop, announcing Grouchy's arrival ... Shouts of '*En avant! En avant!*' greeting this news; but it needed orders, and these did not come! ...

My general was uncertain, anxious, wanting to know the truth of this news, so I asked him if I could go and establish the truth. Crossing the battlefield, I arrived at the extreme right where VI Corps, Lobau's, and the Young Guard were placed *en potence* were ready to oppose the enemy's movement. Was this Grouchy? I asked Servatius, adjutant-major in the Young Guard; 'Grouchy,' he said, 'looks as if he is white [a traitor]!' ... I then saw black masses leaving Ohain by Jean-Loo on Frischermont. It was Bülow and his Prussians marching against us, and who, if their movement on our right flank was not stopped, would arrive on the main Brussels road, before our centre and our left, who would not have time to retreat! ...

Returning to my general, he realised the truth of the news and in his grief he shouted, 'Horrible! Horrible! ... Silence!'

The third cavalry charge again took the plateau; but repulsed, it had to abandon it. At this moment, a brigade of English cavalry made a charge between Marshal Ney and La Haye Sainte, breaking the 4th Division which occupied it; this movement cut our line and caused disorder which spread ... It was mended when the Prussian cannons redoubled their fire. All the eyes of the army turned towards the right, and every soldier was then able to realise the result of Bülow's movement.

Marshal Ney, by a fourth charge, wanted to re-take the plateau and the immense battery of sixty guns, was thrown back again, now had our infantry march; it was too late! ... why did it not march with the second charge! Nevertheless, Guilleminot's [i.e. Joseph's] division remained in possession of the Hougoumont farm; those of Bachelu and Foy, formed in squares, in echelon, moved off, courageously climbed the slopes of the plateau under redoubled fire of the enemy's artillery and infantry, which, seeing themselves rescued, defended the approaches vigorously. The square of Bachelu's division was to our right and a little bit further advanced than that of General Foy. At musket range, the general tapped me on the shoulder and said to me, to show he still had hope, 'Tomorrow in Brussels and promoted colonel by the emperor!' I smiled at these words, and, in response, I pointed out Bachelu's square; it had one of its faces deployed and only formed a triangle, whose base began to drift! ... Keep going and make it better. At this moment, we were struck at close range by infantry fire joined by that of artillery, totally rocking our squares; that of the right broke up, its men taking flight. Ours, ruined by the same fire, followed its example, and, quicker than saying it, all ran off on their own account obliging us to follow them, without being able to stop them! ... All was finished! This was the last effort of infantry, which, employed too late, were no longer strong enough to take the plateau and the sixty guns which defended it.

This fine cavalry, blasted four times, had suffered immense losses and one hoped that infantry could repair its defeat. The impetuosity of Marshal Ney lost all; to provide its last charge, he had even taken the reserve cavalry of the Imperial Guard ... This was not the emperor's intention; when he noticed that it followed the movement of Kellerman's cuirassiers, behind which it was deployed in second line, he sent it the order to stop; but the order arrived too late; it was already engaged and thus Napoleon found himself, at six o'clock in the evening, deprived of his cavalry reserve, this reserve which, well employed, had so many times given him victory!

Close to one of the hedges of Hougoumont, without even a drummer to beat the rally, we re-assembled, under the enemy's fire, three hundred men; it was about all that remained of our fine division. There, gathered up the generals; Reille, whose horse had been killed under him, in the middle of us; d'Erlon, Bachelu, Foy, Jamin, etc. All, sullen and sad as the defeated, said, 'This is all that remains of my army corps, of my division, of my brigade ...'. We had seen fall Duhesme, Pelet-de-Morvan, Michel, generals who had found a glorious death! My General Foy had a ball pass through his shoulder; of his headquarters, two officers remained to him, Cabour-Duhay and I; his nephew (Foy's) had been wounded on the 16th. Fate had spared me in the middle of such dangers; my horse alone, killed by a bullet, had rolled me on the ground; it was at this moment, while I waited for my orderly to bring a second, I noticed on the pack of a dead soldier, some bread. Pressed by need, I took it; a pocket contained butter, I had no need of a knife to spread it; I devoured it, this was the right word, as for two days I had had only beer to nourish me. The men and animals were (particularly in the headquarters) in the same situation; the horse which had carried me had not had its bridle off since the morning of the 17th and had positively only lived off grain that he had grabbed on passing through the fields ... where had he got the energy he maintained? It is necessary to have been in action on a horse to understand; there he animated himself as much as his master: noble animal, his head raised, he inhales, he drinks in the powder smoke; he throws himself forward, like on a hunt and goes on until he falls!

What happened to our divisions on the left wing had also happened along the whole line; the movement of Bülow and his cavalry, suddenly flooding the battlefield, had demoralised our soldiers, who, seeing their retreat cut, retreated without orders.

Hardly, because of the arrival of darkness, had we taken a short rest, than the English cavalry prepared to come down from the plateau; it was eight o'clock. It was necessary to leave this place with what remained of our division. My general sent me forward as a sentry, to come and warn him the moment when this cavalry charged; a half-battery was still in position. The officer said to me:

'I have four rounds of canister; I shall fire them at the enemy then I will come out of action and depart ...'

It was said that there were shouts of 'Save yourselves!' I am sure that I did not hear them, although in the middle of the fugitives; to the contrary, their silence was complete, which was even worse, and I would have preferred some shouts to give life to these masses. Never had the French army been more completely beaten than on this day; it had achieved prodigies of valour, and without the night, the soldier, seeing the emperor, would have rallied. What men! ... how many like the one that I found sitting, at the moment when we tried to rally them: it was a grenadier to whom I appealed, reproaching him for his rest; black with powder, covered in mud, his legs spread, exhausted, soaked with sweat, but still holding his musket; he was motionless. Encouraged to rejoin his comrades he showed me his weapon, his hands, and said to me, 'They have, with this, used more than twenty packets of cartridges; it is more than my share; I have taken those of the dead ... Leave me to die here, on the battlefield! ... I cannot move; it is not courage that I am lacking, it is strength!' At these words, he spread out on the ground saying, 'All is finished! Poor France!' I left him, tears rolling from my eyes. Another, at the first shots, carried back on some muskets, having had both legs taken off by a ball, passed before the division, that was formed in line, shouted out, 'This is nothing comrades; *Vive l'Empereur*! Glory to France!'

Thus the right wing, like the left, had followed the movement of the centre. What remained to cover the retreat after such a collapse?

The four battalions of the Old Guard ... It was in one of its squares that the emperor and his headquarters, Soult, Bertrand, Drouot, Corbineau, de Flahaut, Gourgaud, found a place. Napoleon wanted to die there! ... If he had achieved this, what great sorrow he would have been spared, but Marshal Soult, seizing the bridle of his horse, led him away saying, 'Sire, have they not been happy enough?' He took him away and led him to Charleroi. I got these words from General Gourgaud himself, who was present at this cruel moment. He repeated them to me in December 1839, when he was inspector general and had come to Mézières, where I was in command of the fortress.

It was in this square, commanded by General Cambrone [*sic*], that was made the famous response to the summations of the English and which history has made famous: 'The Guard dies and does not surrender!' The truth, that of the true soldier, a beaten soldier, paints a better picture, in a single word, the anger of the defeat of these colossi of glory, victors until then of all nations and who, in the times to come, had the admiration of the people.

A sergeant of my old regiment (31st *légère*) who had passed into the Guard, told me that it was a lie to cite these words of General Cambrone, that the truth, heard by him, who was close to him, were: '*Merde*, I do not surrender!'

... Was Cambrone a man to make poetry on the battlefield? No, not him, neither has anyone ever done so ...

Lord Wellington and Bülow had become peaceful possessors of the battlefield; they crossed it as masters. But with how much blood was this unjust victory bought!

Never had the French struck their adversaries with more formidable and murderous blows. Eager for blood and glory, despising dangers and death, they threw themselves audaciously on the flaming batteries of the enemy and seemed to multiply in number to go to find it, attack it, pursue it in the inaccessible entrenchments. 30,000 English or Prussians were destroyed on this fatal day, and when one thinks that this horrible carnage was the work of 50,000 men (10,000 of the Guard took no part in the action), after two battles, dying of fatigue and need, and struggling across muddy ground against an impregnable position and 130,000 combatants, one is seized with a painful admiration and give the palm of victory to the vanquished.

This brave and valiant Guard fell on the enemy with shouts of '*Vive l'Empereur!*' It was beaten for the first time, but it made a massacre ... We recognised in its blows the victors of Austerlitz, of Jena, of Wagram, of Montmirail; the English and the Prussians, who suspended their victory songs, united against this handful of heroes and shot them down! . . . Some, covered with wounds, fell drowning in their blood; others, more fortunate, were killed ... Others, finally, who death was still awaiting, shot themselves between them so as not to survive their comrades in arms or to die at the hands of their enemies. If God conserved some, they were the unfortunate ones, witness my brave sergeant, who cried warm tears when telling me of these last moments of combat. This brave soldier, who was thrown out of the ranks as a brigand of Waterloo! Alas! Was he alone? We, officers, were we too not designated as such throughout the restoration?

At eight o'clock in the evening of the 18th, the noble remains of the Old Guard were all the more exposed to total destruction as from second to second the road became more obstructed and despite the order that these braves maintained, they had all the trouble in the world to squeeze a route ...

Infantry, cavalry, artillery, all marched mixed together, closed up in a mass. The drivers of the artillery train and the equipages, in order to flee quicker, cut the traces to their horses, abandoned vehicles and guns, around which the gunners, those model soldiers, still conserved their post, but the situation finished with them having to leave.

Can we imagine 40,000 men on a single road, stopping in masses! It was the rock driving back the torrent, but which, giving in to force, finished by being driven along with it in masses tumbled along by each other, destroying each other in their masses! One could not take this path without danger; also the generals, together close to the hedge at Hougoumont, went across the fields: General Foy alone remained with his three hundred men gathered together on the battlefield, and put himself at their head for the march, leaving me on sentry. It was only towards nine o'clock that the English cavalry descended from the hill, covering the masses of infantry formed in square; it appeared *en fourrageurs* [in a cloud: i.e. not in a formed unit] before the fine brigade of carabiniers, which had not been committed during the day.

From the point that I occupied I could see the infantry that the carabiniers, more in the open, could not see; I rushed to inform them when suddenly I saw them charge all the English *fourrageurs* who, escaping through the intervals between the squares, allowed them to open fire. The carabiniers, arriving on these redoubts made of men, without hesitation, were broken by fire at half range! Forced to turn about to go and reform, their courage was unbroken and successive charges, unfortunately without success, proved it; but they reduced this brigade to less than three squadrons; three hundred men! What a spectacle, seeing these fine men dismounted, wounded, retiring from the battlefield, hampered by their cuirasses, stuck in the mud, where they left their large boots so as not to be taken like birds in glue. The last efforts of the army were made by the carabiniers.

An extraordinary battle, the only one where two sides were defeated, the English first, and then the French! A battle which the Prussians alone won, arriving fresh and rested on the field of the struggle, whereas the French were exhausted by twelve hours of fighting. Chance and the Prussians, here are the true victors. I do not want to speak again of what happened the day before the battle, nor he [Grouchy] that did not come on the day it was given! God will judge!

The battlefield, because of the fatality which had weighed on our army, thus belonging to our enemies; I say enemies because it was not Lord Wellington that won; his defence was obstinate, but he was forced off, beaten, and so positively, that if he had only joined Blücher at the farm of la Belle-Alliance, where he threw himself into his arms like that of a saviour! For it was Blücher who was the master of the battlefield, and him alone, before the English army had descended from their heights.

Thus it was not courage that was lacking in the French army, it was patience; the impetuous audacity of Marshal Ney, brave but rash, who committed, without the emperor's order, all of the cavalry and even the reserves of the Imperial Guard, in order to break the English batteries.

During the first charge of our cavalry, one squadron of the 1st Cuirassiers which had advanced too far, did not turn about like the rest of its column, but continuing its charge, it was obliged to move through the centre of the English army as far as its right! Breaking through everything in its way, it was able to surmount all obstacles and to leave the ground occupied by the enemy to rejoin us at some distance on our left. One suddenly saw smoke rise like that from a haystack or pile of straw that is on fire; one ran there and saw fifteen to eighteen cuirassiers ... men and horses were cut-up ... covered in blood, black with mud, just a shapeless mass ... a *sous-lieutenant* alone had brought these men back along this perilous journey, deadly, through most of an army! The horses were covered in sweat and the smoke that we had noticed was nothing more than the water vapour rising from their bodies ... The officer, when he was questioned, said that his *chef d'escadron*, too closely engaged to turn about, ordered a manoeuvre that offered as much danger as advancing, calling out, 'Victory or death!' ... eighty cuirassiers and three officers as well as himself remained dead on the battlefield! ... But what a terrible charge!

[*He then proceeds to analyse Wellington as a military commander and describe the French retreat. However, before finishing he tells an interesting story that is worth adding.*]

It may be useful to return my readers to our battlefield to indicate the location and situation of the emperor at one o'clock on the 18 June 1815.

Sent back to have the reserve battery of our division moved forwards, I found it like all the others on the main road, the only ground on which they were able to travel before moving onto impractical ground. The time [to move off the road] had come, but the queue of 200 guns with their materiel was long; I thus awaited our reserve and found myself at the foot of a mound on which the emperor was located throughout the battle. A mound to the left of the main road to Brussels, between the farm of Caillou and Rossome [*sic*], opposite Barrière, and for half an hour I was able to watch him and consider him.

Sitting on a chair of straw, before a crude farm table, his map was lying open, his famous telescope in his hand was often pointed at various points of the battle. To rest his eyes, he picked up wheat straws which he used as tooth-picks. To his left, Marshal Soult, alone, awaited his orders and ten paces to the rear was all his headquarters, mounted. To approach the emperor more easily, some engineers had made ramps around the perimeter of the mound.

Never had I seen such great calm, more perfect, than that of Napoleon on the day of this battle; gazing over his army which already, for two hours, had attacked and repulsed the enemy along the whole line; one could see the satisfaction painted on his features, everything was going well and no doubt that at that moment he thought the battle won. I admired him for a long time, my eyes would not leave him, he was a genius of war.

I finally left with our artillery and I never saw him again; I always have this last souvenir in my mind!

Lieutenant Théobald Puvis

Extract from his *Souvenirs du chef de bataillon Théobald Puvis, du 93ème de ligne (1813–1815)*, reproduced in *Journal de route d'un garde d'honneur (1813–1814)* (Paris: Demi-Solde, 2007), pp. 83–6.

In 1815 Puvis served as a lieutenant in the 93rd de ligne which was commanded by Chef de Bataillon *Massot, part of the 1st Brigade (Tissot) of the 9th Infantry Division (Foy), of Reille's II Army Corps.*

Théobald Puvis came from a respectable family in Besancon; his father was a justice of the peace. In 1812, after the disaster of Russia and the rebuilding of the French army, he realised that there was a good chance that he would be conscripted along with his brother. In an effort to spare his brother he volunteered to attend the Saint Cyr military school early in 1813; at that time it was a three-year course. However, the urgency of finding sufficient officers for the new regiments meant that many were taken before they had completed the course. Although he had been a somewhat reluctant volunteer, it appears that he was disappointed not to be chosen amongst those who were sent first to the army. However, due to the losses of the 1813 campaign in November of that year a second group to be commissioned as sous-lieutenant *were called for. This time he was nominated, and, given the option of choosing a regiment, he chose the 93rd de ligne who were in garrison in the town where he went to school. He was subsequently disappointed to find out that those who did not get their preferences were sent to the Young Guard regiments that were being raised. He records that he left Saint Cyr in January 1814, but does not mention any service during the campaign. It seems, although he does not state it, that he was on half pay on Napoleon's return from Elba, as Marshal Ney, who he found at Besacon, told him that the 77th de ligne [the number given to his old regiment after the First Restoration] would arrive the next day. Ney led all those regiments that he had been able to gather to Paris to join Napoleon. The 77th re-took its old number; the 93rd. He says little of Quatre Bras, portraying it as little more than a skirmish. His regiment did not suffer too much at Waterloo compared to many others; on 21 June, of the 2,000 men that made up the four battalions of the regiment, 1,200 were still with the colours, although the 4th Battalion had not fought at Waterloo (they were the guard for the parks) and were therefore probably close to full strength. The regiment made its way back to Paris, was sent south of the Loire after the capitulation of Paris, and Puvis' account finishes with the disbandment of his regiment and his return home.*

Puvis only speaks of his own personal experiences and although there is rather thin detail on his regiment's attacks around Hougoumont, it gives a good feel for how the actions of II Corps seemed isolated from the rest of the battle until the retreat. He gives a good account of how quickly French morale collapsed at the end of the battle.

On the morning of the 18th, soaked by the night's rain, we left our bivouacs and the emperor's proclamation was read out to us; 'The English army is before us and we go to attack it'. The whole army was massed in front of Genappe; the rain did not cease. For six hours we remained in our positions that had the Brussels road on our right and we deployed to march in battle formation. The rye through which we marched was so high that our bayonets hardly rose above it and we could see nothing around us! All the ground we crossed was waterlogged; on the higher ground the enemy's balls began to reach us. On our right we could see a sort of knoll on which the emperor stood, surrounded by his headquarters.

As we advanced, the artillery fire directed against us became heavier. Arriving in a fold in the ground a little lower down, we stopped behind a hedge. General Reille who commanded II Corps under Marshal Ney's command, remained in our midst during the time that we remained stationary in this position. The cannon fire got even heavier. 'We are going to attack the English lines with the bayonet', our senior officers came to tell us, 'warn everyone' it was recommended to us. It was two o'clock when we marched forward; the enemy appeared to be no longer before us.

We were sent out in skirmish order into a tall wood which was to our left; we approached a large building (the farm of Hougoumont), fortified at all points and protected besides by very high hedges with deep ditches. We crossed some ditches, which were rather less wide, and arrived at a hedge that was vigorously defended by the enemy. We tried to get through this hedge in vain. We suffered enormous casualties; the lieutenant of my company was killed close to me. A ball struck the visor of my shako and knocked me onto my backside. The shock was such that I thought I had been wounded; but there was no blood. I recovered my senses immediately. At this moment, I was to the right of the company, the captain followed the movement more to the left.

Marshal Ney rushed up to us on horseback, he was alone, without an escort, and bareheaded. I was the closest officer to him; he sent me with the order for the 100th Regiment that was about a hundred paces behind us, to move to support us; and throughout this movement he stayed with us. We could not take the position. 'It needs cannon', the older officers who had arrived said to him.

Other units had been able to penetrate the position but could not maintain themselves there. The fate of the battle, the prolonged and vigorous enemy action had exhausted us on this flank and allowed him time to receive the support that he had awaited; for without this, over the three hours, the out-come of all the other points of the battlefield had been favourable to us. Relieved by the 100th Regiment who had entered the line in front of us, we had pulled back a little to reform our ranks in a little cover.

Of our three battalion commanders, only one remained. Like the two others, the lieutenant colonel that commanded the regiment had been wounded, as well as General Foy, our divisional commander.

Whilst we reformed our ranks, we heard a lively cannonade on our right and rear. 'That is ominous', our officers said; at the same time we received the order to retreat, to be executed *en échiquier*. We had not marched for a quarter of an hour, when some cuirassiers rushed up to us and pressed us to form square; the English cavalry fell on us. Exhausted and considerably reduced by our losses, the square that our three battalions was able to form did not appear very solid; the English cavalry passed close to us without attacking, but it carried on to fall on the Imperial Guard. Immediately that it had passed us, we pushed on to reach the point where we expected to find our reserves.

The ranks then broke up to get there quicker. There was a terrible dis-order. However, we still thought that it was only our left wing that had suf-fered a check; we could see over on our right deep masses marching ahead. But arriving to link up with the road that we had left in the morning, and where we had our artillery reserve, the same area where our fourth battalion had remained to protect it, instead of the security that we had expected, we were received by a volley from the Prussian army that had arrived on our rear and thus changed the outcome of the battle.

From this moment the ranks broke up; we threw ourselves in disorder across the countryside where we fell into each other in our desperation. It was then eight o'clock and we saw by the light of the fire of the Guard artillery that on this side the struggle continued. But we were pursued relentlessly and rallying even a few men to try and meet these attacks was impossible.

Sergeant-Major Sylvain Larreguy de Civrieux

Souvenirs d'un cadet (1812–1823) (Paris: Hachette, 1912), pp. 166–71.

During the Waterloo campaign, Larreguy de Civrieux served as sergeant-major in the 93rd de ligne, the same regiment as Lieutenant Puvis. The regiment belonged to the 1st Brigade (Tissot) of Foy's 9th Infantry Division, part of Reille's II Army Corps.

Sylvain Larreguy de Civrieux had been born into the minor nobility of the Basque region of France, but the family had been ruined by the French Revolution. Much to the horror of his parents, he volunteered for the army in 1813, aged only seventeen. He describes himself then as 'skinny and weak'. He joined the 116th Line Regiment who were fighting in Spain, but his officers, considering him incapable of bearing long marches, often had his pack carried with their baggage. He fought in the siege of Tarragona and around Villafranca. Although clearly an inadequate soldier, he was quickly promoted to corporal because he could read and write and soon after, for the same reason, to sergeant-major. Part of Suchet's forces, he fought successfully against the British at Ordal in September 1813, where his battalion took a leading role. In 1814 his unit was marched back into France and defended Lyons against the invading Austrian forces. After Napoleon's abdication, the 116th were amalgamated with the 93rd de ligne and re-numbered the 77th. On the emperor's return, Sylvain's regiment was part of Marshal Ney's forces that marched against Napoleon as he approached Paris, and like most of the army, enthusiastically changed sides. In the reorganisation of the army after Napoleon had retaken the throne, the 77th retook their old number, the 93rd and were part of General Foy's division of Reille's II Corps. At Quatre Bras, Sylvain fought in the Bossu wood, but gives little detail of the fighting there. At Waterloo, although only nineteen years old, he was considered an experienced soldier.

Larreguy de Civrieux's account was written long after the event and he has thus included much detail that he would not have known at the time. Like the II Corps' eyewitnesses we have already heard from, there is little real detail on the fighting around the château; but on the ground it must have been impossible to have an overall feel for the fighting much beyond their own location, and in the Hougoumont wood where many of them found themselves, they could probably see little more than just a few yards.

The night of the 17th/18th June was terrible. A violent rain had soaked the ground; it was impossible for us to light a fire, even to cook. Our bivouacs were scattered with beef and mutton cut up by our sabres but that we were unable to cook. The distribution of bread was still awaited; we lay in the water. But such was our fatigue that we slept deeply under torrents of rain.

On the morning of the 18th, the English appeared on the heights, defended by a triple wall of cannon and very imposing forces.

Early, Napoleon called his generals for a council of war. A wide spread of opinion was voiced. The emperor ordered a frontal attack. The enemy, having his centre on the village of Mont-Saint-Jean, was supported on the right by the fortified farm of Hougoumont, to the left of that of La Haye Sainte. From woods, from cuttings, an immense artillery and 90,000 men defended this formidable position.

My division, and that of Prince Jérôme, were deployed in front of Hougoumont. The emperor, with his headquarters, were placed on a small mound close to the farm of la Belle Alliance, from where he could oversee the two armies.

It was an imposing spectacle that affected those of this great duel soon to be joined by 200,000 men, on which history has bestowed the name of Waterloo. I was hardly nineteen years old; but I had endured many ordeals, taken part in some terrible fighting that I had every right, it seemed to me, to range myself amongst the old soldiers of the army. Would I survive this memorable day? I thought affectionately of my mother, of each of my family.

At half past midday, the signal was given by a cannon shot. The division of Jérôme was pushed against the farm of Hougoumont; the fire of artillery and musketry was engaged along a line of more than two leagues. My regiment remained for a long time in a critical position; out of range of the musketry, it suffered from the enemy artillery. The balls reached us after an occasional ricochet from a fold in the ground which allowed us to distinguish the arc the projectiles took before decimating our ranks. Our true courage was there put to a rude proof; and it is very trying to wait in such conditions, death in the most complete inaction, surrounded by death and horribly mutilated bodies. Prince Jérôme, who came for a moment having communicated with the emperor, seeing at every second the bravest officers of his suite succumb around him, Prince Jérôme remarked that much blood would have been spared, if someone would have advanced us several hundred paces towards the enemy. This advice was followed, and from then, indeed, the balls whistled over our heads, always ploughing up the place we had occupied. But this moment of reprieve did not last long. The division of the King of Westphalia [Prince Jérôme] had disappeared under the enemy's fire; Foy's division was sent to replace it under the batteries of Hougoumont. Around this farm were heaps of thousands of dead, wounded and dying, which we soon doubled in number, mown down in our turn by the English and Scottish fusillade from their fortified positions.

Before reaching this terrible butchery, the order was given to leave the eagles in the rear under guard of the sergeant majors. My comrades and I refused to obey this order and this disobedience, in the face of such certain peril earned us the admiration of our regiments.

Here I should be able to describe these terrible scenes of carnage. Soon we had our feet bathed in blood: in less than half an hour, our ranks were reduced by more than half. Each stoically awaited death or horrible wounds. We were covered in splashes of blood; and yet our courage rose to the highest exaltation. Not a wounded man left the field of battle; not a dying man gave his final sign without a thought of devotion to the emperor. My captain, shot through by two balls and losing blood, never ceased to excite us by his failing voice, until when he fell in the middle of this immortal slaughter.

After the most stubborn slaughter, we remained masters of the wood and orchards. A superhuman effort would be required to capture Mont-Saint-Jean and La Haye Sainte, which were taken and retaken a number of times by us and the enemy. Everywhere at last we were victorious when the Prussian corps of Bülow, escaping from Marshal Grouchy, debouched abruptly on our right and changed the situation and the outcome of the battle. The English rallied and attacked in their turn. The most horrible combat started; but Bülow advanced and we were caught between two fires. A new corps, that of Ziethen, appeared behind our right wing. For a minute we believed that it was Grouchy's army; our courage was restored. The emperor demanded a final effort. Labédoyèye came up in his name and directed Reille to fall on the enemy's right wing; Ney hastened up with us and four battalions of the Young [Old] Guard. But suddenly, the Prussian army, which had completed its move up behind us and which we had taken for the corps of Grouchy, opened a terrible artillery fire on us.

The army was struck by a sudden demoralisation. Shouts of '*Sauve qui peut! À la trahison!*' were heard; the rout became general. All discipline disappeared; the regiments fell into an inexpressible disorder, forming disordered masses of men who were ploughed in all senses by the enemy's cannon.

Two or three times, the Prince de la Moskowa [Ney], dismounted, without aides-de-camp, without servants, appeared to us, sword in hand, bare-headed, marching with difficulty, embarrassed by his big boots in this slippery and soaked ground from the rain the day before. His brilliant voice succeeded in rallying a handful of soldiers; but what could this illustrious and unhappy warrior achieve against so many enemies and in this chaos! Vainly he searched for death. Death, so common on this sad day, did not want the brave Ney; it preserved this great victim for French hands.

A single square still remained on this vast field of carnage; it was formed by the Old Guard, and it was in this living bastion that rapidly shrank, that the emperor placed himself. He also vainly wished to die. The entreaties of the generals, as well as the valiant soldiers, determined him to leave. He passed close to us. In the tragic evening which was falling, I saw disappear forever, the conqueror of Europe; he had fallen ...

The rout continued. Our disordered masses fired on each other. The wagons, the artillery, rushed along the main road, crushing and flattening in their cuirasses the dead and dying of a regiment of cuirassiers who, forgotten in their position, had been annihilated without a murmur, along with those of the 4th Battalion of my regiment.

2nd Cavalry Division

Lieutenant J.L. Henckens

Mémoires se rapportant à son service militaires au 6e régiment de chasseurs à cheval Français de 1803 à 1816 (La Haye, 1910).

During the Waterloo campaign, Henckens served as adjutant-major in the élite company of the 6th Chasseurs à Cheval of Piré's division, under command of Colonel Faudouas. This regiment belonged to the 1st Brigade (Huber) of the 2nd Cavalry Division (Piré), part of Reille's II Corps.

Henckens was born in 1780 in a small village near Aix-en-Chapelle (modern Aachen). His father was the mayor of the village which was later integrated into France by the Treaty of Lunéville in 1801. Conscripted into the infantry in 1803, he paid for a replacement so that he could join the cavalry. He was incorporated into the 6th Chasseurs à Cheval in Berne. From 1804 to the beginning of 1812 Henckens was based exclusively on the Italian peninsula. However, he took part in the invasion of Naples in 1806, operated against the Calabrian rebels in 1807 and marched north and fought at Wagram in 1809. In 1812 his regiment finally left Italy and marched into northern Germany to take part in the invasion of Russia. By this time Henckens was adjutant of his regiment. He fought at Borodino and Maloyaroslavetz and despite not being an officer, formed part of the Sacred Squadron formed of unattached officers whose regiments had disbanded. In 1813 he was present at Lützen, but took no part in the battle, but did fight at Bautzen where he had his horse killed under him. In September of that year he was finally commissioned into his own regiment after ten years' service in the ranks. The following month he fought at Leipzig where he was wounded on the first day by a ball which passed through his heel. He was allowed home to recover; the first time he had returned in his ten years of service. He rejoined his regiment in December 1813. In January 1814 he was sent to the regimental depot where he remained until Napoleon's abdication; thus taking no part in the campaign of France. He took part in the grand re-entry of Louis XVIII into Paris and as the colonel (Talhouët) became something of a favourite of the Duke of Berry, the regiment was quickly brought up to full strength. It seems that he transferred his allegiance from the king back to Napoleon without too much soul searching and served with a new colonel (Talhouët chose not to serve Napoleon again and took retirement). In the Waterloo campaign the 6th Chasseurs à Cheval saw heavy fighting at Quatre Bras where they acquitted themselves well and though they were present at Waterloo they held the extreme left of the French army and saw little action. Henckens remained with his regiment during the retreat to Paris and on the 2nd July they took a major part in the defeat of the Prussian advance guard at Rocquencourt. After the regiment was disbanded he tried, but failed, to enter the Netherlands army with his

French rank. In 1817 he was offered a commission as a second lieutenant in the hussars that the government was sending to the Indies; he declined. In February 1818 he joined the cuirassiers as a private as the regiment had a number of officers that he knew. He was made a non-commissioned officer after two months and a month later applied for and got a post as sergeant in the gendarmerie. By the Revolution of 1830 he was a lieutenant in the gendarmerie having served for twelve years. In 1831 the new provisional Belgian government offered him the post of lieutenant colonel of the 2nd Belgian Chasseurs à Cheval, but, unsure about the future of an independent Belgium, he eventually, and reluctantly, turned it down. He retired as a captain of the gendarmerie in 1846.

Henckens' regiment had fought hard at Quatre Bras and had suffered heavy casualties. At Waterloo, they fulfilled the classic light cavalry task of flank protection. After their experiences at Quatre Bras I suspect the regiment was grateful not to have been involved in heavy fighting during the battle and he describes only skirmishing.

[On the evening of 17 June] As it was necessary to await the arrival of the other arms, we occupied the ground that we had arrived on; as we were not able to rely on a distribution of rations, we counted on contributions from the immediate locality; however, these were already exhausted. Towards nightfall we had received enough rations and forage for the following day.

There was no means for us, or our horses, to lay on the waterlogged ground, so that I passed the night of the 17th to the 18th against my horse, which also preferred to sleep standing up rather than lying down. It rained on and off, and the bivouac fires were quickly extinguished.

On the morning of the 18th, the plain was so soaked that, although the weather had become superb, it was not possible to move; we awoke immediately when the dawn and the mists that rose from the ground permitted us to see; men and horses refreshed themselves as well as possible and to scrape the mud off as best they could. We then awaited whatever was asked of us.

The order was given that Piré's division was to be the extreme left of the position at nine o'clock and that we were to come under the orders of General Reille; we were not in a state to make a charge as a complete entity; we only skirmished to disengage the infantry of the I [II] Army Corps; in one of these skirmishes I lost my second horse, so that I had only what the *peloton* had to offer me.

On the evening of the 18th, Piré's division remained level with the Imperial Guard that we supported as much as it was in our ability to do so; there were several sabre blows exchanged, but we were not shaken. Night came, we retreated by Quatre Bras on Charleroi, where we arrived on the 19th between 5 and 6am; General Piré had disappeared during the night.

Chapter 2

VI Army Corps

Introduction

Lobau's VI Corps was the smallest of the three army corps. It had hardly reached the battlefield of Ligny on 16 June and had remained uncommitted in reserve. After Ligny, Teste's 21st Infantry Division was attached to Grouchy's pursuit of the Prussians, leaving the corps with just two weak divisions to fight at Waterloo; it had been the only army corps to have started the campaign without a light cavalry division attached to it. However, during the battle it was supported by two light cavalry divisions (Domon and Subervie) that had been attached to Napoleon's army from Grouchy's force that was pursuing the Prussians. It started the battle in reserve, concentrated behind the centre of the French position closed up in mass astride the main road. Fundamental to Napoleon's accounts of the battle are that he knew of the Prussian approach before the battle started. In his account printed in the *Moniteur* it states, 'VI Corps with the cavalry of d'Aumont [Domon], under the orders of Count Lobau, was designated to move to the rear of our right to oppose a Prussian corps'. However, in Gourgaud's account it says, 'VI Corps was Count Lobau's, formed in close column on the right of the Charleroi road: by this means it was in reserve behind the left of I Corps, and in potence [*en potence*] behind the centre of the first line'. Although Lobau, a fiercely loyal adherent of Napoleon, did not write of the battle, we have two well-placed witnesses to help us understand the deployment and mission of VI Corps; we shall hear from them first.

Adjutant-Commandant Janin

Janin, *Campagne de Waterloo, ou Remarques Critiques et Historiques sur l'Ouvrage du Général Gourgaud* (Paris: Chaumerot Jeune Librairie, 1820), pp. 30–7.

During the Waterloo campaign, Janin served as adjutant-commandant *(colonel), deputy chief-of-staff of VI Army Corps which was commanded by Lieutenant General Count Lobau.*

Janin was commissioned from the École Polytechnique in 1799 and was on the way to join the expedition to Egypt when he was wounded in a skirmish with British ships en route. He fought against the Austrians in 1805 and against the Prussians the following year. After tours in Poland and Spain, he was captured at Wagram. He was promoted chef de batallion *in 1809 and served in command of a march regiment in Portugal in 1810, assisting at the sieges of Ciudad Rodrigo and Almeida. In 1813 he commanded the 3rd and 4th battalions of the 23rd* légère *as major, and was lightly wounded at Lützen and Bautzen. He became chief-of-staff of the 45th Infantry Division and became a prisoner of war at the capitulation of Dresden. Released and put into retirement in 1814, he re-entered service on Napoleon's return. He commanded a division of National Guards for a short time before his move to VI Corps headquarters.*

At Waterloo, Janin served as adjutant-commandant, sous-chef de l'état-major *(deputy chief-of-staff) of VI Corps which was commanded by Count Lobau. He claims to have been the chief-of-staff of VI Corps, but this was only after the true chief-of-staff, General Durieux (or Durrieu), was wounded quite early in the battle, as he describes himself. During the battle he was wounded by three sabre blows to the head, was captured and imprisoned in England. After a period of retirement after the Second Restoration he served in various relatively minor appointments, but eventually reached the rank of* maréchal de camp. *He died in 1847.*

As can be seen from the title of the pamphlet written by Janin, it was written in response to Gourgaud's history of the campaign which was published on his return from St Helena where he had shared Napoleon's exile. One of the key issues in French accounts of the battle is the extent to which Napoleon was surprised by the arrival of the Prussians, which Janin addresses. He clearly describes VI Corps being taken unawares by their arrival and the changing of VI Corps' mission from supporting the attack of I Corps to countering the Prussian advance. Napoleon claims he was well aware of their impending arrival, as described in the first volume of this series, and had taken appropriate measures to counter it; including the early deployment of VI Corps. Of course, it is possible that Janin was unaware of what orders Lobau had received from Napoleon and the extent to which he chose to keep these orders from his subordinates. Janin's account also offers a new and credible reason why the Hougoumont wood needed to be secured; not purely as a diversionary attack as it is so often described.

On the 17th, after having, as I have already said, lost much time in assuring itself of the Prussian retreat, the army that had fought them divided into two parts: the right, under the orders of General Grouchy, went in their pursuit, and the centre, joining the corps of Marshal Ney, moved towards the English, who we attacked in front of Genappe. An affair of the advance-guard, of little importance, marked this day, during which a rain storm rendered the roads very bad and the march very tiring. In the evening the army bivouacked in the presence of the English army which was in the position that General Gourgaud describes perfectly. If Napoleon had been able to attack it this same evening, the chances were in his favour, but the state of the roads and above all, the slowness with which [the army] had left the position at Ligny, did not allow it. However, we cannot disagree that fortune declared against him; the rain continued to fall in torrents throughout the night; this bivouac was extremely painful. A great number of soldiers abandoned it to go to find shelter in the houses which were closest to the camp.

This circumstance, by holding up the assembly of the troops and perhaps also the arrival of the ammunition caissons, contributed to postpone the attack ordered for eight o'clock but which did not start until midday. In the morning I had been sent to the advance-posts to reconnoitre the enemy position. The English line formed a curve whose inside was opposite us, but in a way that, throwing its right forward, its left was refused. The Hougou-mont wood, in front of our left, appeared to me to be strongly occupied. I thought and I said that this post should be taken first. The general, to whom I made my report, told me that the attack would take place in the centre. 'Too bad', I replied to him. These were my reasons: the English, having drawn us up on a battlefield of their own choice and giving their line that direction, appeared to us to set up a trap; in truth, the centre was their weak point, since their line of operations were perpendicular to the rear; but it was strength-ened; first, by the concave line of their position that the English general seemed to like and which he had used several times to advantage; second, by the concentration of the greatest means of defence. An action engaged on this point would in truth lead us to a most decisive result, but it would also be more hard fought, more murderous, and perhaps lead us to employ all our forces, whilst those of the enemy, either contained in, or hidden by the Hougoumont wood, would always threaten our left flank and rear, and would require a corps of observation which would be so necessary for the actual attack in the centre. If I had known of the location of the Prussian army, this reasoning would be still more important, since we would not be able to tackle the English centre without prolonging our right flank opposite that of the Prussians who, moving forwards, would take us in the rear without anyone to oppose it; but this possibility was not known to me.

II Corps, committed first, initially launched several *pelotons* of skirmishers into the wood [of Hougoumont] which were soon destroyed and replaced by others with a similar lack of success, and in a short time we saw an excellent division melt away with no result. At the same moment, in the centre, I Corps suffered a reverse of a different nature: the attack was made in three columns; that of the left followed the road, the two others, either had received a poor direction, or because of unexpected obstacles in the ground, ceased to march parallel and converged on one another so that they joined. This false movement resulted in the greatest confusion. A colonel stopped his regiment to get it back into order; his word of command too forcefully given in such circumstances, was clumsily repeated; the disorder was irreparable; the moment was decisive; they were close to the enemy who profited from the situation; several squadrons of cavalry fell on this disorganised mass, routed it and we lost not fifteen, but forty guns. The cavalry corps of General Milhaud advanced, but too late; however, it overthrew the enemy and covered the infantry as they rallied, which was carried out a little to the rear. The corps of heavy cavalry which did everything that could be expected of this distinguished French arm, covered itself in glory. At first it had brilliant success; supported in its turn, the battle could have been won, *but the infantry reserves, remaining by the attack on the left, were too far off* [his italics]. This cavalry, long exposed to a most violent artillery fire and musketry, was obliged to retire after having suffered irreparable casualties.

Such was the first phase of the affair of Waterloo. Without one of those pieces of luck from which Napoleon had benefitted several times in the course of his long and brilliant military career, or that his genius had bred, this battle was already lost; but it seemed that luck, which was once so lavish with its favours to him, now wanted to overwhelm him with its heaviest blows and have him suffer all the consequences of his inconstancy. VI Corps moved forward to support the attack in the centre: it had hardly arrived on the crest of the valley which separated the two armies when its chief-of-staff, General Durieux, who had proceeded it, returned wounded and announced that the enemy skirmishers extended across our right flank; Count Lobau moved forward with General Jacquinot and I to reconnoitre them and soon we saw two columns of about 10,000 men each emerge; it was Bülow's Prussian corps. The destination of VI Corps was changed by this incident; it was no longer a matter of attacking the English, but of repulsing the Prussians; in short, we were forced into a most unfavourable defensive, the result of which was not in doubt.

VI Corps took position *en potence* behind the right of I Corps and despite the great disproportion in numbers (it consisted of no more than 6,000 men), despite an even greater inferiority of artillery, it stopped the advance of the lead Prussian corps which, however, continuing to deploy beyond our right flank, necessitated the intervention of the Guard, which deployed more or less on the same line as us.

At this point almost the entire army was engaged and, in its general configuration, presented three faces of an irregular quadrilateral whose fourth side was the line of the Dyle cut perpendicularly by the Gennapes [*sic*] defile.

Worthy and honest people have reported to me since that this defile was obstructed by vehicles, baggage and all the embarrassments which so often block the rear of our armies, which render retrograde movements so difficult, and which finally, as at Baylen, as at the Berezina, so often produce such unfortunate results.

Anyone who has even the first notion of war will realise that, in such a position, our defeat was certain. Such was the consequence of the double attack on the right and centre; which followed each other, on the same ground and almost simultaneously, two actions which, however, were un-coordinated or took a diagonal line of battle, forming a very acute angle with our line of operations and thus pushed our centre forward without support and whose right was 'in the air'. From this first concept resulted the impossibility of concentrating our forces at any single point of the enemy line for a great effort, which lowered the chances of success and which alone can decide the victory in battle. For the attack on the wood of Hougoumont, becoming more murderous and prolonged without success, drew the attention of the general in chief who held back at the height of this attack a strong portion of his army, whilst I Corps moved against the English centre, stretching further and further from this reserve which would soon become so necessary to it.

Adjutant-Commandant Jean-Isaac-Suzanne Combes-Brassard

Notice sur la bataille de Mont Saint-Jean, published in *Souvenirs et correspondence sur la bataille de Waterloo* (Paris: Teissèdre, 2000), pp. 15–25.

Like Janin, Combes-Brassard served as a sous-chef d'état-major *(deputy chief-of-staff) of VI Army Corps commanded by Lieutenant General Count Lobau.*

Combes-Brassard was born in 1772 and was commissioned into the 15th Cavalry Regiment when he was twenty. He took part in the campaign of 1792–3 and was wounded twice at the battle of Neerwinden. He then served in the headquarters of the Army of the Sambre and Meuse as lieutenant and then captain until May 1798 when he took retirement because of his wounds. However, by the end of the year he re-took service in the headquarters of the 20th Military District (Angoulême) before becoming captain commandant of the 1st Company of the Dragoons of the Paris Municipal Guard. He became aide-de-camp to General Caffarelli in 1806, serving in Corfu from 1806 to 1810, where he was promoted chef d'escadron. *He next served in Spain from 1810 to 1813 when he was promoted* adjutant-commandant *(colonel on the staff). During the 1814 campaign he served as the chief-of-staff of the 1st Military District (Paris) and returned to this headquarters, but as deputy chief-of-staff, working for General Lobau, on Napoleon's return. In April 1815 he accompanied Lobau to his command of VI Army Corps, becoming the corps deputy chief-of-staff. Put into non-activity in July 1815 he was recalled to work as colonel in the royal headquarters in 1818. He finally retired in 1826 and died in 1860.*

The following was penned on 22 June 1815 at the château of L'Échelle, or Léchelle, near Guise (this is where Combes-Brassard took refuge after the battle), thus giving it some credibility for having been written soon after the battle. However, he is clearly in error on the sequence of the battle in the centre, which he could not have observed for himself or had the time to learn after the battle; he has the French cavalry attacking before d'Erlon's I Corps. He speaks with more authority and interest on the actions of his own corps. His account is also noteworthy as it finishes with a damning indictment of Grouchy's performance which is reminiscent of much later criticism, suggesting that this may have been added after the original account.

On the evening of 17 June, I had supper with the headquarter officers and the emperor's aides-de-camp at the farm of Caillou. The battle was imminent. Our advance posts were in contact with those of Wellington. We chatted after supper and argued over the battle of the following day. Talk of battle came to the ear of the emperor who was in the room next door.

He came out abruptly, his hands behind his back, glanced around the room we were in and said to no one in particular: 'A battle! Messieurs! Do you know what a battle is? There are empires, kingdoms, the world or its end between a battle won and a battle lost!' He returned to his own room after these words. I thought I had heard a judgement of destiny.

On 18 June, the French army attacked the combined armies of the English, Belgians and Dutch. In the first plan, the French army was to attack by its right and centre, refusing the left, destined to push against Brussels and Mons, if we forced the English from their positions.

This plan was wise, since it cut Wellington off from Blücher's army that Grouchy was observing; that, on the other hand, favoured the movement of Grouchy on the Dyle. Finally, it also had the advantage that Grouchy found himself, by this manoeuvre, posted in such a manner to act as the reserve to the French army in case of a mishap, and ready to pursue and dislodge Blücher from the banks of the Meuse in case of success.

The columns were in movement, the army was advancing to attack in accordance with this plan, when the emperor suddenly changed his mind; he refused his right to attack by his left, and moved all his efforts against the enemy's centre.

Wellington had recognised a good position and had fortified it. All his troops were strongly deployed on this ground, which I think had been studied for some time.

The left of the French army approached closely to the English right, which defended itself for a long time, but which was nevertheless forced from their positions with enormous loss.

The extreme left of the French was not led with energy. A body of cavalry which was there was destroyed due to the fault of the general who commanded it.

The success of the left, which had taken the enemy position and which pushed it back vigorously on its centre, was the signal for the attack in the centre.

It was neglected to approach first with infantry. It was thought a quicker and more decisive success could be achieved by launching the reserves of cuirassiers and the Guard with horse artillery.

The young and interesting Labédoyère (what great misfortune possibly awaits him) committed a great mistake. At the moment when the great attack on the centre, at Mont-Saint-Jean, was launched and led with as much talent as audacity by Marshal Ney, he had noticed a pronounced movement to the rear by the enemy's army. Victory beckoned. Labédoyère rushed to the emperor and convinced him to leave it to him to take the reserve of cuirassiers to complete the disorder of the enemy. This cavalry indeed threw disorder into the English army. But this movement was premature and proved unhappy for us. An hour later, the emperor would have drawn all the advantages from his cavalry if he had held it back. Napoleon, despite his eagle *coup d'oeil* for war, often found himself under the charm of officers whom he loved and whose talents he should have employed a little later.

This manoeuvre was executed with great courage and great success. The first and second English lines were broken, their line of artillery taken. The disorder and rout was at its height in the enemy army, but as no one supported this manoeuvre with infantry, which was too far off to assure success and the formation of lines by the French cavalry which had taken the enemy artillery positions, it turned out that the enemy's infantry, which had been broken by the French cavalry, seeing that it was not protected, rallied in the rear and broke it in their turn, when it wanted to reform to support the efforts of the Allied reserve cavalry that Wellington had sent against it.

This capital fault cost us many men and changed the outcome of the day. It was necessary to protect the retreat of our reserves of cavalry by new charges, and soon all the enemy's cavalry found itself engaged in an unequal struggle, since it required a coordinated effort of cavalry and infantry.

It was then that the right of the French army, under the orders of Count d'Erlon, moved forwards to engage.

But the damage was already too great. Our cavalry had suffered enormous losses; it had few means to deliver and decide a new attack.

VI Corps, forming the reserve (I was the chief of staff of this corps) marched to support the attack being made on the right. This corps was entirely composed of infantry.

It was 3.30pm, a terrible fire could be heard along the whole line of the two armies. VI Corps completed its deployment into reserve on the army's right, when, moving over to the extreme right, I recognised the heads of columns emerging from the direction of Wavres, by Ohain and Saint-Lambert.

These columns were Prussian. Their arrival had come without any orders from the emperor. We were outflanked.

Napoleon, it is said, was the first to see the danger. He ordered Lobau to cross the Brussels *chausée* by a change of direction to the right by division, and to move towards the chapel of Saint-Lambert to support the cavalry of Domon and Subervic [*sic*], who had already been sent on reconnaissance towards the Prussians.

We were turned before we were in position. Still uncertain on the nature and intention of these troops, I moved closer to them to observe their movements. Soon I saw that this column was Prussian and cutting the French army's line of retreat on Genappe and the bridge over the Dyle. The Prussians were already moving on our rear.

I rushed to prevent this. There was still time, by taking up the position where the army had bivouacked before giving battle, to prevent the dangers of the position in which we found ourselves. But there was not a moment to lose. The loss would be the loss of the army. Fate had ordered this.

The emperor, persistent in wanting to break the enemy's centre, gave no importance to the movements that were being made on his flanks.

The Prussians had already joined the English left and were deploying in our rear, so that the right of the army and VI Corps found itself forming an acute triangle of which two sides and the tip were the English and Prussian armies.

A terrible fire of artillery and musketry broke out at this moment. English, Prussian and French regiments disappeared like phantoms chased by the wind.

Our rear and flanks were cut by the enemy. VI Corps opened a passage with the bayonet, but we left this position to see the whole French army broken in disorder, making a retreat that was so late that it was soon a terrible rout.

In the middle of the storm, the emperor, almost alone, braved a million deaths which rained down on us.

I saw actions, I heard sublime words; words worthy of the companions of Leonidas.

The General of the Guard Michel was mortally wounded in one of the squares of the Guard. Four grenadiers were ordered to carry him. 'No!' they replied calmly, 'it is here that it is necessary to die; nowhere else will we find so early a death.'

The emperor had been brave to the last moment and was one of the last to leave the battlefield. He was still there at eight o'clock in the evening. It was then that he followed the general movement. I left him half a league from la Belle-Alliance.

On the 18th June, towards nine o'clock in the evening, the emperor left the battlefield. He only left it when disorder had arrived at the point when it was no longer possible to keep four men together. Each looked out for himself.

I remained near the emperor from the moment that VI Corps, of which I was the chief-of-staff, had been destroyed and dispersed in the attack against the Prussians.

... if Grouchy had executed the movements which he had been ordered to do, and that even the least experienced officer could have executed in his position, nothing would have been spoiled by the modification of the general plan of battle. It is to Grouchy alone that belongs all the misfortunes of this day and all the consequences which resulted for France.

20th Infantry Division

Maréchal de Camp Jacques-Jean-Marie-François Boudin Count Tromelin

Lachouque, *Un Gentilhomme d'Aventure: Le Général Tromelin* (Tournai: Bloud & Gay, undated), pp. 227–8.

During the Waterloo campaign, Tromelin commanded the 2nd Brigade of the 20th Infantry Division (Jeanin), part of Lobau's VI Army Corps.

Tromelin was a particularly interesting character, so his biography is rather long ...

Born into the minor nobility in 1771, Tromelin was destined for a career in the military. After attendance at a royal military school, he was commissioned into the infantry regiment of Limousin in 1787. His life was rocked by the Revolution, but being based in Corsica, much of the drama passed him by. In September 1791 he was promoted lieutenant in the 57th de ligne based in Landau; most of his family had fled France for England and Germany. Leaving his regiment, he joined the emigré forces as a simple soldier. Deserted by the Allies after Valmy, Tromelin made his way to Jersey and then to England. There he got involved in various plots and plans to invade France and provoke a counter-revolution. He was a captain in the royalist forces in 1795, the same year all hope of a military expedition seemed lost. In an attempted landing with Sir Sidney Smith in France, Tromelin was forced to surrender and was

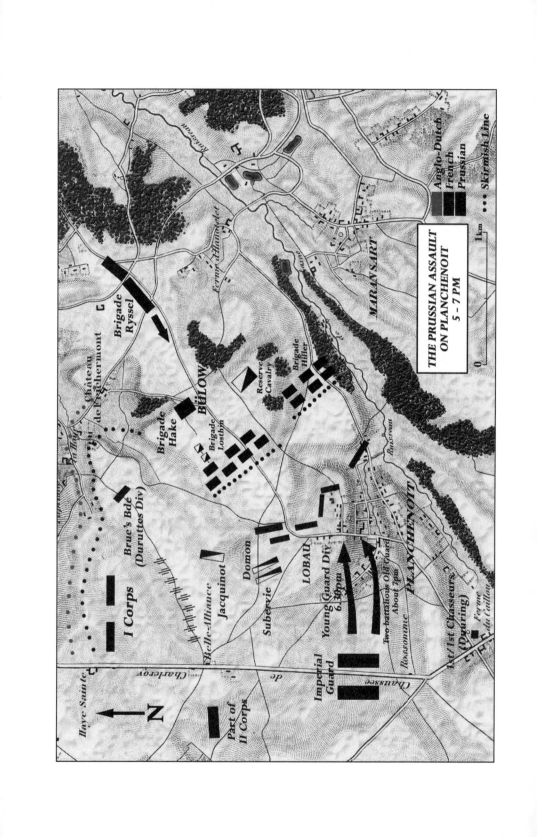

THE PRUSSIAN ASSAULT
ON PLANCHENOIT
5 - 7 PM

Anglo-Dutch
French
Prussian
• • • • Skirmish Line

0   1km

Brigade Ryssel

Château
de Frichermont

BÜLOW

Brigade Hake

Brigade Losthin

Reserve Cavalry

Brigade Hiller

MARANSART

Brue's Bde
(Durutte's Div)

I Corps

Belle-Alliance

Jacquinot

Domon

Subervie

LOBAU

Young Guard Div
6.30pm

Two battalions Old Guard
About 7pm

Imperial Guard

Part of II Corps

N

Haye Sainte

(Charleroi)

Chaussée

de

PLANCHENOIT

Rossomme

1st/1st Chasseurs
(Duhring)

Ferme
du Caillou

imprisoned with Smith. He avoided a death sentence by posing as Smith's Canadian servant, John Bromley, and was eventually returned to England. He was later offered an opportunity by Smith to join the Turks fighting against Bonaparte in the Middle East; in 1798 he became a major in the Turkish army and was transported to Constantinople by the Royal Navy. He maintained the name Bromley. The following year he fought with the Turks against Napoleon's forces at Aboukir; the Turks were thoroughly beaten. In 1800 Tromelin was promoted to lieutenant colonel; he fought with the Turks against the French in close co-operation with Sir Sidney Smith until 1801 and the French evacuation of Egypt. With peace between France and Britain, Tromelin returned to France in 1802. Discovering his association with Sir Sidney Smith, Tromelin was arrested and imprisoned in April 1804, but swearing allegiance to the new order (Napoleon), he was released just two months later. In 1806 Tromelin was formally assigned to the imperial army, becoming captain in the 112th de ligne, *but was soon transferred to the headquarters of the Army of Dalmatia headed by the future marshal Marmont. With Russia a common enemy to both France and Turkey, Tromelin found himself once more as an envoy to the Turks in 1807, though this time on behalf of imperial France. Returning from this mission, Marmont's force was involved in the 1809 campaign against Austria and Tromelin was in combat for the first time in Napoleon's armies at the minor engagement of Göspich. He was promoted* chef de bataillon, *but soon given the provisional rank of colonel to command the newly-raised 6th Croat Regiment. He remained in Illyria as part of the garrison during the invasion of Russia. After this debâcle, Tromelin was recalled as part of the attempt to rebuild the army. In 1813 he became chief-of-staff in General Pacthod's 13th Division and then shortly after in the 14th Division, with whom he took a distinguished part at Bautzen, having three horses killed under him. He fought at the disaster of Dennewitz, again having three horses killed under him. Made* adjutant-commandant *(staff colonel) he was present at Leipzig and Hanau. Tromelin was promoted* général de brigade *in November 1813 and made commandant of Frankfurt, but on its evacuation he was nominated chief-of-staff of IV Army Corps, the garrison of Mayence, where he remained until Napoleon's abdication. His old royalist leanings being well known, he was posted as major* à la suite *of the Royal Corps of Grenadiers. On Napoleon's return and determined not to go into another exile, Tromelin waited for an appointment. He was allocated a brigade command in the 20th Division (Jeanin) of VI Corps (Lobau); it contained only a single regiment (the 10th* de ligne; *the only regiment to fire a shot against Napoleon's return!). At Waterloo he fought against the Prussian incursion on the French right flank and withdrew with his brigade, claiming to be one of the last to leave the battlefield. After his return to Paris, known for his royalist leanings and previous diplomatic experience, he was sent by the provisional government to negotiate with Wellington to see Louis back onto the throne. After the Second Restoration he was put into non-activity for a short while before returning to service. Most of his subsequent appointments were with the inspectorate of infantry, but he commanded a brigade in the invasion of Spain in 1823. After this he became inspector general of infantry and lieutenant general. He was again put on the inactive list in 1836 and died in 1842.*

Tromelin does not reflect on whether the Prussian appearance was a surprise, but restricts himself to describing the deployment of VI Corps and the fighting against the gradually overwhelming numbers of Bülow's corps. Given the numerical weakness of VI Corps, and notwithstanding the reinforcements they received from the Young and Old Guard, they were able to give a good account of themselves for over four hours before they were forced to retreat.

At 3pm, Jeanin's division [in which he was serving], following Simmer's 1st Division [1st Division of VI Corps, but numbered 20th in the army], crossed the main road two hundred metres to the south of Belle-Alliance, passed behind Milhaud's corps of cuirassiers, left Planchenoit to its right and deployed behind the 1st Division on a ridgeline between two streams, a quarter of a league to the northeast of this last village.

The three regiments of the division were divided into two groups: the 10th *de ligne* and Cuppé's battalion of the 107th *de ligne* were put under my orders and occupied a small wood. Before us, two horse artillery batteries of the cavalry divisions [Domon's and Subervie's] were already firing on the Prussian columns which were emerging from the Frischermont wood.

On the left, Milhaud's squadrons were shaken. It was 4pm. The Prussian attack started towards 4.30pm. Our cavalry sabred the enemy squadrons, then we formed ourselves into square by brigade and remained under the fire of forty Prussian cannons which damaged us. No one knew what was going on elsewhere on the battlefield.

At 5.30pm, the enemy received reinforcements of infantry and cavalry; the cannonade became heavy. Resisting firmly, but falling to the weight of shot, the four squares of the *corps d'armée* retired slowly *en echiquier* in the direction of Planchenoit, where finally I established myself, already outflanked by the Prussian cavalry. The debris of my three battalions occupied the gardens and orchards.

It was then that our right was extended by the Young Guard, and then reinforced by my old commander General Morand, at the head of a battalion of grenadiers. The fighting was terrible. This mix of units repulsed several Prussian assaults and even gained ground of several hundred *toises* [a *toise* was a French unit of measurement that roughly equates to 2m] beyond Planchenoit.

But towards eight o'clock in the evening, decimated by the Prussian attacks that were constantly fed with reinforcements, our right was turned by Blücher's cavalry, whose squadrons our own could no longer contain, and our left by the English cavalry launched in pursuit of our army; you could sense that those battalions that remained to us would soon become disordered and the order arrived to abandon Planchenoit in flames and to retire towards the main road.

At the moment when the last brigade of the 1st Division passed mine, I started my own move; my square, pressed on all sides, broke and retired in disorder. Remaining alone on the ground, I had the greatest difficulty in re-mounting in order to rally my men next to a wood in the rear of my position. I found it was occupied by the Prussians which forced me to regain the main road with only those I could gather around me. We rallied some men to the left of a square of grenadiers of the Guard, but, noticing that they began to drift away, I decided to regain the main road where I found the divisional commander and, with him, those men who remained to me ...

Sergeant-Major François Marq

Description des Campagnes de Guerre (Paris: Edmond Dubois, 1901), pp. 44–7.

During the Waterloo campaign Marq served as sergeant-major of voltigeurs in the 107th de ligne (Colonel Druot) which was part of the 2nd Brigade (Tromelin) of the 20th Division (Jeanin), part of Count Lobau's VI Army Corps.

Marq was born in 1792 and entered the National Guard in April 1812 aged twenty, being allocated to the 6th Company of the 56th Cohort of the 1st Ban. Just a few days after joining his unit he was made corporal, being responsible for the distri-bution of rations while his unit was in Utrecht. Napoleon called the cohorts into the line infantry to repair the huge losses suffered in Russia and Marq's cohort became the 2nd Battalion of the 153rd de ligne. He was promoted sergeant in the 4th Com-pany of this battalion. The regiment was sent to Magdeburg where it was put on a war footing. He states that the four battalions of the regiment became Penne's brigade of Lacroix's division of Maison's corps (in fact, Maison was the divisional commander [16th Division] and Lauriston commanded the corps; the 5th). He fought at Bautzen and when Maison's division was surprised at Hainau; here the 153rd suffered over 300 casualties. He was at the battles of Dresden and Leipzig. Marq skates over the 1814 campaign of France without the slightest detail on either his or his regiment's role in it, other than to say that he was promoted to 'sergeant-major of voltigeurs' after Napoleon had abdicated. Once his regiment had been amalgamated with others as the size of the army shrank, it became the 88th de ligne. Marq spent much of the duration of Napoleon's absence on leave and returned to his regiment almost as his emperor entered Paris. On the reorganisation of the army, Marq found himself in the 107th de ligne and fought with them at Waterloo where he was seriously wounded and left on the battlefield for two days before being picked up and having his wounds treated. He remained in hospital in Brussels until 10 August and when he was fit enough to be moved he was then sent to Britain as a prisoner. He arrived back in France on 1 January 1816. Having to use vehicles to return to his home department, he reported to the local military commander. After a medical inspection he was given a full discharge, but his application for a pension, as he was unable to work, although agreed, allocated him just 270 francs per year with which he was clearly dissatisfied as he describes it as 'in no relation to my rank or wounds'.

Marq states that his account was written in 1817. He restricts himself to describing his own personal experiences during the battle fighting against the Prussians.

About 10am (18 June), the regiment left its encampment to move to Waterloo, where the battle was already lively. The regiments that made up our corps (VI of Observation) were all concentrated and they marched in column up to the area of the battle. We were held in this position until we fell-in at 3pm, and having been exposed for a long time to artillery fire which fell in our ranks, we were marched in closed columns into the middle of the battlefield. Whilst marching to this place, several men were killed in the ranks and having arrived, we were deployed into regimental squares because the English [Prussian] cavalry were close to us and fought with the cuirassiers. It [the Prussian cavalry] came several times to try and break our squares, but it did not succeed. Cannon balls and canister fell in our squares like hail; we had been ordered not to fire our muskets and having our bayonets fixed, many men were killed in this position.

After several hours being in square, the battalion commanders received the order to send their voltigeurs in skirmish order. I was sergeant-major of the 3rd Company, and immediately this order was given we were led by our officers and arriving close to the enemy we were deployed here and there close to a small wood which was on the right of the Brussels road, being very busy and supported by columns of cavalry which were behind us, we forced the enemy to retire; but immediately on our pursuit, 40,000 enemy suddenly emerged from the wood and opened fire on us; the skirmishers that had been in there had all been killed or wounded; first I was wounded by a ball which passed through my body, passing by my left kidney and which exited after an incision was made, in the right buttock. It made me fall on my stomach and I was picked up by my two sergeants who were nearby; they picked me up and put me on an artillery horse; but I had hardly gone twenty paces on horseback when I was obliged to allow myself to slip off because I could not stand the march; I remained on the battlefield on the 18th, 19th and 20th June, when I was picked up by some local people and taken to Brussels where I was attended to for the first time. I was put into a convoy of 1,600 wounded men. The battle was terrible for the French; they were completely routed; the artillery parks, the munitions caissons, the rations, all remained in the hands of the enemy. The retreat was so hurried that there was hardly time to cut the traces of the horse teams to save them. Finally, I cannot give a complete account of this unhappy retreat as I became a prisoner; but remaining on the field of battle I saw a large part of the enemy which marched in pursuit of the French. I remained where I fell, bathed in my own blood, and despite this cruel position I took the precaution before the enemy passed by us, to undo my trousers and my *calcons* [underwear] and to lie face down on the ground to make it look as if I had been killed and pillaged. This proved to be a wise precaution; there was a cavalryman who wanted to see if I was dead, who prodded me with the point of his sabre on my neck, but I had enough self-control not to move, for if I had made the least movement, I think that he would have finished me off, and even in my sad state I had been sensible enough to keep a little money that I had taken the precaution of hiding in my mouth.

Chapter 3

The Heavy Cavalry Reserve

Introduction

Leaving aside the Imperial Guard, the two heavy cavalry corps commanded by General Kellerman (3rd) and General Milhaud (4th) were generally considered the élite of the army. The regiments that made up these corps were mainly of the famed cuirassiers, who had made a devastating impact on many battlefields of the empire, and although they had been almost entirely rebuilt from scratch after the disastrous 1812 campaign, they retained their high reputation.

The two corps (see order of battle in the Appendix) were each of two divisions; each division containing four regiments in two brigades. Whilst the infantry corps contained 15,000 to 20,000 men, the cavalry corps were relatively weak; Kellerman's corps started the campaign about 3,600 strong and Milhaud's about 3,100. Kellerman's corps was not exclusively of cuirassiers; l'Héritier's division (the 11th) included a strong brigade of dragoons and d'Hurbal's (the 12th), a brigade of carabiniers; Milhaud's regiments were all of cuirassiers.

Many of the regiments were well below their established strength, as much a shortage of horseflesh as it was manpower. Guiton's brigade of l'Héritier's division contained only five squadrons in its two regiments and had made a gallant, if essentially fruitless, charge at Quatre Bras where, although capturing a colour of the British 69th Regiment, they were finally routed with a loss of 300 men. The weakest of Guiton's cuirassier regiments, the 11th, had only two squadrons and had not been equipped with cuirasses before the campaign opened.

Milhaud's corps had been present at Ligny on the 16th. Remaining in reserve until the closing stages of the battle, only Delort's division (the 14th) had been engaged in support of the final advance of the Guard and made a number of successful charges against the Prussian cavalry as darkness fell.

At Waterloo, Kellerman's corps was deployed in the second line behind II Corps to the west of the Brussels road; Milhaud's corps was in the second line behind I Corps to the east of that road. Both were heavily engaged in the great cavalry charges during the battle which are well described by the following eyewitnesses.

3rd Cavalry Corps

Lieutenant General François-Étienne Kellerman

Témoignage inédit du Général François-Étienne Kellerman sur la Campagne de 1815, reproduced in *Souvenirs Napoleonien*, No. 438, December 2001/January 2002. Kellerman's essay was entitled, *Observations sur la Bataille de Waterloo en réponse à un Écrit Intitulé Campagne de 1815 fait à Sainte-Hélène et publié sous le nom de Général Gourgaud*, pp. 29–35.

During the Waterloo campaign, Kellerman was commander of the 3rd Reserve Cavalry Corps.

François Kellerman was the son of Marshal Kellerman, the victor of Valmy. Despite his poor health, he was commissioned into the Colonel General Hussars in 1785 aged just fifteen. In 1791 he went to the United States to work with the embassy staff, but was re-called in 1793 and posted to the 2nd Cavalry Regiment. Although he saw little action he was promoted steadily, reaching lieutenant colonel in the Kellerman Legion that same year. Before the end of 1793 he was recalled to France and promoted again, to chef de bataillon *at just twenty-three, into the Hautes Alpes Chasseurs, but instead of joining his new regiment he moved to be an aide to his father who was then commander of the Army of the Alps. He spent a short time in prison for showing 'a lack of zeal'! In 1794 he joined the 1st Hussars and made colonel the following year. He joined Napoleon's staff on the latter's arrival in Italy with the rank of* adjutant général chef de brigade. *After success in minor operations in Italy he commanded the 4th Chasseurs against the Austrians and fought at Castiglione, Bassano and Arcola, enhancing his reputation at each action. He fought at Rivoli early in 1797 and distinguished himself under Napoleon's eye at the crossing of the Tagliamento. For these actions he was promoted to* général de brigade. *He filled a number of brigade command appointments, including one of infantry, in Italy until his health broke down in 1799. Recalled to command by Napoleon he played the decisive role at Marengo for which he would ever be remembered. Although his role in the battle was acknowledged by Napoleon, Kellerman was disgruntled not to get promoted for his feats that day. In fact he was promoted soon after, but his criticisms had been noted and until 1805 he held posts that gave him no opportunities to excel. In the Austerlitz campaign he at last commanded a division on campaign. At the battle of Austerlitz he experienced mixed fortunes, but came out of the battle with credit and a serious wound. He missed the campaigns in Prussia and Poland and was posted as commander of a light cavalry division for the invasion of Portugal in 1807. At the end of operations he was made governor of Alemtejo province; on the landing of the British force, with no cavalry command available, he was given command of the army reserve consisting of four battalions of grenadiers. He commanded these at Vimeiro, but his assault at the end of the battle failed. As one of only a few French officers who spoke English he helped to negotiate the Cintra Convention which finally took him back to France. He soon returned to Spain at the head of a dragoon division, but was tied down to a large area trying to combat the guerrillas. Drawn to support operations commanded by Marchand, he won a brilliant personal victory at Alba de Tormes, where his 3,000 cavalry thrashed three Spanish infantry divisions. On Massena's invasion of Portugal he commanded the small army that protected Massena's northern flank. However, it seems that the responsibility of this post went to his head and he ignored Massena's orders and concentrated on plundering the countryside. Seeing the writing on the wall, he resigned citing ill health and returned to France in May 1811. His poor health prevented him from taking up a number of commands and on the point of resigning he was ordered to report to Ney's III Corps in Saxony in 1813. He fought without distinction at Lützen and again at Königswortha, and was wounded at Bautzen. In June 1813 he became commander of the Polish cavalry brigade and fought at Leipzig. Struck once more by ill health he was forced to give up his command and took no further part in the campaign. As Napoleon was short of experienced cavalry commanders in 1814 he was recalled to command the 5th Cavalry Corps composed of veteran dragoon regiments. His corps took a prominent role in the victory at Mormont and then saved Oudinot's army from destruction at Bar-sur-Aube, though at heavy cost. Although somewhat mauled at Malmaison, he again made a sizeable contribution at Saint Dizier, his last battle in 1814. He quickly ingratiated himself with the Bourbons and was rewarded with a number of prestigious posts. Stopped from confronting Napoleon on the latter's return from exile by the mutiny of his men, he retired to his estates and awaited the turn of events. Although reluctant to employ him, Napoleon, once again short of experienced cavalry commanders, recalled him to command the 3rd Cavalry Corps. He led a brigade of his corps in a desperate charge at Quatre Bras and led his corps in their charges at Waterloo. He stayed with the army in its retreat to Paris and was employed by Davout to negotiate the submission of the army to the returning Louis. Later placed on half pay, he was recalled in 1818, but not trusted with a command he was retired in 1831 and died of a stroke in Paris in 1835.*

This account was written by Kellerman to challenge aspects of Gourgaud's book named in the title of his account. Kellerman was a reluctant Bonapartist and his writing is more a critique of the battle and Napoleon than a true account of his experiences. However, it concentrates on the cavalry action that Kellerman witnessed for himself and this adds real value and interest. Unlike many other French writers, he does not claim that Wellington was saved from defeat by the appearance of the Prussians. He does, however, speak of the reluctance of the cavalry to retire from the Allied ridge in order to avoid dragging the rest of the army back. He laments the useless destruction of the carabinier brigade and praises the action of Lobau's corps and the Young Guard. His account is written in the third person.

The engagement started on the left of the French army. The author [Gourgaud/Napoleon] even admits that he was not able to capture the wood and the fortified château of Hougoumont before which II Corps was uselessly committed the whole day. However, the arrival of Bülow on our right flank towards three o'clock, had forced Napoleon, by his own admission, to divert 10,000 men to face this attack.

Hoping to fool the public, and perhaps himself as well, and to cover over his desperate enterprise, he assures us that he had taken sufficient precautions against this enemy corps of 30,000 men and that he was able, in all security, to execute the attack that he had planned and that he dared to venture against the enemy's centre.

It is more than probable that Bülow's arrival and the danger in which this placed Napoleon, convinced him to launch his attack in the hope that a prompt success against the English would save him from what was menacing his right flank and that, in a situation that was becoming increasingly desperate, it was necessary to risk all. It is difficult to explain otherwise his recklessness that did not justify the so-called enthusiasm of the troops, which had appeared to us to be cold.

Either way, the attack on the centre was ordered, but instead of being properly co-ordinated, with that imposing order that inspires confidence and promises success, to reserve the great effort for the critical moment, General Milhaud's cavalry was launched too early and it was followed by the cavalry of the Imperial Guard. The right of the cavalry reserve of the 4th Corps was drawn forward imprudently by the imbecile general that commanded it [General l'Héritier] and whilst not awaiting the orders of the Comte de Valmy [himself], his immediate commander, they all arrived mixed up, in disorder and out of breath, on the ridge that was occupied by the English artillery line. The guns were actually abandoned for a short time, but we did not have the horses to take them off.

Besides, behind them was a double line of infantry formed in square. It was necessary to stop, to re-impose order, despite the problems, under enemy fire, but it was not possible to force the cavalry, excellent as it was, into new charges: it found itself in the cruellest of positions, without infantry or artillery support.

The enemy squares reserved their fire, but were covered by a cloud of skirmishers whose each shot counted. It was in this awful position that almost all our cavalry remained for several hours between the Hougoumont wood and La Haye Sainte, not wanting to retire in order not to risk dragging along the army with it, nor able to charge because it had no quarry, receiving death without being able to fight back, and, besides, exposed to the fire of our own batteries that it had already passed.

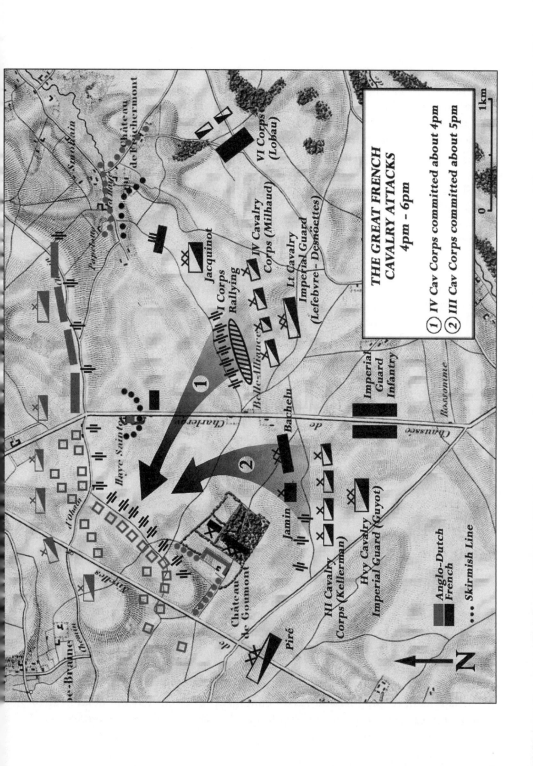

THE GREAT FRENCH
CAVALRY ATTACKS
4pm – 6pm

① IV Cav Corps committed about 4pm
② III Cav Corps committed about 5pm

VI Corps (Lobau)

Jacquinot

I Corps Rallying

IV Cavalry Corps (Milhaud)

Lt Cavalry Imperial Guard (Lefebvre – Desnoëttes)

Belle-Alliance

Bachelu

Imperial Guard Infantry

Chaussée

Chaussée de Charleroi

La Haye Saint

Papelotte

Château de Frichermont

Smohain

Rossomme

Jamin

Château de Goumont

Hvy Cavalry Imperial Guard (Guyot)

III Cavalry Corps (Kellerman)

Piré

de

d'Ohain

Nivelles

Mont-St-Jean

de

Anglo-Dutch
French

.... Skirmish Line

N

1km

0

Napoleon himself recognised the fault and bad timing of this charge of all the cavalry, too far from infantry [support]. This was the main reason for our failure. The Count of Valmy was of the same opinion. He held back the brigade of carabiniers, of close to 1,000 men, from this fatal drive. He located it close to a battery of the Guard, with the express order to make no movement without the immediate agreement of the Comte de Valmy.

He moved himself into the line where General l'Héritier had so wildly driven his division. He had wanted to retire his cavalry from this unsustainable position, but fearing to cause a general flight if they made the least retrograde movement, the generals, resigned to maintaining their troops in position through their own presence, were condemned to watch defenceless men and horses fall around them.

Suddenly one noticed in the distance the red headdresses of the carabiniers in movement. The Comte de Valmy, sensing a disaster, rushed to stop it. He was unable to arrive in time. This superb corps, in no time, was almost destroyed. One is tempted to say that the sad destiny of France steered all the false measures of the day. The brigade of carabiniers had been in the plain and the marshal [Ney], noticing it, rushed over to it, indignant at its inaction. He ordered it to fall on seven or eight English squares placed in echelon on the slope of the ridge, close to the Hougoumont wood, and flanked by numerous batteries of artillery.

The carabiniers had to obey. Either through impotence, or clumsiness, their charge had no success. Most of the brigade was left on the ground. Several hours later, if it had remained intact and in position, this corps would have been able to repeat the miracle of Marengo on the English Guards, or at least to have saved the army from a complete rout.

The exhausted infantry could do no more. The cavalry was reduced to nothing, inevitably submitting and giving ground little by little. One could foresee the result of the day. A disaster appeared inevitable whose consequences would be more or less terrible. The cannon balls of Bülow's corps were falling on our rear and it was at this moment that Napoleon used deception, pretending that it was Grouchy's fire and had announced everywhere the arrival of this marshal and victory in the battle.

The deception was all the worse because they feared they were cut off, and it is very surprising that Bülow's corps had not in fact closed the road to Charleroi. But Count Lobau and General Duhesme saved the army from misfortune and succeeded with their feeble means and a vigour worthy of the greatest praise, not only to contain, but to repulse Bülow's corps. This was a very important service and perhaps the finest feat of the day.

Napoleon, to support and revive courage, thus circulated the news of the junction of the corps of the right, but Grouchy, had he arrived at this moment, would not have been able to change the state of affairs. It is thus not true to suggest that 60,000 Frenchmen had until then fought with advantage against 115,000 English and Prussians. Whatever the author of the relation says, we think it can be said that at no time during the day can we reasonably flatter ourselves by thinking we were winning it.

However, with prudence, it might have been possible to avoid a catastrophe. The natural caution of the English left us this chance. But prudence was not a distinctive quality of the commander of the French army. Whilst a single battalion remained to him, an *ecu* to bet, it could not be doubted that he would risk one or the other.

It cannot be denied that the account is very deceptive and that for those that were not present at this battle, it is not obvious that Napoleon did not act with coherence and responsibility. Today he arranges his defeats, as before he arranged his victories. To hear it said that the time had come to make the decisive attack and to complete the day, one would think that with one last effort and we would be singing victory. And yet the enemy had not been broken down and our troops, reduced to less than half, were continuously losing ground.

However, the Old Guard remained intact to Napoleon. The day was drawing to its end, the fighting was fading away, but everyone was giving up; there was one more step that could be taken. It was not possible to win, but we could hope night might come before disaster and we could retire behind the Sambre, conserving the only precious reserve which remained, the only body that had not been committed.

He admits himself that a fresh Prussian army and a division of English cavalry had arrived. He confesses that a part of his right retired, although he encouraged it to re-take its position. And it was then that Napoleon judged that the time had come to strike a decisive blow! He committed the few troops that remained to him as if a handful of braves, suddenly and un-expectedly, as at Marengo, would be able to overturn the inevitable and prevail with order, numbers and bravery combined.

With what address was this last attempt presented; one cannot but sense that it was thoughtless, desperate, and did not offer the least chance of success. And here we must deplore the imprudent charge that destroyed the carabinier brigade. It had been precisely on the point where the division of English cavalry had arrived to which Napoleon attributed the retreat of his Guard. It is possible that it would have stopped or overthrown this cavalry or would have been able to throw itself on the right flank of the column of English Guards that pursued the grenadiers of the Imperial Guard.

We did not hear that our troops fought amongst themselves, but, if this is true, it would increasingly prove that no arrangements had been made in case we had been forced to retreat. Also, from when this had been determined on and night had fallen, it was impossible to establish order and to stop the fugitives. It was just confusion, a terrible rout, without remedy, but such is what happens when you engage everything that you have; when you don't even maintain a weak reserve.

Chef d'escadron Dieudonné Rigau

Souvenirs des guerres de l'empire (Paris: Librairie des Deux Empires, 2000), pp. 110–15.

During the Waterloo campaign, Dieudonné Rigau served as chef d'escadron *in the 2nd Dragoon Regiment (Colonel Planzeaux). This regiment was part of the 1st Brigade (Picquet) of the 11th Cavalry Division (l'Héritier), part of the 3rd Reserve Cavalry Corps (Kellerman).*

Rigau was born in Maastricht in 1789 to a serving cavalry officer who fought throughout the Napoleonic Wars and died in exile in the United States after being condemned to death after the Waterloo campaign. The young Rigau joined the 16th Cavalry in 1803 (aged just fourteen), which was to become the 25th Dragoon Regiment. Despite his tender years he became brigadier-fourrier, *then* maréchal des logis, *then* adjutant sous-officier *by the end of the same year! The following year he was commissioned; it is hard to know how much his father was able to influence these promotions, but it is little surprise to learn that he served in the same regiment! He was present at Ulm and fought at Austerlitz, where he was nominated for the* Légion d'Honneur. *He next fought at Jena in 1806, after which he was promoted lieutenant, and then at Pultusk and Eylau the following year. Made aide-de-camp to General Lorge, who commanded a dragoon division, he went to Spain and was present at the battle of Corunna. In 1809 he was promoted captain and posted to the infantry, the 47th de ligne, with whom he took part in the disastrous invasion of Portugal of that year. During this campaign he had two horses killed under him; one at Oporto against the British. At the end of this campaign he travelled back to France to become aide-de-camp to his father in 1810. In 1812 he was re-assigned as a staff officer in imperial headquarters for the invasion of Russia; no doubt his father still had some influence! He was present at Borodino and entered Moscow; during the occupation he commanded a sector of the city. He survived the retreat and in the 1813 campaign he was present at Lützen and Bautzen. Having passed to the 59th de ligne in July he became chief-of-staff of the 43rd Division (Claparède) in St Cyr's XIV Corps, with which he fought at the battle of Dresden. Left as part of the garrison of that city, he missed the battle of Leipzig. After a determined defence, St Cyr was forced to surrender Dresden and Rigau went into captivity with the rest of the corps. Somehow Rigau escaped from Prague, crossed the Rhine with a fisherman and was able to rejoin the French army for the campaign of France in 1814. He was sent to general headquarters where he submitted a detailed report on all he had seen of the Allied armies and was questioned by Napoleon on this subject. He was promoted to* chef d'escadron *and attached to general headquarters, being sent on a number of missions during the campaign (during which his father commanded a dragoon brigade). On Napoleon's return he was appointed* chef d'escadron *in the 2nd Dragoons and fought with them at Waterloo. He stayed with the regiment in its retreat to Paris, was present when it was disbanded and went onto the inactive list. In 1828 he was called back into service and was posted to the 4th Hussars which he later commanded. After further service with the 9th Chasseurs, in 1833 he was nominated to command the 3rd Regiment of* Chasseurs d'Afrique. *He commanded this regiment on operations in Algeria for two years, before moving to the 5th Chasseurs in 1839. He retired as a colonel later that year.*

Rigau seems to think that the 2nd Dragoons were re-numbered the 1st for this campaign, although this does not seem to be official. Martinien's lists of officer casualties for the Napoleonic Wars records them as the 2nd, as do most orders of battle. However, as will be seen, they were referred to as the 1st Regiment by the other dragoon regiment in the brigade, the 7th. Rigau suggests that the great cavalry charges were the result of other units following a charge made by his regiment against British cavalry charging some guns that were deployed just in front of them. He makes no mention of infantry action which for much of the battle he would not have been able to see.

As for the premature movement of the French cavalry on the heights of Mont-Saint-Jean, which is a big question in several military works, nobody ordered it; it was made spontaneously by the 1st Regiment of Dragoons, commanded by the brave Colonel Planzeaux. I was a part of this intrepid regiment, in which I was a *chef d'escadron*. We arrived on the ground alone very early in the morning; it was still raining a little. Without orders and without generals the regiment formed up on the slope of Mont-Saint-Jean with an isolated house thirty paces to our right which was on the main road; we were in closed column. A random cannon shot passed between the squadrons; the regiment deployed into line.

Towards eleven o'clock the battle commenced; we were in the front line; General l'Héritier arrived, but at the same moment that he was speaking to me, he was struck by a ball which went through his shoulders and he had to retire; it was at this moment that we lost our *sapeurs*.

The 7th Regiment then arrived, commanded by Colonel Leopold, and deployed to the left rear of the 1st Regiment. Two guns of small calibre, commanded by a *maréchal des logis*, were deployed a few paces from our squadrons. They had hardly opened fire than the English cavalry charged them. It was then that without a command or order, the two closest squadrons, that I commanded, moved off, in front of these guns, to meet the enemy cavalry with the same shout on all our lips, a shout so familiar to our brave soldiers, '*En avant! En avant!*' ...

This movement was followed by our other two squadrons, and then by Leopold's regiment. We remained on the heights of Mont-Saint-Jean, where the Lion is situated ... the whole day, until the moment when we had to retreat, continually charging the enemy squadrons that we fell on as soon as they presented themselves. Never were cavalry mêlées so long and so close since they were continuous; our squadrons were kept at bay by the English squares anchored on the main road and with their backs to the village, who did not dare to open fire the whole day; these troops were so tired from holding the position of 'ready' that the whole time you could hear their officers warning the men that had sunk to the ground to get up.

Marshal Ney has taken the blame for having given this order for this premature movement, while I have explained that it was spontaneous.

Our misfortune has prevented the glorious actions of the regiments from being known. Thus, in the 1st Dragoons, an officer named Graffin was killed after having two horses killed under him, and, whilst mounting a third, a horse from the artillery train; *Adjutant-Major* Laussate, who retired to Pau, did not hesitate, in the middle of a mêlée, to jump from his horse in order to give it to the colonel who had been dismounted; Henry, captain, who was cut to pieces; Rivaux, who carries the scars on his face and who served in the gendarmerie; Hurtant, captain in retirement, today mayor of his village in the Department of Allier; and Suchet, captain, who has become an object of curiosity for the local people that we pass, because he was covered from head to toe in sabre blows. The eulogies merited by all these brave men should never end; nearly all the officers and NCOs were wounded and several were killed; glory to them and their families.

On this day I had the honour to lead (my comrades will recall) the squadrons twelve times to the charge at full tilt. Major Collet, who retired to Saint-Germain, was among these brave men. I regret not being able to name all those that I saw act as heroes, but I saw all their dangers, their faces, their actions, without being able to recall all their names. These dangers were the price of glory and immortality; electrifying consolation, for the warrior does not go into battle on the condition of victory; he could be wounded; all is not sadness in these wounds; he also has some sweetness to fulfil his need and to spill his blood for *la Patrie*.

The disorder of this unfortunate day has been exaggerated; a retreat is not executed like a parade; but it must be mentioned that the enemy were so surprised by their success, that in their pursuit they only attacked the soldiers in disorder on the plain to the left and right of the road.

I retired last from the battlefield with a squadron and always at the walk, without the enemy daring to come near us, despite surrounding us on all sides. Arriving close to the emperor's position, I stopped, and distinctly heard Napoleon say, 'Deploy the eagle of the battalion of the *île d'Elbe*', which was in its case. *'Vive l'Empereur!'* was shouted, but destiny had given its verdict; he was forced to retire.

King Jérôme, who was ordered to attack the farm of Hougoumont on our left flank, covered himself in glory; the fire at this point was always the most lively and murderous.

Never did General Cambronne nor any French general pronounce the response, although very French, that has been attributed to him; I had it from himself and, I believe, he also told General Drouot. The retreat of the Imperial Guard nor any élite unit would be reduced to such, and I have never heard it said that an English officer boasted of suggesting such an insolent proposition as to surrender; it would have been long known if this had taken place, but, I repeat, the enemy kept away from those bodies who kept their order. Thus, any regiment which, like the Guard, gave everywhere a great example, would not have suffered such a humiliation, which was not made to any other units. My body of men passed the night in a farm, next to the battle-field, where the enemy did not come to bother us, and it was only the next day, the 19th, at 9am, that we re-joined Kellerman's cavalry corps, of which we were a part, at Charleroi.

In the emperor's memoirs he says the Imperial Guard retreated in good order and could not, therefore, have been summoned to surrender. Napoleon, with his headquarters, remained for a long time in the middle of its squares. These old grenadiers, these old chasseurs, the model of the army in so many campaigns, covered themselves in glory again on this battlefield.

General Friant was wounded; Poret de Morvan, Devaux and Michel found a death to envy there.

General Duhesme, made prisoner, was basely massacred the next day by a Brunswick hussar, a crime that remained unpunished . . . The army achieved prodigies of valour; but several commanders led badly. Without the arrival, as night approached, of the 1st and 2nd [*sic*] Prussian Corps, victory would have been ours; and 120,000 Anglo-Dutch and allies would have been beaten by 60,000 Frenchmen.

Chef d'Escadron Létang

From the Archives de la Guerre at Vincennes, reproduced in *Les Carnets de la Campagne*, Number 5, *Les Vertes Bornes* (Brussels: Tondeur Editions, 2002).

During the Waterloo campaign, Létang served as a squadron commander in the 7th Dragoons (Colonel Léopold). This regiment was part of the 1st Brigade (Picquet) of the 11th Cavalry Division (l'Héritier), part of the 3rd Reserve Cavalry Corps (Kellerman).

Writing in the third person, Létang's account is clearly very self-serving. However, his description of the feeling of his men as they charged the British line is of particular interest.

The Hougoumont farm, although attacked, was still in the possession of the English. The French infantry, deployed between this farm and that of la Ste. Alliance renewed its attacks. L'Héritier's heavy cavalry division were in closed columns and the men dismounted behind the infantry, waiting for the English to evacuate their fortified positions so they could charge them or at least to interfere with their retreat. However, the English artillery fired on us and several balls flew over the infantry and fell among l'Héritier's division, striking men and horses, but without causing disorder. This however, prompted the line to mount up quickly. The English had seen us take up our attack positions; they took the offensive and advanced their infantry which formed a line behind the farms, without other deployment (and this was a big fault).

The squadron which formed the head of the column of l'Héritier's division, launched itself against this infantry and was followed by the other squadrons; but the distance that separated us from the English allowed them time to see this movement and to form into square to receive the charge. The squares resolutely awaited the cavalry and held their fire until point blank range. The powerful impact of the infantry fire on morale, being greater than its physical effect on the cavalry, was never better illustrated. The steadiness of the English infantry was more remarkable still by the absence of the volley that we awaited and were greatly surprised not to hear; this disconcerted our troopers. Realising that they would be exposed to a fire that would be that much more murderous from being at point-blank range, panic seized them, and probably to escape such a fire, the first squadron wheeled to the right and caused a similar movement by all the squadrons that followed it. The charge failed and all the squadrons only rallied next to the fortified farm of Ste-Alliance [probably La Haye Sainte], which was still occupied by the English whose fire killed and wounded many in an instant. General l'Héritier, commanding the division, General Picquet commanding the brigade, Colonel Leopold

(**Above, left**) Reille commanded the II Corps. He wrote only a brief description of the battle and seems to have used it primarily to deflect blame for the failure around Hougoumont onto his subordinates.

(**Above, right**) Trefcon served as chief of staff to General Bachelu. He gives a rather uncontroversial account of the battle but is notable for having abandoned the army after the battle.

(**Left**) Napoleon's brother Jérôme was a divisional commander in the II Corps and was primarily responsible for the French action around Hougoumont. He appears to have abandoned his division sometime during the battle to join the emperor.

(**Above**) Foy commanded a division in the II Corps. He made little contribution to the action around Hougoumont, but his description of his attack on the British ridge is interesting.

(**Opposite, above left**) Tromelin commanded a brigade in the VI Corps. His brief account describes the fighting against the Prussians on the French right flank.

(**Opposite, above right**) Kellerman was an unenthusiastic supporter of Napoleon but accepted the command of the 3rd Cavalry Corps. He gives us some interesting detail on the French great cavalry attacks.

(**Opposite, below left**) Delort commanded a cuirassier division at Waterloo and gives an interesting account of the battle in general and the cavalry charges in detail.

(**Opposite, below right**) Ordener inherited the command of a cuirassier brigade early in the battle after its original commander was wounded. His account concentrates on the great cavalry charges.

(**Above, left**) Pelet commanded the 2nd Regiment of Chasseurs à Pied of the Imperial Guard. He gives a long and detailed account of the fighting against the Prussians in Planchenoit.

(**Above, right**) Guyot commanded the heavy cavalry division of the Imperial Guard. He describes the actions of the division during the battle before he was wounded.

(**Right**) De Brack served as a captain in the lancers of the Imperial Guard. He gives some interesting detail of the attacks against the Allied squares.

This famous painting of the battle shows the fighting around Hougoumont. French accounts prove that far fewer troops were committed to the fighting here than is generally portrayed in Allied histories.

This rather romanticised print shows Ney leading the great French cavalry attacks against a British square. The accounts of these charges are some of the most detailed of the French participants.

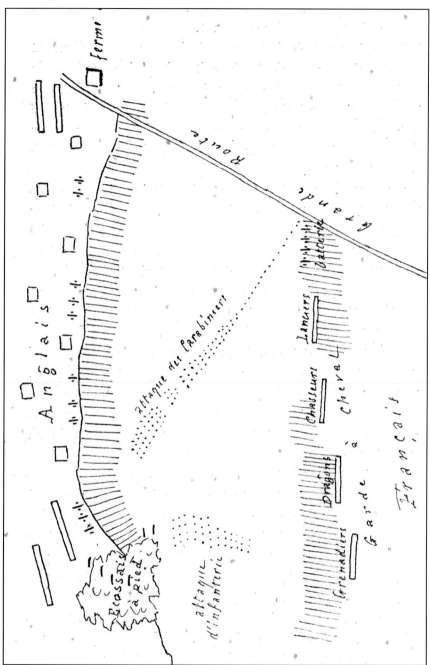

This sketch was drawn by Captain de Brack to show the futile charge of the carabiniers which is described by Kellerman in his account of the battle.

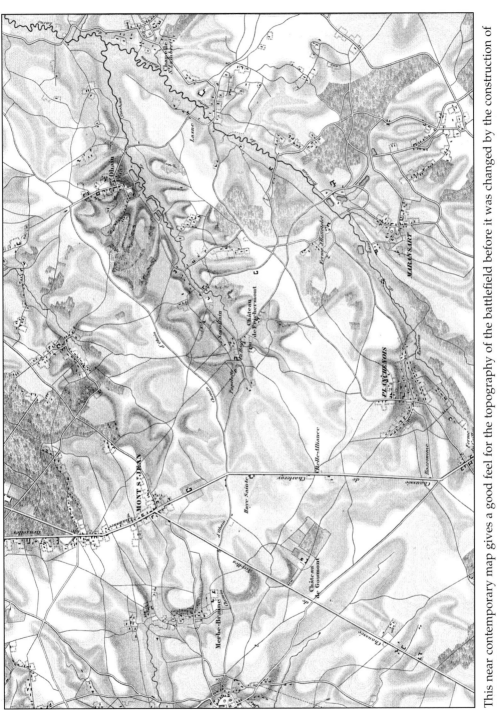

This near contemporary map gives a good feel for the topography of the battlefield before it was changed by the construction of the Lion Mound.

commanding the 7th Dragoons, and two *chefs d'escadron* of this regiment were all amongst the wounded. The command of the 7th Dragoons fell to *Chef d'Escadron* Létang at the moment when they rallied near la Ste Alliance.

At this time, the emperor, informed of the danger of our position, ordered la Ste Alliance [once again he clearly means La Haye Sainte] to be taken at any cost. Ney placed himself at the head of the infantry which marched on this fortified post and took it. Only then did l'Héritier's division cease to suffer from the murderous fire to which it had been exposed for so long.

Forced from their fortifications, the English left the farm in disorder to retire to the rest of the army. They presented their flank to our cavalry that remained close to the farm, allowing them to charge with success. This opportunity did not escape the experienced eye of *Chef d'Escadron* Létang commanding the 7th Dragoons. He put himself at the head of the 1st Dragoons who were formed in front of his own regiment and pointed out the opportunity to the commander of the 1st Dragoons for a charge, encouraging him to move his troops off and assuring him that he would vigorously support him with the 7th Dragoons in echelon to the right of the 1st and at the foot of the slope, the crest of which was occupied by the 1st. But the commander of the 1st Dragoons had no orders and would not take the advice of the commander of the 7th. In vain did Létang point out that since the generals were wounded and absent, there were no orders to await, but that he should take the initiative; the commander of the 1st Dragoons remained where he was. That of the 7th then declared that he would charge and seeing there was no time to lose, for the 7th to climb the distance of the slope which separated the two regiments, he then asked to be supported in the attack that he was going to undertake.

Quick as lightning, *Chef d'Escadron* Létang rejoined his regiment and set off at the trot so as not to exhaust the horses in order to mount and then push the charge with vigour. But time was lost; the English infantry, in flight a few moments before, had re-formed and were supported by fresh troops that were rushed forward. However, the charge of the 7th Dragoons succeeded and the English squares hardly formed were sabred as well as other troops that advanced to their support. An unexpected event annulled the result of this great feat of arms. The 1st Dragoons, having appeared to have set off in support of the 7th, at the very time that they had started their charge, made a retrograde movement in order to occupy the position that the 7th had just vacated.

Whatever the reason for this movement, it was certainly inopportune for the 7th Dragoons, engaged with the English; seeing the 1st Dragoons turn about instead of supporting them, believing that our line had been turned, and abandoning the infantry that had become their prisoners, they followed the 1st Dragoons, close to whom it rallied and ceased its own rearward movement. Thus, this unfortunate move denied it the brilliant success of the charge commanded by *Chef d'Escadron* Létang, who after having loudly and energetically condemned this unnecessary and precipitous retreat, returned his regiment to the advance. But the English infantry had received reinforcements and was formed in good order; the 7th Dragoons had been weakened after having broken the ranks of this infantry and many men of the regiment had not been able to rally to the 1st Dragoons and had been stuck amongst the squares. Thus it was not possible to usefully execute another charge. It was only possible to maintain a good bearing.

At this moment, an artillery battery of the Imperial Guard deployed in front of the 7th Dragoons and in a short time fired off all its remaining rounds. It then withdrew; when *Chef d'Escadron* Létang ordered it to remain in position where it had been, saying to the commander that at least the enemy might think that it had more ammunition and that moreover it [illegible]; however, he could not stop it retiring after it had attracted enemy artillery fire at this point.

4th Cavalry Corps

Lieutenant General Baron Jacques Antoine Adrien Delort

Stouff, *Le Lieutenant Général Delort (d'apres ses Archives et les archives du Ministère de la Guerre)* (Paris/Nancy: Berger-Leverault, 1906), pp. 147–58.

During the Waterloo campaign, Delort commanded the 14th Cavalry Division of the 4th Reserve Cavalry Corps (Milhaud).

Delort was born in 1773 and enlisted in the 4th Battalion of the Jura aged eighteen. He rose quickly through the ranks and in 1792 was commissioned into the 8th de ligne. After fighting at Valmy, he spent the next four years as a staff officer before retiring due to ill health. However, he returned to duty later in the year and served in the Army of Italy, finishing in Venice and a transfer to the 22nd Cavalry Regiment. He fought against the Austrians in northern Italy and was promoted to chef d'escadron *in 1800. He remained in Italy until promotion to lieutenant colonel and the disbandment of his regiment in 1803. He transferred to the 9th Dragoons with whom he fought throughout the 1805 campaign against Austria, distinguishing himself in command of the regiment at Austerlitz, where he was wounded by two lance thrusts. In 1806 he was promoted colonel and commander of the 24th Dragoons in Naples. He took his regiment to Spain at the end of 1807 and distinguished himself at many battles against the Spanish, being promoted to* général de brigade *in 1811. At the end of 1813 he was recalled to France for the 1814 campaign. Promoted to* général de division *in February of that year, he led a desperate charge with his raw troops at Montereau on the 26th and took command of the division. Not an avid Bonapartist, he was decorated by the returning Louis XVIII, but was put on the inactive list. In 1815 he only reported for duty after Louis had left the country. Against the advice of many, he was given a command on the recommendation of Suchet, with whom he had served in Spain, and commanded the 14th Cavalry (Cuirassier) Division in Milhaud's 4th Cavalry Corps. He was present at Ligny but took little part in that battle, but his division took a prominent role at Waterloo where he was wounded. He safely extracted the remains of his division after the battle but led them back to Paris. He was suspended from duty in August 1815, reinstated in 1820 and then put into retirement again in 1825. He was recalled once more after the July Revolution of 1830 and served in various posts before his death in 1841.*

Unlike like Kellerman, Delort was an admirer of Napoleon and his account seems to follow those of his emperor, including Napoleon's excuses for the loss of the battle. Although written quite soon after the battle, it is riddled with facts that he could only have learnt from other histories and not directly from his own experiences. He suggests that the great cavalry charges were launched to support the counter-attack against the British Household and Union Brigades by a brigade of cuirassiers. He also claims that squares made up of the British Guards were broken, which is clearly wishful thinking.

Drawn from a letter to an unknown maréchal de camp *who was involved in the compilation of* Victoires et Conquêtes ..., *dated Arbois, 19 September 1820.*

It [the enemy] was, besides, favoured by his great superiority of his forces, by the dominating ground on which it was deployed, by some farm buildings which offered strong points and finally, by the rain that fell in torrents throughout the night of the 17th/18th. The soaked and muddy ground made offensive cavalry manoeuvres and artillery movement extremely difficult, and thus favoured, by these new obstacles, the defence over the offensive.

From dawn on the 18th, the English army was deployed for battle in front of Mont-Saint-Jean, covering the main roads from Brussels and Nivelles. Its right was anchored on a ravine, near Braine-la-Leud, and its left on the height which dominated the hamlet of la Haye. All the defensive deployment of the English general are exactly described in his official report on the battle of Waterloo and it coincided very closely with the account in the memoir just cited [of Napoleon]. This memoir describes truthfully the detail of the emperor's attack order and leaves us, in this report, with nothing to be desired.

The two armies, ready to come to grips, presented an imposing spectacle. Their attitude promised a bloody and desperate battle. The courage of the troops on both sides had been stimulated to the highest degree. They did not know that the pre-eminence of the nations was attached to the terrible struggle which was to come. The French fought for the honour and independence of their country and to avenge the defeats of the last campaigns. They showed a boiling ardour and their bearing made the enemy fear French fury which was irresistible. The calm of the English displayed this cool boldness which could brave the most threatening dangers and against which our brilliant impetuosity had been checked more than once. The commanders of the two armies, in very different ways, inspired an equal confidence in their soldiers.

The French general, endowed with immense powers, an active genius, enterprising, daring, let no obstacle stand in his way. He had been heard to say that the word 'impossible' should be taken out of the French dictionary. The character of the English general was slowness, foresightedness, timidity and a kind of defiance. One spread with pomp his superiority and did not reduce his anticipation to a complete domination. The other hid his pride under an outer bonhomie and simplicity ...

Already the enemy line had been scouted by General Haxo. It had not been reinforced by any fortification, but the English occupied the château of Hougoumont and the farm of La Haye Sainte with élite troops to cover the centre-right and their centre-left.

Towards nine o'clock in the morning, the army divided into eleven columns and set off. From all parts, trumpets sounded, drums beat 'to battle' and music rang out the cherished music of victory. At 10am., this great movement was complete. A profound silence reigned. All the troops were ranged in admirable order, occupying the positions that had been assigned to them. Immediately, the emperor passed down the line and his presence excited the greatest enthusiasm everywhere. The soldiers' ardour was for him the presage of victory. He placed himself on the heights of Rossomme, from where he could easily discern the movements of both armies. The reserve occupied, close to imperial headquarters, a central position, ready to move anywhere its support was deemed necessary.

These preliminary deployments were efficiently completed. The most perfect order presided in their execution. But the English army, having its left flank guaranteed by the Prussians and supporting its right on a valley, covered its centre by small woods and houses where élite troops were hidden. Ranged in line on a dominating plateau which had strong points on its extremities, the English army, limited within a small space, its right at Braine-la-Leud, its centre towards Mont-Saint-Jean and its left at La Haye Sainte [la Haie/Haye], was in a position to successfully repulse all our attacks. Nevertheless, one could rightly reproach the English general of having committed a capital fault by choosing a battlefield which had defiles through the Soignes forest behind it. Indeed, if the plan to force his centre had succeeded, his retreat would have been very difficult, or even turned into a rout.

After the defeat of the Prussian army at Ligny, the English general would without doubt have directed his army in a manner more conforming to the interests of the Allies, to the rules of wise prudence and above all, to the laws of war, by concentrating his army much closer to Brussels. It is there that he could, it seems, have chosen a battlefield, rallied there the Prussian army, which if not disorganised, was at least shaken by its losses from the 16th, and awaited in this position the reinforcements recently disembarked at Ostend.

Close to ten o'clock in the morning, the division of Prince Jérôme attacked with the greatest vigour the wood and gardens of the château of Hougoumont, but the brigade of the English Guards, under the order of General Bing [*sic*], bravely maintained itself there for several hours. Foy's division moved to support that of Prince Jérôme, and it was only by the sustained and repeated efforts of the most determined bravery that the wood and the avenues of Hougoumont, scattered with the bodies of the intrepid English, that they remained in our hands. But the fortified château, defended by a battalion, was only taken a long time after with the aid of a battery of howitzers which set fire to the stables and rooftops.

During this determined combat which, by a strong diversion, drew all the attention of the enemy and occupied the élite of his troops, the emperor made the preparations for the principal attack on the enemy's centre. The goal of this attack was to capture Mont-Saint-Jean, a crossroads of the great roads from Nivelles and Charleroi to Brussels and thus to separate the English left from its right, where the greater part of its forces were, and to prevent the Prussians joining them, should they escape from Marshal Grouchy who we expected to see at any moment. It is evident that this plan was well conceived and brought together all possible advantages. But before putting it into execution, the French general should have had positive information on the location of Count Grouchy and have been sure this marshal was well placed to contain the Prussian army and to prevent it from throwing itself on our right flank and rear at the height of the action. The extreme slowness with which Count Grouchy had set off in pursuit of Blücher after the battle of Ligny should have inspired in the emperor an uncertain confidence in his conduct. Should he have given up at the slightest uncertainty, the possibility of a co-operation so necessary and potentially so decisive? On the other hand, could one reasonably have had doubts that a general who, until then, had given such guarantees of his talents, of his activity and his experience, would misinterpret his instructions and his duty in such an essential manner, and to misunderstand to the point of ignoring entirely the direction taken by a beaten army which he was to follow, 'sword in his kidneys', up to the moment of a second battle?

Nevertheless, this concern of the emperor's had been reinforced because, already, before eleven o'clock in the morning, one could see in the distance, in the direction of Saint-Lambert, troops which were heading towards the left flank of the English army. Everyone was on tenterhooks. Some confirmed that it was a detachment of Marshal Grouchy, others that it was the advance-guard of the Prussian army. This disagreeable uncertainty did not last long. A Prussian hussar, carrier of a despatch for the English general, and made prisoner by the light cavalry that covered the area between Vavres [*sic*] and Planchenoit, informed of the arrival of Bülow's corps of 30,000 men. This corps was intact and all the more redoubtable because it had taken no part in the defeat of Ligny. Soon this report was confirmed by Generals Domont [*sic*] and Subervie, whose divisions of light cavalry had been immediately despatched a few thousand metres to our right. They informed us not only that they were in the presence of the advance-guard of the Prussian army, but that patrols sent in all directions had found no information on the movements of Marshal Grouchy. This event forced the emperor to detach Count Lobau's corps to support Domont's light cavalry and contain the Prussians. He hoped, with perhaps too much confidence that 10,000 French, advantageously posted, full of enthusiasm and devotion, led by a commander of proven firmness, would resist all the efforts of Bülow whilst awaiting the arrival of Marshal Grouchy, while the English centre would be broken by an irresistible impet-uosity. But the English army was strengthened in its resistance by the means that had been lost to the attack, and we have already noted the advantage of their position and that it had an immense superiority in forces.

However, a lively fire fight was engaged along the whole line. It was mid-day. The Emperor had ordered Marshal Ney to attack La Haye Sainte and the village of la Haye vigorously, to chase the English out of these two posts and then to establish himself between them and Bülow's corps. Eighty guns supported this attack. It could not have been confided in a better general who, by his sang-froid, his keen *coup d'oeil* and a consummate experience, had, on many battlefields, decided the victory. But it is claimed that, based on the events of 1814 and 1815 in the situations which put all the sentiments, all the affections and all the duties of a brave soldier and a man of honour in the most deplorable dilemma, his motivation was no longer the same and that the emperor relented, but too late, in having given him the most important missions. Either way, the enemy skirmishers were repulsed on all points, several important positions were abandoned, the English reserves were con-centrated on the left, entire masses were exterminated by a terrible fire of musketry and artillery, La Haye Sainte was taken by I Corps under the orders of General Reille [*sic*: it should read General d'Erlon], a great confusion in the middle of the equipages, convoys and a crowd of wounded which encumbered the road to Brussels, the stupor and concern of the English general, the immobility of his troops, the enthusiasm of the French, all announced the entire and profound rout of the English army. In this truly critical situation, the Duke of Wellington had the brigades of Generals Sommerset [*sic*] and Ponsonby. These brigades, formed of the 1st and 2nd Household Guard Cavalry, the dragoons of the Guard and the 1st, 2nd and 3rd Regiments of English dragoons, fell impetuously on the division of General Durutte. This division was sabred, dispersed, lost its eagles and all its artillery. But the 2nd Brigade of cuirassiers of General Delort having been ordered to advance against the English cavalry that covered the plain, profited by this disorder and made them pay dearly for the success they had obtained. In a moment, this brigade, consisting of the 6th and 9th Regiments, having *Maréchal de Camp* Farine at their head [Farine actually commanded the 1st Brigade, the 2nd Brigade was commanded by General Vial], and with Lieutenant General Delort and Lieutenant General Dejean, who had carried the emperor's orders, launched itself against the English cavalry, overthrew it, and scattered the battlefield with its dead. Two élite English regiments were almost destroyed in this vigorous charge, and despite the inferiority of numbers and the disadvantage of attacking an enemy encouraged by a brilliant success, the cuirassiers did not lose a single man and hardly any wounded. The guns were retaken and the infantry promptly rallied.

The success of the battle then appeared certain. The emperor was close to achieving his goal. He was going to separate the two armies and clear the main road to Brussels. It was three o'clock. But the II and IV Prussian corps, which had started their march at dawn, had crossed the narrow defile at Saint-Lambert and had taken a position hidden by the Frischermont forest in order to attack the rear of the French army at the most opportune time, while I Corps advanced by Ohain to attack our right flank simultaneously. III Corps was to follow this movement. Thus the whole Prussian army, less III Corps under the orders of Thielman [*sic*], who was forced to hold at Vavres [*sic*], was before us, outflanking our right and by an inconceivable fatality this decisive movement was conducted quietly through extremely difficult defiles without Marshal Grouchy, with more than 30,000 infantry, half our cavalry and a hundred guns, thinking to threaten it.

Lobau's corps, which had repulsed Bülow several times, was not strong enough to stop an army. The emperor was obliged to send Generals Duhesme and Morand to his support with two divisions of the Young and Old Guards and a strong battery of artillery.

The English, doubly favoured by the approach of the Prussian army and the reduction of the troops sent against themselves, re-took their courage. The light cavalry of General Jacquinot, who conducted a lively pursuit of the enemy cavalry on the plateau of la Haye, was charged and thrown back in disorder by a large part of the English cavalry. The cuirassiers of General Milhaud (divisions Vathier [*sic*] and Delort) moved quickly to his support and with shouts of '*Vive l'Empereur!*' everywhere the English cavalry was repulsed and broken. The intrepid cuirassiers pursuing their success, charged the squares of the English Guards, broke them, covering the ground with their dead, but were not able, because of the terrain, to profit from all the advantages of these brilliant charges, in which *Fourrier* Isaac Palan, of the 9th, and *Maréchal des Logis* Aubert, of the 10th Cuirassiers, each took a flag.

Forced to withdraw a few paces, these two divisions, charged by the English cavalry, turned about and forced it to seek its salvation under the protection of its infantry. But placed at the extremity of the plateau where they were exposed to the shock of the entire English army, it became an urgent necessity to reinforce them by the cuirassier corps of Lieutenant General Kellerman, formed of the divisions of l'Héritier and Roussel d'Urbal, and by the cavalry division of the Guard, commanded by General Lefèbre des Nouettes [*sic*]. This united cavalry, after having broken several squares, sabred thousands of infantry, repeatedly repulsed all the cavalry charges, maintained themselves, hardly supported by a few battalions, against all the repeated efforts of the English army. General l'Hériter fell seriously wounded from a shot through his body. The chief-of-staff of General Milhaud was killed. Lieutenant Generals Milhaud and Delort both had horses killed under them, their uniforms and hats were riddled with bullets. The latter had, besides, been wounded by a musket ball and several blows from a sabre. Nearly all the superior officers were *hors de combat*. The dead covered the ground where the cavalry operated; but its heroic steadfastness could not be shaken, either by the many charges of the English cavalry, nor by the terrible fire of their artillery and musketry. The circumstances were such that any retrograde movement would have compromised the French army, and these 10,000 élite cavalrymen had to face, for more than three hours, a most imminent death to maintain themselves in face of the whole English army on the ground that they had conquered. We can contend that our military splendours do not present, perhaps, such an example of devotion amongst the prodigies which render ever memorable the courage of French soldiers. The emperor then rode along the entire line under a hail of balls and canister. The brave General of Artillery Deveaux [*sic*], who escorted him, was struck by a ball at the moment when the services that one hoped for in such a distinguished officer rendered his loss even more painful. He was replaced by General Lallemand who was wounded soon afterwards. All these circumstances held up the prompt and effective support that we awaited from the reserve artillery.

This great movement of cavalry, where so much bravery was deployed with sheer loss, had been ordered by Marshal Ney. It was certainly a great mistake. It seemed to us that the enemy's progress on our right and rear then directed that this élite cavalry, supported by several battalions of the Imperial Guard, should have been placed in reserve towards Planchenoit. In a position where this cavalry could have been allowed to operate with freedom, it is probably sure that it would have re-established affairs, repulsed the English and the Prussians and repaired all our setbacks. The devotion which it had shown proves this assertion. With this invincible cavalry, the emperor would have remained master of the battlefield and as the Allied armies had suffered losses triple those of our own in killed and wounded, as Marshal Grouchy would have been able to join us at dawn the next day with his army corps which had not been broken down by the most bloody of combats, it appears likely that the enemies would have affected their retreat and that, if they had wanted to re-new the battle, all the chances of success would this time have been in our favour. Marshal Ney was not only wrong to commit the cavalry prematurely, but he had made it charge again on hilly ground, little favourable for its manoeuvres and where, not being supported by infantry, it was unable to benefit from its initial success. The price of this false manoeuvre was to have put it in a position where it sacrificed itself uselessly without being able to advance or retire.

[*Here, Delort adds a footnote*: Without anticipating the progress of the Prussians on our rear, I stopped *Maréchal de Camp* Farine's brigade, which, on the order of Marshal Ney, and without reference to me, was advancing towards the great plateau. I pleaded with him not to separate himself from the division and explained that I had not received an order from the corps commander. Whilst this protest held up the brigade, Marshal Ney himself came over, bristling with impatience. He insisted not only on the execution of his first order, but demanded, in the name of the emperor, both divisions. I still hesitated … I explained that heavy cavalry should not attack unbroken infantry on heights which was well prepared to defend itself. The marshal cried, '*En avant*! The salvation of France depends on it!' I obeyed with regret, praying that such an unwise manoeuvre would not result in its loss.]

However, the entire Prussian army advanced in the direction of La Haye Sainte and Planchenoit, favoured by a ground in the form of an amphitheatre, where his artillery, moving progressively down on the mounds which dominated it, protecting the infantry brigades which formed up one after the other to move forwards in echelons. It is fair to say that these combined movements were executed with order and precision. Already, Prince Blücher had arrived at la Haye, where the 4th Division of I Corps [Durutte], the same which had been broken towards midday by the English dragoons, only offered weak resistance. It was even said that some traitors uttered the sad cry of '*Sauve qui peut!*' This division, although struggling against much superior forces, could have stopped the progress of the enemy for much longer. The disorder started to spread throughout the right when the emperor had the shout 'Victory!' announce Grouchy's arrival. This false news, strengthening the spirit of the soldier for a moment, did not take long to be contradicted and produced a discouragement even greater than the frustration of our last hope. The enemy had entirely turned us and he was close to penetrating into the village of Planchenoit.

The emperor, at this eminently critical moment, wanted to attempt one last effort; he had the reserve of his Guard formed into attack columns, but the English moved to the threatened points with reinforcements and a formidable artillery and this Guard, advancing, had such a discharge of balls and canister to suffer that its ranks were broken and it became impossible for them to be reformed. This terrible fire could only be compared to violent storm in which the lightning criss-crosses the heavens, where the continual detonations of a thunder which sows devastation and death with a horrible crash, which mixed with a torrent of hail and rain. Vainly the cavalry of the reserve of the Imperial Guard, under the orders of General Guyot, attempted, by a vigorous charge, to protect the foot Guard; this division was overwhelmed by superior forces. The cuirassiers themselves abandoned the battlefield conquered with so much courage and defended no less valiantly. ... The Prussians took on the Imperial Guard who defended themselves in the village of Planchenoit with their accustomed valour and the whole English army marched forwards. The enemy generals met each other at the farm of la Belle-Alliance. The battle was lost. The soldiers of all arms fled pell-mell, mingled together, indifferent to the voices of their leaders and officers. The roads, perhaps obstructed deliberately through treason, left almost all our guns, our caissons and our baggage in the hands of the enemy. Even the emperor's carriage became the prey of the Prussian hussars. Finally, the rout was complete and the losses of France irreparable. Everywhere bad Frenchmen augmented the confusion and excited the soldiers to desert. The most terrible disorder reigned in the French army until its arrival under the walls of Paris.

Colonel *Comte* Michel Ordener

Lot, *Les Deux Généraux Ordener* (Paris: Roger et Chernoviz, 1910), pp. 91–5.

During the Waterloo campaign Michel Ordener commanded the 1st Cuirassier Regiment. This regiment was part of the 1st Brigade (Dubois) of the 13th Cavalry Division (Wathier St-Alphonse), part of the 4th Reserve Cavalry Corps (Milhaud).

With Dubois wounded early in the battle, Ordener took command of the brigade, which consisted of the 1st and 7th Cuirassiers, and led it in the great cavalry charges.

Michel Ordener, not to be confused with his brother Antoine (who was to be killed at Waterloo), was born in 1787, son of a then maréchal des logis-chef. *In 1802 he joined the 11th Chasseurs à Cheval and became a student at the Special Military School at Fontainebleau the following year. He was commissioned into the 24th Dragoons at the end of that year. In 1805, as lieutenant, he became aide-de-camp to his father who was then general, commanding the Grenadiers à Cheval of the Imperial Guard, and took part in the Austerlitz campaign. He was present at that battle where he charged with the Guard cavalry and where he won the* Légion d'Honneur. *The following year he became aide-de-camp to General Duroc and served with him in Prussia and Poland in 1806–7, being present at Jena, Eylau and Friedland, at which his bravery earned him promotion to captain. He served with Duroc in Spain the following year and was promoted* chef d'escadron *in a provisional regiment of chasseurs, then the 7th Cuirassiers in 1809. He took part in the campaign against Austria in that year and took provisional command of the regiment when the commanding officer and senior* chef d'escadron *were wounded and led it during the battle. Advancing with the 7th Cuirassiers into Russia in 1812, he was wounded by a lance thrust to the head at Polotsk. In November 1812 he was promoted colonel aged just twenty-five years. He commanded the 7th Cuirassiers at the crossing of the Beresina where he distinguished himself and was wounded. Named colonel of the 30th Dragoon Regiment in 1813 he was present at Lützen and Bautzen, and fought at Dresden and Leipzig. In the campaign of France in 1814, at the head of a provisional regiment, he charged at Montereau, was present at Laon and Sommesous, and was later wounded during the battle of Paris. He remained in service after the First Restoration and became commanding officer of the 1st Cuirassiers for the Waterloo campaign. He was wounded at that battle. After the Second Restoration he was put on the inactive list and did not serve again until after the July Revolution in 1830 when, for the second time, he commanded the 1st Cuirassiers. Promoted to* maréchal de camp *in 1831 he fulfilled less active posts before promotion to lieutenant general in 1846. He commanded several military divisions and filled inspectorate positions before being retired in 1852. He died in Paris in 1862.*

Ordener gives us an interesting and detailed account of the counter-attack against Ponsonby's brigade and the great cavalry charges.

On 18 June Milhaud's division was deployed three hundred metres to the rear of the line formed by the corps of d'Erlon to our immediate right, from the château of Frischermont as far as La Haye Sainte; points occupied by the English.

Hardly had the battle started than the strange marching order came to the regiments of d'Erlon which delivered them to Wellington's artillery and the sabres of Ponsonby's dragoons. Our infantry fell by the hundred and the enemy cavalry sabred them to the mouths of our artillery which knocked them down. At this sight, the 7th and 12th Cuirassiers threw themselves on Ponsonby's dragoons, swept them away laughing and destroyed them; then they returned to their initial positions.

Then started the furious battle for La Haye Sainte. Impatient of the losses suffered by our troops and of the delay caused to the movement of the corps by the resistance of the enemy at this point, *le maréchal* Ney ordered me to take an English battery located close to the farm of Mont-Saint-Jean, whose fire was having great effect in our lines. I set my regiment off at a trot, in column, by squadron, at deploying distance. The Hanoverian battalion Lüne-bourg and the 2nd German Light Battalion were encountered en route; we passed over them, I overthrew three officers with my own hand, their colour remained in our possession, we reached the English battery out of breath, took the twenty-four pieces that composed it, which I had spiked, and I pursued the charge which took us to the edge of the Soignes forest. There I found myself ten paces from a square, a face of which opened a murderous fire on us; my horse was killed, I was struck by a ball in the neck. Protected by my cuirass, I was able to get away. I re-joined my men and returned with them to our lines where after being bandaged I remounted and retook my command.

From this moment (it would have been about 2.30pm), it was, I cannot help but think, a great fault to support my successful charge with the whole cavalry. The plateau of Mont-Saint-Jean had been taken, without great loss, the English army cut into two pieces, and strongly compromised because it could not have retreated by the Brussels road. Instead of exhausting our infantry with fruitless efforts against Hougoumont, a point which we could have ignored without great risk, it could have been directed against the important position of Mont-Saint-Jean, where it could have replaced us and allowed us to wipe out the enemy before the arrival of the Prussians. Later, the possession of this plateau cost us an enormous loss of blood and it was impossible to maintain ourselves there.

Having witnessed the way that I had executed the orders of the Prince de la Moskowa, General Milhaud confided in me the command of one of his brigades, composed of my regiment which I had previously commanded in the campaigns of Austria and Russia; the 7th Cuirassiers. [The original commander of this brigade, Travers, had been wounded.]

It was necessary to take Mont-Saint-Jean at all costs, a position whose possession would decide the battle. D'Erlon's corps had been half destroyed and completely disorganised so that it was incapable of achieving this. Napoleon understood this; he passed close to our ranks, he saluted us with his magical smile. The enthusiasm was general. Our four superb lines were still almost all fresh; they moved off together with a shout of '*Vive l'Empereur!*' I do not know if there is another example in history of such a mass of cavalry launching itself into combat at the same time. For me, who had taken part in the celebrated charges of Austerlitz, Jena, Eylau, Friedland and Wagram, I had never seen such a fight. There was nearly 5,000 of us. Ney put himself at our head. It was 4pm. Our first shock was irresistible. Despite a rain of iron that struck our helmets and cuirasses, despite a sunken road above which were established the English batteries, and into which I tumbled with the front ranks (I got out by hanging onto the tail of the horse of one of my cuirassiers), we crowned the crest of the heights, we passed like a bolt of lightning through the guns, and approached the English infantry; we threw it back in disorder on the squares formed in haste by the Duke of Wellington. These redoubtable squares were attacked in their turn and decimated. To give himself a moment of respite, the English general called to his aid all that remained of his cavalry; but the Dutch brigade that he sent against us was broken; its debris fled, spreading terror everywhere. We could already clearly see the enemy equipages and the mass of fleeing men running pell-mell down the Brussels road. A few infantry battalions in support would have seen the end of the English army. Ney searched for some everywhere, he cried out loud, but there were none anywhere. Already, far off was ringing out sinister cannon that none of us could understand [we must presume he is speaking of the Prussian guns]. However, the squares still held; the fire from their flanks caused heavy casualties in our ranks. It was absolutely necessary to resign ourselves to retreat or triumph in a final effort against British tenacity.

The Prince de la Moskowa advanced our last reserves. Dragoons, carabiniers, grenadiers á cheval, joined the cuirassiers, lancers and chasseurs. Milhaud and Lefebvre-Desnöuettes were joined by Kellerman, the victor of Marengo, and Guyot, the friend and replacement of my father. Ney had eighty [*sic*] squadrons under his orders. What did they accomplish? The charges followed one after another without interruption. We were almost masters of the plateau. But the English, although three-quarters destroyed, were rooted to the spot; it was necessary to kill every last one of them. Exhausted, our cavalry could do no more. Exposed without shelter from artillery and musketry, their supreme part in this great drama, maintaining their position, condemned them to death. They were the only salute of the army. The disaster commenced; my brigade had suffered enormous losses; it was at this moment that my unlucky brother, already wounded in the morning by one of Ponsonby's dragoons, received his death-blow; a ball, ricocheting, struck his helmet and smashed his skull. It was nearly 8pm.

We still had a glimmer of hope. A heavy weight of fire suddenly came from La Haye Sainte; this was d'Erlon's regiments who had been encouraged by Marshal Ney's voice. Several of our cavalrymen dismounted and acted as skirmishers to support this movement. Further away, the regiments of the Guard were advancing; the Prince de la Moskowa who was everywhere, led their first battalions; the emperor himself, we were assured, commanded the others. We were now going to have a little of that infantry which we had lacked for such a long time.

This illusion was short-lived. Deploying out of the Soignes forest, the Prussians appeared on our flank. From Mont-Saint-Jean we saw their masses advance preceded by eighty guns; at the same time, Wellington added the brigades of Vivian and Vandeleur to the first of Ziethen's squadrons, two or three thousand cavalry launched themselves against our line of retreat. At this sight, the commotion penetrated our ranks; the devotion of our cavalrymen was finished, the sense of self-preservation overwhelmed it. In vain did we make our final efforts to keep them in line; they went down the slopes in disorder, swirled around the squares of the Guard and dispersed under a hail of musket balls. Swept along by this flight, I rallied some of my cuirassiers, and followed with my brother [a 22-year-old lieutenant in the 7th Cuirassiers who was wounded at Waterloo and died of a *fièvre cérébrale* (a fever of the brain) at Cambrai on 10 July] the debris of the Guard as far as Genappe and Charleroi. There the scenes of Vilna were repeated under my eyes. But it is necessary to render justice to this heroic and unfortunate army; the demoralisation of which it gave a sad spectacle was due to the wild savagery of the Prussians.

Étienne-Nicholas Pilloy

In a letter dated 24 June 1815 from Reims, published in *Carnet de la Sabretache 1907* (Paris: Leroy, 1907), pp. 506–20.

In the Waterloo campaign, Pilloy served as a cuirassier in the 9th Cuirassiers (Colonel Bigarne). The regiment was part of the 2nd Brigade (Vial) of the 14th Cavalry Division (Delort), part of the 4th Reserve Cavalry Corps (Milhaud).

Pilloy entered the 13th Cuirassiers in April 1813. Amalgamated with the 9th Cuirassiers in 1814 after the First Restoration, he was promoted to brigadier *(the equivalent of corporal in the cavalry) on 9 August 1815. He took part in the campaigns of 1813, 1814 and 1815. He charged at Ligny and Waterloo. After the Waterloo campaign he was admitted into the Cuirassiers of the Royal Guard and served until 1821.*

One of the few French accounts from the lower ranks, Pilloy gives us a little detail on his experiences in the great cavalry charges.

... then we arrived at Fleurus; there we engaged the first battle [Ligny] which was very hard fought; it started at eleven o'clock in the morning and finished at eight o'clock in the evening. The next day, only our light troops pushed back the enemy for six leagues and we were only four leagues from Brussels, in Brabant. There we gave a terrible battle; there with me were veterans of twenty-five to thirty years' service who said they had never seen anything like it. It started at nine o'clock in the morning and finished at nine o'clock at night. The cannonade never slackened; everything trembled. At nine o'clock in the evening, the grenadiers of the Guard charged by divisions on our left; as they arrived where the English were well hidden, they fell like flies; the few that remained turned about and escaped and then in quarter of an hour the whole army was in rout; everyone just looked out for themselves.

This whole affair started on the 16th, at Fleurus; on the 17th, our light infantry pushed them back six leagues to the rear as far as a very advantageous position for them and which caused our loss. On the 17th, I was part of a group of twenty men selected to be the escort of General Delort. At some time during the 18th, when it [the fighting] was very warm, he left us at the gallop and I did not see him return.

At that moment, I found myself very embarrassed, not knowing where to find the regiment. The 5th regiment came into view in line, ready to charge an English battalion square. Unwisely, I put myself in their ranks; we charged three times and it was only at the third attempt that we entered the square. As you would expect, there remained cuirassiers and horses on the ground. I retired and a little time after I noticed our regiment which was about to charge some English dragoons. Then I found myself once more in the action. We again charged three times; in the last, we routed them. You will understand that by then my horse had had enough. It is true that a heavy rain had fallen in the night of the 16th to 17th and that our horses were continually in the mud up to their stomachs. At the time when the infantry were routed, the enemy were already there, but the disaster determined that the situation changed from a march and all the cavalry followed the infantry. In an instant, all were mixed up; cavalry, artillery and infantry; and even many infantrymen were crushed by the cavalry or caissons. All night we heard the trumpet sounding the rally, but everyone was scattered.

Chapter 4

The Artillery

Throughout the Napoleonic Wars the French army had enjoyed a very high reputation not only for the quality of its artillery arm, but also the number of guns it fielded, only the Russians coming near to challenging them. Due to the relatively low battle casualties they suffered, the efficiency of this arm did not reduce significantly as the wars progressed and it seemed that whatever the state of the army, it was always able to field a well-manned and well-equipped artillery arm. There may have been a shrinking pool of manpower, but there was never a shortage of guns and rarely a shortage of limbers and caissons; in the later campaigns the main problems seemed to be the sufficient supply of ammunition and finding sufficient horses and manpower for the train. In 1813 and 1814, Napoleon drew heavily on the naval artillery for both manpower and ordnance and did so again in 1815. Although much of the credit for its efficiency is given to Napoleon as a gunner by trade, he also had a large pool of very competent senior artillery officers to ensure the artillery maintained its standards. At Waterloo the French enjoyed a considerable advantage in artillery over Wellington's Allied army (246 guns to 157), although the arrival of the Prussians reduced this disparity considerably. Due to the mud and sudden collapse of the French army at the end of the battle, most of the guns were abandoned on the battlefield and overrun.

Much controversy still surrounds the exact deployment, composition and numbers of the grand battery at Waterloo; indeed some modern historians even claim there wasn't one. There is also some uncertainty as to whether the grand battery deployed to a more forward position and around how much French artillery was deployed forward onto, or close to, the Allied line to the west of the main Brussels road later in the battle. Unfortunately, we have only two artillery eyewitnesses to draw on to try and get a clearer picture. One of these, Lieutenant Pontécoulant, served in the Imperial Guard, so we will examine his account in the next chapter; he deployed forward with his battery and the deployment is described by a number of British and other Allied accounts. Luckily, the other witness, Colonel de Salle, was well placed to give more information on the grand battery

Colonel Victor-Albert, Baron de Salle (or Dessales)

Extract from his *Souvenirs*, originally published in the *Revue de Paris* on 15 January 1895, and reproduced in *Souvenirs et correspondence sur la bataille de Waterloo* (Paris: Editions Historiques Teissedre, 2000), pp. 51–6.

During the Waterloo campaign, de Salle served as the commander of the artillery of the I Army Corps (d'Erlon).

De Salle was born at Versailles in 1776. He volunteered as an artilleryman in a volunteer battalion in 1792 and was elected sergeant the following year. He took part in the campaigns with the Army of the North in 1792–3 and the Army of the Sambre and Meuse in 1793–7, during which time he was commissioned as lieutenant, and then captain. In 1798 he served in the Army of England and then the Army of Italy in 1799. He was taken prisoner at Peschia in 1799 but released soon after and served with the Army of the Rhine in 1800–1. Promoted chef de bataillon *in the artillery in 1805 he took part in the campaigns of 1805, 1806 and 1807 with the* Grande Armée. *From 1808 to 1809 he served in Spain and then in the 1809 campaign against Austria, being promoted colonel after the battle of Wagram. He then successively filled the posts of Director of Artillery at Grenoble, then Saint-Omer and finally commandant of artillery at the camp of Boulogne before rejoining the* Grande Armée *as Director General of Military Bridging. He took part in the invasion of Russia and then became Director of Artillery at Metz in March 1813, then of bridging with the Army of the Main. In April 1813 he became the commander of artillery in VII Corps for the remainder of the campaign before joining the garrison of Magdebourg as chief-of-staff to the governor, General Lemarois. Although provisionally promoted to* général de brigade *by this general, the promotion was not confirmed by the First Restoration, who initially posted him to the artillery staff and then put him on the inactive list. Recalled on Napoleon's return, he was again promoted to* maréchal de camp *and made commander of the artillery of I Army Corps under d'Erlon. He fought at Waterloo and once again found his new rank not confirmed after Napoleon's abdication. Employed by the new government in 1815 as colonel, he was returned to the inactive list the following year. Recalled to duty in 1817 he was finally promoted to* maréchal de camp *in 1823 and commanded the artillery school at Rennes until formally retired in 1831. He died in 1864.*

We will see that Napoleon appointed de Salle as the commander of the grand battery, although he does not use this title to describe it until the end of his narrative. In fact, de Salle's rather muddled account, however interesting, gives little clarification on the points in dispute. Firstly, his maths in calculating the number of guns in his battery appears to be awry and while he describes a move forwards it appears never to have been completed and he is rather quick to condemn it (perhaps with the benefit of hindsight). He suggests the Imperial Guard artillery were only used to replace the losses caused by the British cavalry charge; many historians have Guard artillery in the initial battery. He seems to have made little effort to co-ordinate the withdrawal of his guns at the end of the battle. He clearly feels the advance of the battery was a mistake and worries that many have blamed him for ordering it.

[On the 17th,] His Majesty . . . addressed his orders to me: 'Have all the horse artillery go ahead and pursue the enemy without respite'.

I mounted a horse as quickly as possible, rushed down the columns and sent two horse artillery batteries to the advance-guard with which I pursued the enemy relentlessly. We drove him from height to height until night. He stopped at the farm of la Belle-Alliance [La Haye Sainte?] where he held firm.

The emperor wanted to push on; to support my horse artillery, I had to put one of my foot batteries of eight guns in battery, the light artillery was no longer able to continue on their own. But hardly had I opened fire than a formidable artillery, which we were [not] expecting, despite appearances, replied overwhelmingly. In a few seconds I lost men and horses; we would have been completely dismounted if I had not ceased fire. Everything was then quiet until morning. A ball passed so close to the rear of my horse that this last took me into the plain; I had to work hard to take control of it and it was only when I dismounted and stroked it that I was able to calm it.

It rained heavily the whole night. I gave up my lodgings to Count d'Erlon and thus passed the night in bivouac. By morning I was soaked and without my vehicle, which was in the park, it was impossible for me to change, which made things very uncomfortable for me.

The fatal 18 June arrived. The ground was waterlogged, although the weather was fine. The Emperor made a reconnaissance in the morning. He still did not believe the English wanted to fight a battle; he ordered several movements on the right to reassure himself. I had to go and look at the road that entered the forest to reassure myself that it was practical for artillery. The two armies watched each other. Our soldiers were ordered to eat.

Towards ten o'clock, the emperor ordered I Corps to close up towards II Corps, who occupied the left of the Brussels road. We occupied the right of this road, which was steep sided at this point. Two divisions of the V [VI] Corps and the Guard formed the reserve.

I was close to Count d'Erlon when M. de Labédoyère, *Génèral* aide-de-camp to the emperor, came to tell me that he [Napoleon] had given me the command of a battery of eighty guns, which was to be composed of all my six-pounder batteries, my twelve-pounder reserve battery, and of the reserve batteries of II and V [he means the VI] Corps, which would actually give me fifty-four guns, of which twenty-four would be twelve-pounders. First I ordered all these guns to be put in battery on the position we now occupied, mid-slope, in a single line and to open fire all at once to surprise and unsettle the enemy's morale. I was going to execute this order [to organise the grand battery] when General Ruty, commander-in-chief of the artillery, came to me and told me to make a forward reconnaissance of a more advanced position that could be occupied later. As an old soldier, knowing that in theory and practice that all movement on the battlefield is risky, and that above all a movement of a large quantity of artillery is dangerous, I stared at him for a long time, examining his demeanour to be certain that he spoke seriously. When I was sure, I made my reconnaissance quickly, then on my return I opened fire which suddenly shook the ground.

I wanted to confer the command of the twelve-pounder reserve to Colonel Bernard, my chief-of-staff, a wise and prudent officer. Unfortunately he informed me that having lost an eye at the siege of Saragossa he would not be able to fulfil this responsibility very effectively. I therefore spoke to General Ruty, who sent me Lieutenant Colonel *** [sic], chief-of-staff of II Corps [although this officer's name not given in de Salle's account, in the army returns the II Corps artillery chief-of-staff is named as Bobillier]. I placed Bernard on the right, close to General d'Erlon, and Colonel *** [sic] in the battery with the twelve-pounder reserve. I spread the rest of the superior officers along the rest of the line. I placed myself at the centre of the line, close to Marshal Ney, informing the officers that I could always be found in this position.

The enemy, whose artillery was entrenched, opened a lively fire on us, which did not let up in either rapidness or accuracy. I paid close attention to the enemy's position, I examined alternately his masses. *Chef d'Escadron* Waudré, who commanded my horse artillery, came to warn me that on the enemy's extreme left, considerable masses of cavalry were forming,[1] enquiring if it was necessary to inform the emperor.

I replied to him, 'Return to your post, the emperor is not a man to leave things to chance; he has an excellent telescope and will doubtless have noticed this cavalry'.

At this moment, the enemy's fire increased in intensity, a swarm of shells, balls and even Congreve rockets fell about us; a shell exploded close to me and wounded all those around me. I received a fragment in the collar of the coat I wore over my uniform, but which only made my arm numb for a time. I thought about the movement I was to carry out [move the grand battery forward] and that I proposed to execute battery by battery, firing as we went. I approached Marshal Prince de la Moskowa [Ney] who had complete confidence in me, to inform him of what I intended to do and to take his instructions, when I noticed Lieutenant Colonel *** move off with the reserves and go, without any precautions, to the second position. He arrived there and intended to establish them in battery. At that instant, the marshal shouted to me, 'You are charged!' Indeed, the enemy cavalry, profiting from the slackening of our fire, charged the 1st Division of I Corps which formed a single square in a fold in the ground below us.

At the time my reserves re-opened their fire, I did not want to leave a large interval between them and my six-pounders. I sent my aide-de-camp to tell their commanders to join the left of the battery. It was too late! The infantry, charged from behind by a formidable cavalry, was broken. They arrived all mixed together with the enemy on the reserve artillery whose fire was paralysed by the fear of killing their own men. I only had time to order a change of front, the right wing on the rear on the left-hand gun.

I was successful for the reserve of my own *corps d'armée*, commanded by *Chef de Bataillon* Saint-Michel, a brave officer full of *sang-froid*: but the two others were dragged along by the general disorder. The remainder of the battery found itself in the middle of the enemy cavalry, charged and forced to flee, pulled along in its movement.

I mounted my horse and galloped into the middle of this mêlée to try and bring back this alarmed multitude to my side, that is to say near the sunken road at the side of which I had succeeded in arranging my twelve-pounder reserve. Vain effort! I could no longer be heard, commanders and soldiers of the artillery and train fled as best they could. I re-opened the fire of Saint-Michel with renewed energy. The officers I had sent to the rear were not able to rally a single battery, although the charge had been repulsed and honourable men would have been able to return to their post, since no gun or caisson had been taken by the enemy. There were only men and horses killed. This check was grave.

The emperor sent to demand who had ordered this movement. I had a reply sent to him that I was too experienced to have ordered it and much pained not to have been able to prevent it. He sent Colonel Duchant [*sic*] of the artillery of the Guard, to replace the losses I had suffered. Then the battle continued after this bloody episode, as if it had not taken place.

The French cavalry made several beautiful charges. The infantry had taken and re-taken the farm of la Belle-Alliance [La Haye Sainte], nothing had been decided.

Marshal Ney said to me, 'Have you ever seen such a battle? How fierce!' However, he invited me to have supper with him in Brussels that evening. Ah, Destiny!

Finally, the enemy's fire eased; everything appeared to be inclining to our favour; the emperor had us informed that Grouchy was deploying onto our right when guns were heard in that direction.

The emperor had been deceived, or had deceived us. We later learned that it was the Prussians that passed between our right and Grouchy's left to out-flank us. The V [VI] Corps only had time to form *en potence* and to resist the troops which threatened our communications. However, the fire continued on the line of battle and for a long time, although becoming much reduced; we sensed that already much artillery and many troops had ceased to take part in the fighting. I have since learned that the artillery, a Belgian battery nearby, was lacking ammunition. I thus estimate that if the emperor had tried to break the last square that crowned the heights and appeared destined to protect the retreat of the English, the battle would have been won despite the arrival of the Prussians which the next day would have found themselves between us and Grouchy's corps.

It is claimed that Napoleon, pressed by the young men that surrounded him, took this desperate decision. What is certain is that it was this that decided the fate of the French army.

I continued my fire. I then saw a part of the Guard shake out into columns and descend into the valley then climb up to the attack on the famous English square. There was neither hesitation nor wavering, the charge was made admirably. But it was received calmly. The guns of a Belgian battery joined the terrible fire of the English. The Guard was astonished by such resistance. It hesitated, started to drift to the right and left; it resisted for a few more minutes, after which it was shaken and forced to retreat. Finally, it suddenly turned about in disorder and was carried off in flight which accelerated more and more, all that which still held behind it until the height from which we had first opened fire.

I had not left the advanced position from where I supported this charge. I wanted to continue to hold it, for the victor is he who remains last on the battlefield. When General Dalcambre, sent by General d'Erlon, came to find me and to inform me that all the enemy troops were falling on us, my twelve-pounders, although well drawn, could withdraw only slowly back up the slope, with the result that, as we reached the top, the enemy cavalry was on us. I only had time to throw myself into the last square of the Guard. The grenadiers whose bayonets still faced the cannon invited me to close in on them. It was at this moment that I found my general-in-chief and his head-quarters in the middle of the most dreadful fight I have ever seen in my military career.

Hardly had the enemy charge been repulsed than I was re-united with my general-in-chief, to his chief-of-staff, surrounded by his aides-de-camp.

As for myself, I was absolutely alone; not even an orderly. Each had abandoned me to flee in the rout. I could not complain, for the post that I had occupied all day had hardly been agreeable. When we set off in retreat, Count d'Erlon and us, we made, on twenty different occasions, efforts to form a weak nucleus with which to be able to march. Useless effort! The terror was painted across every face. An unceasing panic gave legs to these unhappy soldiers to flee, but their heads were lost . . . The soldiers were not able to get over their fright. Dalcambre and I took turns to lead the columns in order to give them more confidence. Well, at the least noise the soldiers were ready to disperse again. I made them form a circle around me when I noticed that a sound or some marauders had thrown terror into their ranks. I thus reassured them for an instant, but soon panic took over again . . .

[*In a footnote to this last passage, de Salle wrote*;] I have said in the course of this narration that Lieutenant Colonel ***, who had, without my orders, inadvertently hurried the movement of my grand battery, had been the cause not of its loss, but the dispersion of these useful forces. What I must add still annoys me as I write it. This officer, full of honour, had been promoted at the passage of Napoleon through Grenoble (4th Foot Artillery). He became excited and had followed part of the battery in its flight. He had made vain efforts to bring back several guns into the fight, but having not succeeded, he came to find me to inform me and to confess his mistakes. I was so furious that at first, not fully realising what the consequences would be, I received him with these exact words, 'Monsieur! When someone commits such a military fault, one does not re-appear, one gets themselves killed!' The poor young man! He left at the gallop. I never heard him spoken of again.

My heart beats faster at this story and I sense that at my last supper the thought will be heartbreaking, for I cannot cease to recall the wickedness of this kind of condemnation of a commander irritated by his subordinate.

I know that 'good souls' have accused me of ordering the movement in question, but no one has dared to write it.

Chapter 5

The Imperial Guard

The Imperial Foot Guard[1]

As his elite, battle-winning force, it was clearly vitally important for Napoleon to build up the Imperial Guard before the inevitable campaign opened. Consequently, on 8 April 1815 he published a decree outlining its new organisation. The following direction was given for the formation of the Foot Guard.

The corps of the grenadiers and chasseurs were each to be composed of three regiments of Old Guard and six regiments of Young Guard.

Each infantry regiment was to be composed of two battalions, each of four companies, each of which were to be of 150 men including officers.

In times of war, the companies were to be raised to 200 men including officers.

To be admitted into the first regiments of grenadiers and chasseurs, the men required twelve years' service, including campaigns. To be admitted into the second regiments it was necessary for them to have eight years' service, including campaigns. To be admitted into the third regiments, they were required to have four years' service including campaigns.

Grenadiers had to be 5 *pieds* 5 *pouces* tall. (A *pied* was only marginally longer [1.066] than a British foot and a *pouce* was only marginally longer [1.066] than an inch.) Chasseurs had to be 5 *pieds* 3 *pouces* tall.

The first regiments were to be completed from men drawn from the second regiments. These men were to be presented by the colonel of the corps and examined by the commandant of the corps.

When the first regiments had been filled, the second regiments were to be filled either from soldiers drawn from the infantry of the line or from men chosen from the third regiments.

The third regiments of the Old Guard were to be completed from men drawn from the infantry of the line, or men drawn from the regiments of tirailleurs or voltigeurs (grenadiers and chasseurs of the Young Guard).

In each regiment of line and light infantry, the colonel was to nominate two officers and thirty non-commissioned officers and soldiers to be placed into the second and third regiments of the Old Guard. These men were to be inspected by the commandant of the military division. They were to be divided into two classes:

The first class was to be of men who had eight years' service including campaigns.

The second class was to be of men with four years' service. These men were to be placed into the second and third regiments by the Ministry of War.

The second and third infantry regiments of the Old Guard were to have the same uniform as the first regiments.

A call was to be made in all the departments to former non-commissioned officers and soldiers of the Old Guard who had retired and who wanted to resume service in their old regiments. They were to be incorporated following their old seniority in the first or second regiments of their units.

The same call was to be made to all former members of the Young Guard. They were to be placed into their units according to their seniority or their *qualités* in the Young Guard, or in the three regiments of the Old Guard.

The first regiments of the Old Guard infantry were to be composed of men who, before 1 April 1814, were part of the first regiments of grenadiers or chasseurs; the second regiments were to be composed of men belonging to the second regiments; the third regiments were to be composed of men who belonged to the regiments of fusiliers (the old Middle Guard). The ministry of war was then to complete the regiments according to the lists provided by the regiments of the line/light.

The officers were to be provided from the officers who were currently serving in the Guard, among those who were on half-pay and those who were on the lists provided by the line/light.

The companies of the Old Guard who accompanied Napoleon to Elba were to take the head of the first regiment of their arm (grenadiers or chasseurs). The companies of grenadiers were to form the first two companies of the first regiment, and the chasseurs of the first chasseur regiment.

The fourth regiments of grenadiers and chasseurs were established by a further decree of 9 May and three days later the Young Guard was increased from six regiments each of voltigeurs and tirailleurs, to eight of each, though only four of each were completed before the end of the campaign.

So many non-commissioned officers and sergeant-majors who had been discharged presented themselves for service that there were more than required to provide cadres for the Young Guard regiments. Some of these were put into the Old Guard. On 13 April, Napoleon ordered that the companies of the Guard infantry were to be raised to their war establishment; that is from 150 men to 200. These surplus non-commissioned officers were now required to provide the cadre for these extra men. However, none of the battalions came close to filling this requirement of 800 men (see figures in Petit's account below). Even Napoleon doubted whether this could be achieved. From the time of his decree of 8 April, Napoleon took a very close interest in the organisation, equipping and uniforming of the Guard, and constantly demanded reports from General Drouot (who served as the Guard's *aide-major*) on progress. Napoleon had nominated Marshal Mortier to command the Guard, but on his falling sick with sciatica, he was not replaced. Drouot, as *aide-major*, became the *de facto* commander of the Guard.

It will be noted in Napoleon's decree that all three regiments of grenadiers and chasseurs (increased later to four) counted as Old Guard, although each regiment's place in the hierarchy was clearly established by the seniority of the manpower in each. The decree of 8 April did not re-establish the regiments that made up the former Middle Guard; essentially the Fusilier-Grenadiers and -Chasseurs. However, many French accounts of Waterloo describe the 3rd and 4th Regiments of grenadiers and chasseurs as Middle Guard. In his accounts, Napoleon himself describes them this way and it appears certain that they were considered Middle Guard by the two senior regiments. In fact, they may even have been considered as Middle Guard by the men themselves; if a British account is to be believed (Macready), after the attack of the Guard at the end of the battle one of the wounded and one of the prisoners, asked what unit they belonged to, replied '*Moyenne Garde*'. Others wish to interpret the use of 'Middle Guard' by the French as an attempt to downplay the defeat of the guard at the end of the battle and to maintain the aura of invincibility of the Old Guard.

There is plenty of evidence to show that the apparently strict qualifications for each regiment were often ignored in an attempt to ensure the regiments were fully manned.

Having stood in reserve and out of sight of the battlefield for most of the day, those in the Guard were not in a position to describe the whole battle, only their personal experiences. The Guard infantry were involved in two actions; the fighting in Planchenoit against the Prussians (the Young Guard and just two battalions of the Old Guard) and the final attack on the Allied ridge. The attack and repulse of the Imperial Guard at the end of the battle is one of a number of unresolved controversies of Waterloo. Accounts from the two sides absolutely contradict each other and even amongst British units there remains considerable disagreement on not only who should take the credit for their defeat, but also the form and point(s) of the attack. Funnily enough, in British accounts there is less disagreement on the form that the attack took, but this is not the end of the story. Two of the units that claim to have repulsed the Guard, the British Guards and the 52nd Light Infantry, seem to agree that the Guard advanced in narrow, but very deep, columns.

However, those historians that have recycled this account of one or two very deep columns have clearly not read any of the French accounts. For not only are the columns they describe contrary to all French tactical practices, but no French eyewitness accounts describe the attack being made in such a ridiculous formation. We will leave those who witnessed, or actually took part in this attack, to describe it for themselves.

The Grenadiers à Pied

Maréchal de Camp Jean-Martin Baron Petit

General Petit's account of the Waterloo Campaign; The Morrison Collection – published in *The English Historical Review* 1903.

During the Waterloo campaign Petit commanded the 1st Regiment of the Grenadiers à Pied of the Old Guard; the senior regiment of the Guard.
  Petit was born in 1772 and joined the 2nd Battalion of Paris Volunteers as a soldier in 1792. Within two months he was sergeant-major and then served in the Army of the North and was wounded at Saint-Amand in 1793. He was commissioned lieutenant in 1794 and served in the Army of the Sambre and Meuse. He was then transferred to the Army of Italy in 1797 and became aide-de-camp to General Hector, then General Mireur and finally General Friant in 1798, having been promoted captain earlier in that year. From 1798 to 1801 he served in Egypt and was wounded at the combat of Aboumana and again at the siege of Cairo. He was chef de bataillon in 1802 and served in the armée des Côtes *from 1803 to 1805. He joined the* Grande Armée *in 1805–06. Major in the 15th légère, he served in Portugal until promoted colonel in 1808; he then took command of the 67th de ligne and fought at Aspern and was wounded at Wagram in 1809. He served in Catalonia in Spain from 1810 to 1813 until nominated major in the 1st Regiment of Grenadiers à Pied in November 1813. Adjutant General of the Imperial Guard by the end of that year he was present at Château-Thierry and Montereau in 1814. He famously commanded the Guard troops at Napoleon's farewell at Fontainebleau before his exile on Elba. He continued to serve with the (Royal) Guard and became major-colonel (the commanding officer) of the 1st Regiment of the Grenadiers à Pied of the Old Guard for the Waterloo campaign. Put on the inactive list at the end of 1815, he retired in 1824 but became honorary lieutenant general in 1825. He re-entered service after the July Revolution of 1830, serving in an administrative post until again going onto the inactive list in 1837. He remained in the reserve until 1840 when he became deputy commandant of the Invalides hospital where he was buried on his death in 1856. As the commander of the senior regiment of the Guard at Waterloo, it is*

noticeable that Petit's fighting record is a poor shadow of many of the other senior commanders that served with him in the Guard.

As Petit's account is such an interesting insight to the Foot Guard of 1815, I felt that it would be of interest to include the whole account, rather than restrict it to Waterloo. Most French histories of the battle base their account of the attack of the Guard on that of Petit, but the truth is, as Petit commanded the 1st Regiment of Grenadiers à Pied, he did not actually take part in the attack he describes, although he may have put himself in a position to observe it and would certainly have spoken to officers who did take part.

The infantry of the Old Guard was formed for the campaign of 1815 in two divisions, of three regiments each and a reserve composed of the two senior regiments of grenadiers and chasseurs. Each of these two regiments formed the reserve of the division composed of the corps of its arm; the chasseurs formed one division, the grenadiers the other. The two divisions were commanded by Generals Roguet and Michel.

M. le lieutenant-général Comte Friant commanded the whole, as well as the infantry of the Young Guard, and he had under his orders for the Old Guard *M. le lieutenant-général Comte* Morand.

It was standard in the Old Guard to always march with the 'left ahead'; thus, the chasseurs always marched in front of the grenadiers, and the last regiments were grenadiers, so that the regiments of chasseurs marched with the 4th in the lead, then the 3rd, then the 2nd. It was the same with the grenadiers. Often it happened that they arrived mixed up, but in this case the 1st Regiment of Chasseurs and then the 1st Regiment of Grenadiers always came last.

The strength of the corps was:

4th Regiment of Chasseurs – 1,000
4th Regiment of Grenadiers – 800
The 3rd and 2nd Regiments of the two arms – of 1,200 or 1,300 each.
The 1st of Chasseurs and Grenadiers – each of 1,400 and 1,500 men.

Two twelve-pounder batteries, each of eight guns, were attached to the infantry of the Old Guard.

The Guard left Paris in different columns; it was concentrated at Beaumont on 14 June where it took position, part in the town and part in front of the town.

On the 15th it set off on its march to Charles le Roy [Charleroi]. General Vandamme's corps were to have preceded it to this point, but the orders that had been sent to him had been delayed and it was the *Sapeurs* and *Marins* of the Guard that forced the bridge and were first to penetrate into the town; they suffered little loss.

Towards 3pm there was an hour's engagement about a league from Charles le Roy [at Gilly] where the service squadrons were engaged, [Footnote: They broke two infantry squares that were placed on the heights and on the edge of the wood which is found in front of the right of the village of **** where the road separates. These charges resulted in the capture of several hundred prisoners.] but the infantry of the Guard remained in position on the heights before Gilly. The 1st Regiment of Grenadiers and the 1st Regiment of Chasseurs re-entered the town in the evening where the *quartier-général* was established.

On the 16th, all the infantry of the Guard was reunited towards 9am and set off; arriving in the plains of Florus [Fleurus] towards 2 o'clock in the afternoon. There it formed into columns of deployed battalions and then in deployed regiment. It broke up its column to pass through Florus, then re-took the same order (that is to say, in column of deployed regiments) until the area of the mill of ... [Naveau] where the corps of grenadiers supported their right and the Chasseurs were in front of the mill.

During the battle, several corps were engaged successively: the three last regiments of chasseurs (4th, 3rd, 2nd) marched in the direction of St Amand in reserve to the corps of the line who were all engaged and even obliged to make a retrograde movement. It supported them there to advantage.

The two junior regiments of grenadiers (4th and 3rd) marched on Ligny. In the evening all the units of grenadiers with the first of chasseurs, concentrated on the heights in the rear of this village which was soon forced and taken from the enemy, who had defended it with vigour against the different corps of the line since the beginning of the affair. The 4th and 3rd Regiments of Grenadiers formed the head of the column; the 2nd marched behind. It was these three regiments which, after having chased the enemy infantry from its position on the other side of the village, received a brilliant cavalry charge which was repulsed by them with a great loss of men and horses.

The service squadrons[2] and the squadron of *Gendarmerie d'élite* [Footnote: that is to say the squadron of lancers and grenadiers and a company of the *Gendarmerie d'élite*] deployed from Ligny almost at the same time as the 4th, 3rd and 2nd Regiments of Grenadiers, pursued the enemy cavalry and forced back an infantry square which retired in good order. During this time, the enemy cavalry rallied and charged the service squadrons in their turn and, when the enemy were stopped by the fire of the three last regiments of grenadiers (who were formed in battalion squares), they retook the charge with the greatest vigour, although inferior in number.

The 1st Regiment of Chasseurs and the 1st Regiment of Grenadiers, having also deployed out of Ligny, formed up on the right of this village, facing and observing the enemy forces which still occupied the heights and the route leading to Wavre until the arrival of Count de Lobau's corps which arrived as night fell. This army corps formed up in front of these two regiments.

Several Guard batteries had been advantageously employed against Saint-Amand and Ligny. A battery from the grenadiers passed through the village with the last two regiments (4th and 3rd) and caused the enemy great damage.

The result of the day at this point had been the taking of seven guns 'of 13' [this is almost certainly a mistake and should read '12'], several caissons and also a good number of prisoners.

The grenadiers slept in their position ahead of Ligny with the 1st Regiment of Chasseurs. The three last regiments of chasseurs were placed close to Florus, where the headquarters was established.

At 10am on the 17th, the Guard was completely concentrated in front of Ligny. The infantry started its march, gained the main road from Brussels to Quatre Bras, passed through Genappe and slept at *** [Glabais] where the head of the column only arrived at 11pm.

We had left the main road to take a back road a little before it got dark, in order to avoid getting mixed up with the cavalry and artillery. During the night the weather was terrible. The tracks were in such a state of decay that it was impossible to keep any sort of order on the march. The troops, searching for easier routes, or marching across the fields, were mostly separated. It was only during the 18th that they were able to rejoin their colours. The weather had then calmed a little and the morning was employed in cleaning the arms which were in a very poor state.

At 10am we re-started our movement along the main road. The eight regiments of the Old Guard (4th, 3rd, 2nd Regiments of Chasseurs, 4th, 3rd, 2nd Regiments of Grenadiers, 1st Regiment of Chasseurs and 1st Regiment of Grenadiers) took position behind the centre of the army in front of the Caillou farm. The combat was already strongly engaged. General Friant formed the Guard in column by deployed regiment, first to the left of the road, then to the right; having before them a ridge which hid them from the enemy. They remained thus until about 4pm.

The enemy had made some progress on our right which was completely outflanked. The Young Guard, which had been sent there at two o'clock, having been forced to make a retrograde movement from the village of Planchenoit, the 2nd Regiment of Chasseurs and the 2nd Regiment of Grenadiers each detached a battalion to this village. The enemy was chased out with great loss. They were pursued with the bayonet onto the plateau.

The Chasseurs and Grenadiers marched right up to the Prussian batteries which were temporarily abandoned. This movement took place towards 6pm.

During this movement, the 1st Regiment of Grenadiers formed in two squares, one per battalion. One was placed to the right of the *chaussée* (facing the enemy) on a small height which dominated the small road which came from Planchenoit and which led to the main road. It threw some skirmishers towards the extreme right of this village to observe the enemy there, who were in force. Several men were taken with an *adjutant-major* who got too close.

The other square was placed to the left of the road on the mound which the emperor had first occupied. It was joined there by an eight-pounder battery of six guns and by the companies of *Sapeurs* and *Marins* of the Guard.

It was about seven o'clock in the evening, the corps of the Guard had suffered horribly [presumably he means through frustration, not through loss], when the 4th and 3rd Regiments of Chasseurs and the 4th and 3rd Regiments of Grenadiers were ordered to march off. They passed to the left of the main road where they were formed into battalion squares with the exception of the 4th Regiments which, because of their weakness, only made one square each.[3] They formed up and were deployed thus; the 1st Battalion of the 3rd Regiment with its right against the main road. The 2nd Battalion was detached to more than a cannon's range to the left to observe and contain a movement that the enemy seemed to make on this point. The emperor himself took it there and this battalion formed his Guard.

A little to the rear in echelon and to the left of the 1st Battalion of the 3rd Regiment, formed successively the two 4th Regiments of Grenadiers and Chasseurs and the 3rd Regiment of Chasseurs. They were, as has already been said, in square, but closed up to one another. It was in this order that they all advanced; the 1st Battalion of the 3rd Regiment of Grenadiers as has been said, close to the road, marching parallel to the road, the other units following the movement in good order, conserving their distances. These troops went at the *pas de charge* to the area of La Haye Sainte which they passed, pushing vigorously before them all the enemy, despite the greatest fire of artillery and musketry.

At this moment, General Friant, who commanded the whole attack, was seriously wounded and General Michel, commander of the Chasseurs, was killed. The death of this latter officer caused a certain amount of excitement amongst the troops. They came to a halt. But soon, at the voice of General Poret, commander of the 3rd Grenadiers, the 1st Battalion resumed their vigour and resumed the advance, marching at the *pas de charge* with loud shouts. Marshal Ney, whose horse had been killed, was on foot at the head of this battalion with his sword in his hand. The other battalions of chasseurs also resumed their advance. Each followed on; all was well. The enemy was frightened off; the first formidable enemy battery was overrun and in our possession.

New enemy columns, infantry and cavalry, appeared. Entire ranks of our men were knocked down by a most terrible artillery fire (from the second line) and of musketry which wiped out our squares. There was disorder and we retired.

At this juncture the two second battalions of grenadiers and chasseurs of the 2nd Regiments, had come forward at the *pas de charge*, commanded by Generals Christiani and Pelet [here he is certainly in error; Pelet was deployed in Planchenoit]. We wanted to reform and return to the attack, but the enemy continued his progress and there was disorder. It was necessary to retire.

During all these mishaps, the 2nd Battalion of the 3rd Regiment of Grenadiers, with whom the emperor was stationed, remained in position. General Cambronne arrived at the same position with the 2nd Battalion of the 1st Chasseur Regiment and took position there. General Roguet, *Colonel en Second* of the Grenadiers was also there. The efforts of the enemy at this point denied them any movement to the left. General Cambronne was wounded. Thrown from his horse, he was thought to be dead. A great number of officers and soldiers fell on the battlefield. We had to retire, unable to resist such great numbers.

The emperor retired at the gallop and placed himself in the square of the 1st Battalion of the 1st Grenadiers. The entire army was in the most terrible disorder, infantry, cavalry, artillery, all fled in haste in all directions. Soon the only order was in the two squares formed by the two battalions of this regiment placed to the right and left of the main road. The emperor ordered General Petit to have *La Grenadière* beaten to recall all Guardsmen who were swept along in the torrent of fugitives. The enemy followed closely. In the fear that they would break into the square, we were obliged to fire on the men who were being pursued and threatened to throw the square into disorder. It was an evil necessary to avoid an even greater one.

It was almost dark. The emperor himself gave the order to abandon our position which was no longer tenable and which had been outflanked to left and right. The two squares retired in good order, the 1st Battalion across the fields, the 2nd on the main road. Halts were made to give time to the skirmishers and fugitives to rejoin us.

Half a league from Genappe the two squares joined on the main road on which they marched in columns of sections. We collected up all those that belonged to other regiments of the Guard. The enemy followed up this movement but without causing us any anxiety. This was when a panic seized the soldiers of the artillery train, who cut the traces of their horses and overturned their guns and caissons which blocked and encumbered the route, caused by the left of the column coming under a lively fire. This caused little harm, but much augmented the disorder which was already at its height.

In this state of things it was not possible for all there was of the Guard to go through the town; we succeeded to go round to the left of the road and this place. There was no longer any means of conserving order or to reform.

The troops marched scattered on different tracks that it was felt ran parallel to the main road. One large group retired on Florus and then to Charles le Roy. Everything was in confusion. They spread out in the town without it being possible to concentrate them. It was only at Beaumont and at Philippeville that their units started to reform. General Roguet, General Morand and the different generals of the Guard did everything they could. Leaving Beaumont in the evening of the 19th, a little order had been restored and small marches were made as far as Laon, where the greater part of the Guard that had escaped the unhappy day and night of the 18th were reunited.

On the 21st, they stayed there; the next day morale had been fully restored, the men found their courage again, then the news of the emperor's abdication came to once more discourage the men.

Petit's second account was written in response to General Pelet's appeal for information from former officers of the Imperial Guard, the responses to which form the majority of the Guard accounts. Regrettably, unlike the British responses to Siborne's request, and excepting Petit's and Pelet's own accounts, the French Guard officers concentrate almost exclusively on the final attack of the Guard.

In: *L'Infanterie de la Garde à Waterloo*, by Vicomte A. d'Avout, *Carnet de la Sabretache, 1905* (Paris: Leroy, 1905), pp. 105–10.

Letter to General Pelet, dated Bourges, 18th May 1835
[The 1st Regiment of Grenadiers] ... did not have more than 1,500 bayonets when we crossed the Sambre.

At the affair of the 16th, the 1st Regiment of Grenadiers left the village of Ligny behind the other grenadier regiments towards 7pm. It formed up with the 1st Regiment of Chasseurs, forward and to the right of the village, facing the enemy that still occupied the heights and who only evacuated them during the night when the arrival of Count Lobau's corps took position in front of these two regiments. The 1st Grenadiers lost only a few men.

. . .

On the 18th, at 3pm, the eight regiments of the Old Guard, as well as the *Sapeurs* and *Marins*, were in position behind the centre of the army, in front of the Caillou farm; first to the right, and then to the left of the road, formed in columns by deployed regiment [*colonne par regiment déployé*].

The 1st Regiment of Grenadiers formed the left of the column.

The Guard remained like this until four o'clock. At this time, the enemy made progress on our right where we were outflanked by the corps of General Bülow. The whole of the Young Guard, under the orders of Generals Duhesme and Barrois, having made a retrograde movement, the regiment of chasseurs and grenadiers each detached a battalion that marched on the enemy and chased him from the village of Planchenoit.

This movement took place about 6 o'clock.

At the same time, the 1st Regiment of Grenadiers formed in two columns by division, then, later, in two squares, one per battalion, were positioned; the 2nd Battalion to the right of the main road, on top of the position dominating the small track which ran between the village of Planchenoit and the main road. It had to throw out skirmishers to the extreme right of the village to observe the enemy. Several of these men were with *Adjutant-major* Farré, whose horse fell into a ditch; this officer was wounded.

The square of the 1st Battalion formed on the left of the main road, on the mound that the emperor had first occupied. There it was joined by six eight-pounders and by the *Marins* and *Sapeurs* of the Guard. At 7pm, the order was given to advance the two last regiments of chasseurs and to form in battalion squares on the left of the road. A battalion of grenadiers was detached to a cannon's range to the left, to observe from there the enemy who threatened a movement from this side. The emperor himself positioned this battalion forming his left.

The 1st/3rd Grenadiers had its right anchored on the main road; behind and to its left, the 4th of Chasseurs and Grenadiers, and then the 3rd Chasseurs.

Thus formed in squares in echelon, they moved forward. General Friant at the head of the 1st/3rd Grenadiers, marching parallel to the road, the others following in the best order, conserving their distances as far as La Haye Sainte which they bypassed, pursuing the enemy at the *pas de charge*, despite the losses from heavy artillery fire and musketry. At this moment, General Friant was seriously wounded and forced to retire. General Michel was killed a few moments later, which occasioned some hesitation in the ranks. They stopped, but at the voice of General Poret, they continued their advance to shouts of '*Vive l'empereur!*'

Marshal Ney was on foot, sword in hand, at the head of the 3rd Grenadiers. The enemy retired in disorder, his forward battery was then in our hands. However, the English general (Wellington) advanced fresh forces of infantry, cavalry and artillery, which soon inflicted heavy losses on our troops.

General Roguet then arrived with the two 2nd Battalions of Grenadiers and Chasseurs; as you found yourself there, the result of this movement is known to you [Footnote: Error: General Pelet was at Planchenoit with the 1st Battalion of his regiment, the 2nd Chasseurs.[4]]

Whilst this was happening, the divisions of the Young Guard, on our right, had been forced to abandon its positions; General Duhesme, their commander, remained on the battlefield; General Barrois, seriously wounded, had been evacuated.

Ahead, on our left, the 2nd/3rd Grenadiers had been joined by the 2nd/1st Chasseurs, but the efforts of the enemy obliged them to retreat, General Cambronne being left for dead on the battlefield.

The emperor then arrived at the square of the 1st/1st Grenadiers.

At this fateful moment, only the two squares of this regiment retained any order, placed as I have said above, to the left and right of the road. Everyone was fleeing from all parts.

By the emperor's order, I had the drummers beat the *Grenadière*; a great number of men of the Guard rallied to my squares. From the three ranks in which they were formed, they found themselves in eight and finally ten. The eight-pounder battery opened fire, but could not stop the enemy.

The emperor then gave the order to retreat, which was carried out in the best order; making frequent halts or marking time as if they were drilling to allow people to catch up, or the skirmishers that covered us. Further on, the two squares were brought together on the road and formed up into columns. The enemy followed, but without worrying us much.

As the 1st Regiment arrived at Genappe, a panic had seized the soldiers of the artillery train. They had cut the traces of their horses, overturned their guns and caissons, fired on us, so that the village and the horses were so much of an obstacle that it had to bypass the village by its left. The 1st Regiment marched across the fields, along the tracks and byroads throughout the night.

... The loss of the regiment on the battlefield was not serious; it only lost a lot of men in the evening ...

Maréchal de Camp Baron Joseph Christiani

In: d'Avout, *L'infantrie de la garde à Waterloo, Carnets de la Sabretache 1905* (Paris: Leroy, 1905), pp. 111–13.

During the Waterloo campaign, Christiani commanded the 2nd Regiment of Grenadiers à Pied of the Imperial Guard.

Christiani was born in Strasbourg in 1772. At eighteen he enlisted in the Boulonnois infantry regiment (later the 79th de ligne). A year later he was made corporal;

his regiment was in the Army of the Alps (1792–3), becoming caporal-fourrier *and then* maréchal des logis. *He then moved to the Army of the Eastern Pyrenees (1794–5) and then the Army of Italy (1796–7), having been commissioned in 1794. He served throughout Italy over the years 1796 to 1800 and was wounded and taken prisoner at the battle of Trebbia in 1799, but released on parole the same year. He became* chef de bataillon *in the Army of Batavia in 1804 and then part of the* Grande Armée *in 1805, being present at Austerlitz. From 1806 to 1808, he served in the Army of Dalmatia as major in the 56th* de ligne *and took part in the Wagram campaign, after which became colonel of the 8th* légère. *Later the same year he was posted to the grenadiers* à pied *of the Guard. In 1810 he became colonel commandant of the Guard school of instruction and then colonel-major of the fusilier-grenadiers (Middle Guard) and commanded them in Russia. In 1813 he took over command of the 2nd Regiment of Grenadiers à Pied and fought in Friant's 1st Guard Division throughout the Saxony campaign of that year, during which he was promoted to* général de brigade *major-colonel. In 1814 he commanded a brigade of the fusiliers and vélites of the Guard before taking over command of the 2nd Guard Division at the combat of Château-Thierry when Michel was wounded. He commanded them at the combats of Vauchamps, Laon, Fère-Champenoise and the battle of Paris. After the First Restoration he served with the Grenadiers of the Royal Guard. On Napoleon's return he commanded the 2nd Regiment of Grenadiers à Pied as major-colonel with the rank of* maréchal de camp *and fought with them at Ligny and Waterloo. After the Second Restoration he was put on the inactive list, but quickly brought back into service the following year and he filled a number of inspectorate and administrative posts until 1834 when he retired. He died in 1840.*

Christiani's regiment sent one battalion to the fighting in Planchenoit, and the other to support the assault on the Allied ridge. As the regimental commander, he led the battalion forward to support the assault on the ridge. His order of events is a little mixed up; he describes the attack of the Guard taking place before he sent a battalion into Planchenoit. In fact these actions took place the other way around as Napoleon attempted to secure his right flank before launching part of his Guard against the Allied ridge. For a comparatively senior regiment of the Guard, his battalion seems to have broken up rather easily at the end of the battle.

The order was given to prepare our arms for the attack. Later, we took position to the rear of where the emperor was, on a height to the right of the Brussels road. Here, I do not recall the movements of the other regiments of foot grenadiers, but I recall receiving the order to move forward with the 2nd Regiment and take position to the right of the Brussels road. I had to my right a very deep gully. I remained in this position the whole day. I saw the return of the debris of the four regiments of the Foot Guard which had been sent under the orders of General Friant to take the position that was occupied by the Allies, which, protected by a deep valley and by a numerous entrenched artillery.

Like me, you know the sad result of this attack.

Between five and six pm, perhaps later, I received the order to send a battalion of the regiment to the village situated to the right rear of the position that I occupied to drive off the Prussians who had come to seize it (Planchenoit). It was M. Golzio, *chef de battalion* of the 2nd Battalion of the regiment that I tasked with this mission; I only saw him again in the evening during our retreat. I do not recall if he had lost many men, but only that he told me that he had done much harm to the enemy.

Finally, towards 7pm I think, I left with the 1st Battalion that remained to me, to go to join the emperor who was to the left of the road, a little distance from the position that I had previously left. He was alone, on foot, with General Drouot. I had my battalion form square. The emperor remained there observing for some time, I think, the rearwards movement of artillery made in the plain to the left of the road, and then mounted up to retire.

At this time or close to it, the enemy made a cavalry charge along the main road and found itself mixed up with our own cavalry and infantry that was retiring in disorder. The English skirmishers appeared and opened fire. Then I began my own retreat with my battalion in square; several balls fell amongst us that caused some confusion in the ranks. The voices of the officers were unfamiliar and arriving in the vicinity of the 1st Regiment of Grenadiers, my soldiers left the ranks and it was impossible to rally them. I joined the road towards Genappe; I also saw General Roguet there. We endeavoured to rally as many as possible before night, but we were abandoned.

The Chasseurs à Pied

Maréchal de Camp Baron Jean-Jacques-Germain Pelet-Clozeau

In: d'Avout, *L'infantrie de la garde à Waterloo*, in *Carnet de la Sabretache 1905* (Paris: Leroy, 1905), pp. 37–53.

During the Waterloo campaign Pelet was Major of the 2nd Regiment of Chasseurs à Pied of the Imperial Guard.

Pelet was born in Toulouse in 1777. He enlisted into the 1st Battalion Auxiliaire de la Haute-Garonne in 1799 and became sergeant the following year. He was part of the engineers in the Army of Italy from the beginning of 1800 and was commissioned into the ingénieurs géographes *in 1801 and became lieutenant the following year. He joined Masséna's headquarters in 1805 and became his aide-de-camp; he was wounded by a shot to the head at Caldiero. He then served in Naples in 1806 and became captain in 1807. He was wounded again in the Wagram campaign at Ebersburg. He became* chef de bataillon *the same year and served at Essling and Znaïm. He moved with Masséna to Portugal for the disastrous invasion of 1810 and was promoted colonel in 1811. He then became adjutant-commandant (staff colonel) in Marchand's division for the invasion of Russia, where he served at Smolensk and Borodino. In September 1812, before the retreat started, he was put in command of the 48th* de ligne, *part of Ricard's division. He was wounded in the left arm and both legs at Krasnoe in November. Promoted* général de brigade *in 1813 he served under Marshal Marmont in the 6th Army Corps before moving to command the 3rd Brigade of the 4th Young Guard Division under Roguet in August that year. He was then transferred to the 2nd Brigade of the 3rd Young Guard Division (Decouz) and fought with them at Dresden and Leipzig. He then served as* adjutant général *of the Imperial Guard during the 1814 campaign. He was present at Brienne and took over command of Decouz's division when the latter was wounded. He commanded the division at La Rothière, Champaubert and Montmirail before returning to brigade command in the 1st Old Guard Division at Vauchamps and Montereau. He then commanded the brigade of chasseurs à pied of the Old Guard at Craonne, Laon, Reims and Arcis sur Aube. He was retained in the Royal Guard after Napoleon's abdication as major of the chasseurs royaux de France. On Napoleon's return he became major to the 2nd Regiment of Chasseurs à Pied of the Old Guard and served at Ligny. At Waterloo he was detached with one of his battalions to Planchenoit where he co-ordinated a heroic defence of that village against the Prussians that he describes in great detail below. When the army had returned to Paris he became major to the first regiment of chasseurs, but was put on the inactive list after the Second Restoration. He returned to duty in 1818 and served in a number of administrative appointments until 1830 when he was promoted lieutenant general. He was seriously wounded by Fieschi's* machine infernale *in the latter's attempt on the life of King Louis-Philippe in 1835. He retired in 1848 and became involved in politics. He died in 1858.*

Pelet's account of Waterloo is by far the longest and most detailed of the accounts written by officers of the Imperial Guard and therefore holds the most interest. Unfortunately, he did not take part in the attack on the Allied ridge, but fought in Planchenoit, of which he gives some fascinating detail of the fighting. However, whilst he also describes the attack on the ridge, it must be remembered that this is based on the accounts of others and is therefore not so trustworthy. He actually wrote two accounts of the Waterloo campaign; the first was his journal which he wrote during the campaign, and the second formed a part of his memoirs written later in life, but based on his journal.

I have presented Pelet's account here in the same way as d'Avout in L'infantrie de la garde à Waterloo, *in* Carnet de la Sabretache *1905. This maintains the correct sequencing of the fighting and includes some useful comment from d'Avout which I have retained. The square brackets at the beginning of the paragraphs show from which account the next phase of the narrative is drawn. Pelet claims that only chasseurs were involved in the first wave of the attack and the grenadiers were some way behind. This contradicts Petit's accounts.*

[d'Avout starts with the following:] General Bachelu, who commanded one of the divisions of this corps (Reille's II), wrote, on 22 May 1835 (a letter in my possession [Vicomte A. d'Avout's]), that the division of Prince Jérôme *was alone* engaged [at Hougoumont], whilst his and that of General Foy remained inactive, – that, moreover, artillery ammunition started to run short from 3 o'clock and could not be replenished; that his division only moved towards 8 o'clock in the evening, after Ney's great cavalry charges, in order to support the attack of the Imperial Guard.

Pelet's Account

[*Memoirs*] The emperor had slept at the farm of Caillou. The service there was made by the 1st Battalion of the 1st Chasseurs, who had the order, the next morning, of remaining in this position. The Guard was concentrated during the night in a camp situated in front of a village called Glabais; the ground was extremely waterlogged, the soldiers sank up to their knees. The artillery could not move. This circumstance meant that they were only able to start their move towards nine o'clock.

We started our march towards nine o'clock and stopped for a long time in the area of the Caillou farm, between the road and a wood through which the troops of VI Corps passed. We then crossed the road to move to the northeast of the Callois observatory, between the wood and the road, behind a knoll where the emperor stayed for a long time. This was about the time, towards midday, that the attack on Hougoumont wood was started by II Corps. Soon after we saw the attack of I Corps to the right of the road, and that on its extreme right on the houses of Smouhen [Smohain], la Haye and Papelotte.

The weather was still misty ...

As the line advanced and gained ground, the Old Guard set off in column, following the valley that ran along the road between Rosomme and la Belle Alliance.

The emperor was on the top of a hillock to the left of the road, in front of the Guard and of la Belle-Alliance. We then occupied Hougoumont, La Haye Sainte [d'Avout notes in a footnote: 'There is an error here concerning La

Haye Sainte, which was only definitively occupied towards six o'clock in the evening; as to Hougoumont, it was only ever partially conquered'.] and Smouhen.

The infantry of the Guard was normally deployed in the following order: in deployed regimental columns, the Young Guard forming the head of the column, then the Chasseurs, in reversed order, the left ahead, 4th, 3rd, 2nd and 1st Regiments. The Grenadiers followed in the same order.

[*Journal*] We set off in movement to move onto the right of the road, revealing the farm (of la Belle-Alliance) ... After having a little look around, I fell asleep; then I ate a little and offered a drink of Madeira to General Morand [*Colonel en premier* of the Imperial Guard Chasseurs] who had joined me. Towards four o'clock, I mounted my horse and went forward onto the plateau between La Haye Sainte and Smouhen [*sic*]; I found an immense battlefield, but scattered with English cavalrymen, uniformed in red, edged in silk. After having made a tour, I looked back towards the enemy and saw several masses with shouldered arms; I was unsure whether they were their troops or ours. It was a counter movement and I thought after what I had seen I should return to my post where they would probably have need of me.

Arriving back I found nothing new, but a little later we were attacked on our right flank. The Young Guard rushed onto the heights north of Planchenoit and, hardly had they arrived at the last houses of this village, than they found themselves face to face with the enemy who had passed out of a wood at the end of a small valley. It formed up, sent out skirmishers and stopped the enemy for some time, but these deployed some batteries whose balls soon reached us.

The Guard infantry were then put in movement. Towards five o'clock, the 4th (Chasseurs) moved a few hundred paces ahead of the farm, a little behind and to the right; the 3rd mounted the crest and formed a single square or two. I received an order to form in square where I was and I formed them by echelon as at Nancy [their previous garrison]. At the same time, some cuirassiers and then some chasseurs formed up on our flank, facing the Prussians; the chasseurs à cheval were to the right of the cuirassiers. Some Prussian balls fell and even some English, but they were 'overs'; they struck down several files of the 1st Battalion. I toured the square laughing and chatting with the soldiers, making them laugh and talk; I got them to sing patriotic songs and said to them, 'Now my friends, shout "*Vive l'empereur!*" as much as you want and above all, when those beggars come, we will keep them on the end of our bayonets'. They did not stop shouting out and singing. I believe that all the cavalry in the world could have come but that it would have done nothing against us, so well disposed were we. The 2nd Battalion was less exposed to the balls and so I stayed with them less. I ordered my 1st Battalion to move a short way; someone came to argue a little and I put it back in its place. It seemed to me that a little later the emperor came and put himself to the right of my 2nd [Battalion], facing Planchenoit and that soon after Jérôme came to ask after him; I pointed him out. A small, very young (although grey) engineer officer came to me who despaired of losing his first battle and who wanted to die, to get himself killed. I sent him off gently, but from then on no one thought any longer of going to Brussels.

Some artillery of the Guard was established on the ridge above Planchenoit; it silenced the Prussian guns, but it did not stay intact for very long. The enemy was reinforced and pushed forward; the Young Guard was pushed back and their men started falling back. I received the order to send M. Lepage [First Lieutenant, 2nd Chasseurs], with fifty men, to the first houses of Planchenoit. These first houses were too far from the village, and separated from it, for them to stop there. This officer found there not only a number of soldiers [sheltering], but also some officers. Soon, I had to send a new detachment forward to support the Young Guard; I sent off M. Gourhel [First Lieutenant, 2nd Chasseurs] who went forward like a 'crow' [sic] and so that I had to go myself and place it.

We remained in square, the grenadiers behind me, the 3rd and 4th (Chasseurs) in front. I remember that there was a lack of order in the squares and I am not sure if the grenadiers did not then cross to the other side of the road. Finally, General Morand [commander of the Guard Chasseurs] said to me, 'Go with your 1st Battalion to Planchenoit, where the Young Guard has been beaten. Support it, hold that point, as there is only you and the 2nd Battalion of the 1st Chasseurs as a last reserve. The emperor goes to march with all the rest of the Guard to attack in the centre; if this does not succeed, you are here as a last reserve'. This, it seemed to me, is what he said to me, or what I thought I heard, and I took the necessary measures. He also said to me, 'Keep your men together and under control; if you engage the enemy, attack with a single division [two companies] and with the bayonet'.

[*Memoirs*] The second battalions of the 1st Chasseurs and 2nd Chasseurs were close to La Belle Alliance, thus forming the pivot of the movement. The 1st Battalion of the 1st Regiment [of Chasseurs] remained at the farm of la Caillou, ordered to guard imperial headquarters. It had already advanced close to the Chantelet wood by which the Prussians were advancing. The centre was thus formed by the 2nd/2nd Chasseurs which had moved to the crest under the orders of the emperor, then by the 2nd/1st Chasseurs under Cambronne and which was in the rear of the preceding battalion, then by the two regiments of grenadiers (1st and 2nd) which had crossed to the other side of the road [the left], but level with them. Finally, the left of this change of front, or the 'hammer' of this oblique movement, was destined for the attack on the English, on the main ridge where the bulk of their remaining forces were deployed. The 3rd and 4th Grenadiers held themselves back on the height, halfway along the road.

The Guard cavalry, which was with us in the second position level with la Belle Alliance, was also to advance at the same time on the other side of the road. The brave General Jamin shook my hand and said to me 'We are going to make space for you'.

Sixteen battalions[5] of the best infantry in the world, which had not been committed up until now on this day, and that totalled about 9,000 men, went, simultaneously, to execute and mark out a manoeuvre on a front of some 1,200 *toises* [2,400 yards]. The forces were distributed very unequally on this line, for the largest part were on the left; the masses on the centre and right had long gaps between them which were to be filled by the other corps of the army reforming behind this formidable barrier.

[d'Avout notes: It is important to clearly understand how the movement of the infantry of the Old Guard took place and also to be specific about the division of its forces at this moment. Until then, it followed, as we have seen, the progress of the action, moving along the Genappe to Brussels road, or at least parallel to this *chausée*, which ran perpendicular to the English lines. In detail, the three masses of which Pelet speaks were divided thus; to the right, at Planchenoit, the 1st Bn 2nd Chasseurs, which was joined by the 2nd Bn, 2nd Grenadiers (see letter of Christiani); in the centre, the 1st and 2nd Battalions of the 1st Grenadiers maintained in reserve towards Decoster's house, between Rosomme and la Belle Alliance, to cover the communications and counter the unexpected, as well as the 1st Battalion, 1st Chasseurs, which remained at the Caillou farm with the *quartier-général*; then the 1st/2nd Grenadiers, the 2nd/1st Chasseurs and the 2nd/2nd Chasseurs which, all three, formed the second attack. Finally, to the left, the 3rd and 4th Grenadiers, 3rd and 4th Chasseurs, which formed a mass of eight battalions ready to act, but in reality reduced to six, the two battalions of the 4th Grenadiers having been joined into a single one, the same for the 4th Chasseurs, due to the losses that they had suffered at the battle of Ligny.]

[*Journal*] From then on, I devoted myself to, and went with, the 1st Battalion to Planchenoit. It was about six o'clock, perhaps seven; indeed, I do not know how long I remained there, but it seemed to me a long time. I recalled Gourahel to me and, finding M. Lepage in the first houses, I told him to move to the last houses of the village and to occupy them strongly. Entering there, I encountered the poor General Duhesme, who was being carried dying or dead on his horse, then the voltigeurs [of the Young Guard] completely broken up, then Chartran [commander of the 1st Brigade] who told me that he could do nothing more, and finally Colonel Hurel [Colonel of the

3rd Voltigeurs of the Young Guard], with a lot of men but all retiring. I promised them I would stop the enemy and asked them to rally behind me. Indeed, I moved to the centre of the village and there, seeing the men of M. Lepage coming back pursued by the Prussians, I gave the order to M. Peschot (captain in the 2nd Chasseurs) to march with the 1st Company and to fall on the enemy with the bayonet who were coming along the road opposite ours. His sergeant, Cranges, a lively man, gave the order to the first *peloton* [a *peloton* was a company-sized tactical unit] and marched with him. He executed my order, but hardly had the enemy turned his back on us than the men started to skirmish and he lost control of them. The enemy sent fresh forces; Peschot could not gather his *peloton* together and he was pushed back. I sent forward another, it skirmished: I pushed it forwards myself and the enemy fled. But this *peloton* dispersed and, with each charge that I made, the same thing happened. The men of my last companies shouted '*En avant!*' breaking down into skirmishers and were thus also dispersed. I had the church occupied with some men that I led there and I again found myself face-to-face with those *messieurs* [the enemy] who fired at me at point blank range, but who dashed off. Then, seeing how many resisted them, they launched a multitude of shells into the village and tried to outflank it by the valley of the Lasne and the woods which were around there. I sent an officer there, I believe it was M. Auguis (captain of the 2nd Chasseurs). In all these attacks we grabbed them; our soldiers were furious and cut their throats. I rushed to them to prevent it and, as I got there, I saw them perish in front of my own eyes (they faced having their throats cut with *sang froid* and hung onto my men). I was revolted; overcome with fury, I took several under my protection, including an officer who prostrated himself, telling me of his French friends and those of his family. I put him behind my horse and then handed him over to my *sapeurs* [engineers] saying they would answer to me for his safety. I sent Captain Heuillet to the left, to occupy and defend the church; he went well ahead and next to the wood opposite the enemy; from the rear came some men of the Young Guard who covered the outside of the village.

However, the combat, having gone on for a long time, had dispersed all my men as skirmishers. I could not rally a single *peloton*, the enemy did not enter the village, but he deployed on all sides and, in each interval between the gardens, I saw muskets aiming at me from forty paces. I do not know why I was not struck down twenty times. I went to and fro on Isabelle [his horse]; I had taken off my riding coat and yet our men did not seem to recognise me as a general officer. Certainly, I still held the village; I came, I went, I had the charge beaten, the rally, then the drum roll; nothing brought together even a *peloton*. Finally, at the moment I was most embarrassed, most pressed and at the same time totally exposed, a platoon of Grenadiers [of the 2nd Battalion of the 2nd Regiment] arrived, sent by whom I do not know, but then I was content. I stopped it and used it to rally some chasseurs, then I had it charge with the bayonet without firing a shot. They went forward like a wall and overthrew everything they encountered. I remained there in the middle of this hail of shells, lit up by the fire that had started to burn in a number of houses, in a terrible and continuous fusillade; the Prussians surrounded us with numerous skirmishers. I didn't care, we held like demons; I could not form up my men, but they were all hidden away and laid down a murderous fire on the enemy that contained him; they were stopped despite the numbers that should have overwhelmed us.

Here, Pelet rather unhelpfully cuts away from the fighting at Planchenoit to describe the attack of the Guard on the Allied ridge. However, we will jump forwards to continue his account of his own experiences before looking at his description of the attack of the Guard on the ridge.

[*Journal*] Whilst I came and went continually between the entry and exit [of the village], animating and holding in place all those in the middle of this skirmishing, I encountered Colomban (*chef de bataillon* of the 1st Battalion of the 2nd Chasseurs) who appeared to me a little pale and I noticed this with regret, for perhaps he was thinking the same of me, although I certainly felt as calm and tranquil as I had only a few times before in my life, even in the middle of these enemies that I believed bore me a particular grudge. My major told me that everyone had made off and that the enemy already had cavalry at the entrance to the village [behind him], that we were outflanked on all sides, and in particular by the wood [the Chantelet Wood] on the side of the [river] Lasne. I then gave the order to rally everyone who could be found. I ran round the whole village, where the enemy had entered on all sides.

[*Memoirs*] I had the drums beat the rally and I retired with what remained of the battalion and the company of grenadiers, about half of my men, by the road that ran from Planchenoit to the Caillou farm.

[*Journal*] The entry (to Planchenoit) had already been blocked by the enemy. It was between eight and eight thirty. Out of the village I found myself in a terrible confusion of men saving themselves in rout whilst shouting 'Stop! Stop! Halt! Halt!' It was those who shouted loudest that ran the fastest. These sounds were accompanied by cannon shots, which hastened even the slowest. The enemy accompanied us with his skirmishers, especially by the wood that stretched from Maransart, from where these rascals outflanked me. I had rallied all the men I could around me. I met the poor Langlois [Lieutenant of the 2nd Chasseurs], then the eagle bearer of the 1st Regiment,[6] Baric [Lieutenant of the 2nd Chasseurs] and recall that I embraced the eagle with great emotion in finding it and raising my hat shouted, 'My friends, we must defend it to the death!' This animated them and united them. When we were in a fold in the ground where the enemy artillery could no longer hit us, I said, 'Put your eagle there Martin!' This was the name of the officer who carried the eagle, and then, 'To me Chasseurs of the Guard, rally to your eagle and your General!' I rallied only a few men. I held firm again and found myself surrounded by a body of men; one could not see more than four paces. I thought that they were French, I was told they were our lancers; then I realised they were enemies on which we fell with the bayonet. We fired on them without considering if it was for better or for worse.

I continued to retire little by little. A short time later, I found myself close to the unfortunate Ney, who was also at the head of a handful of men. I went to him and shouted, 'Well! *Monsieur Maréchal?*' I wanted news from him, for him to bear witness to my satisfaction of seeing him ... A little further, still accompanied by my eagle, I came across a great crowd; it was said it was the foot grenadiers. I went to check and told Martin to wait there for me, in case it was the enemy, because everyone was mixed up and you could not recognise anyone at ten paces. When I was sure it was them, I called Martin and shouted to him: 'We must go round to the right!' I do not know what had happened to him. Not seeing him come, I ran over to where he had been, but I could not find him. I roamed around for a long time without finding him, neither him nor the chasseurs that had remained with us. Then I ran back to the body of grenadiers; they were nearby, I think they were marching in square on the right of the road where the ground was more even. I recall seeing Roguet and Petit and I marched with them for a long time; then, having met *Monsieur* Duuring, I went to him.

[*Memoirs*] As it got dark, Major Duuring, close to Caillou with the 1st Battalion of the 1st Regiment of Chasseurs, saw the arrival of the emperor followed by some generals and a few chasseurs à cheval. At this moment, the skirmishers of his regiment were engaged with the enemy [the Prussians]. The emperor asked the major the strength of his battalion, giving him the order to close up in mass and to follow him, adding, 'I am counting on you'. The battalion followed for an hour, in the very tall corn, probably as far as Genappe.

Broken up each moment by the necessity of crossing sunken lanes, through woods, ditches, the battalions of the Old Guard finished by dispersing completely at the passage through Genappe. But they finally re-united at Charleroi, where the army would have been able to rally if the emperor's orders had been executed. In this sad night, we noticed from afar the bivouac fires of Marshal Grouchy, who had rendered us no other service than to warn us to keep away from the direction that he had followed, for us to maintain ourselves on that of Charleroi, the army's line of operations.

We now return to Pelet's account of the attack of the Guard against the Allied ridge. We must remember that he did not witness this for himself, but will have based it on the no doubt many discussions he had with his fellow Guard officers in the days immediately following the battle. It is on these apparently dependable, but distinctly second-hand, accounts that his own account is based and we cannot therefore be absolutely sure of its accuracy.

[In his comment, d'Avout tells us: 'We leave Pelet in Planchenoit holding head against the Prussians and we return to the attack of the infantry of the Old Guard directed against the plateau of Mont-Saint-Jean against the centre of the English line. This attack, as we have said, was composed of *six* [his emphasis] battalions, the only ones which at this time had arrived in the dead ground around la Haye-Sainte; the emperor deployed one, the 2nd Battalion of the 3rd Grenadiers, on a small mound to the left, halfway towards the farm of Hougoumont. Thus only *five* [his emphasis] battalions marched against the enemy; that is, the 1/3 Grenadiers, the 4th Grenadiers reduced to a single battalion, the 1/3 and 2/3 Chasseurs and 4th Chasseurs also reduced to a single battalion'.]

[*Memoirs*] These regiments had already suffered two days earlier and their strength was hardly 500 men per battalion, giving a total of 4,000 at the most.

It appears that the chasseurs were then to the right of the road, the grenadiers to the left. The chasseurs who were on the right of the column formed march divisions, closed up. In this order, they crossed the road and moved one or two hundred paces from la Haye Sainte in a fold in the ground where they stopped a short time, having to their right, between themselves and the road, a body of cuirassiers. It appears also that all that remained of the Guard, infantry, cavalry and artillery, came to take part in this attack and that the cavalry, or at least part of it, had followed and were also pressed into the same fold near la Haye Sainte; perhaps only the service squadrons of which the emperor speaks. It seems also that several artillery pieces had followed and protected this attack by their fire.

Napoleon followed the movement of the column until halfway between la Belle Alliance and la Haye Sainte, where he remained to the right of the road.

The English general, favoured by the ground, which it must be admitted was skilful, and we are all the more willing to offer this eulogy that he rarely merited otherwise, the English general, that we have seen continually located on a mound which dominated the ground, allowed him to examine our movements at this critical moment. He had been able to follow, in all its developments, the march of the battalions of chasseurs, descending the slopes of la Belle Alliance, crossing the main road and directing themselves towards the centre of his line, on the point where he found himself. More than a quarter of an hour had passed between the start and end of this manoeuvre. Wellington had had the time to call all his battle-worthy troops forwards, batteries which were still able, cavalry that he called from the wings, for the arrival of the Prussians had brought him all kinds of support. As at Fuentes d'Onoro, he piled up his lines one behind the other and rendered the success of this attack impossible.

The majority of the men that made up the 3rd and 4th regiments of chasseurs during this attack agreed that these regiments suffered from only little musketry and artillery which came from their left. This attack was led by General Michel, *colonel en second* of the chasseurs. Marshal Ney and General Friant [commandant of the grenadiers] accompanied him. After several minutes of rest employed in reforming and during which *they should have deployed their masses* [his emphasis], these regiments climbed in a single column the steep slopes of the plateau that was already covered in a great quantity of English dead and was crowned by the enemy. They advanced firmly towards them and pushed back the first line of skirmishers, seizing and passing through the advanced batteries that were only able to fire two or three rounds and which the enemy had unlimbered at the approach of our battalions. Consequently, these guns remained abandoned on the ground without it being possible to drag a single one off at the first moment.

When the head of the column had passed the crest of the position, it was stuck by a most violent fire of infantry and artillery. This head of column were wiped out; Generals Michel and Mallet [commander of the 3rd Chasseurs] fell dead with their lead divisions; Friant was seriously wounded. One can sense too late the serious fault that was committed and the ravage this fire produced in the depth of the column; it attempted to deploy by the centre under this fire of iron. The masses of the 3rd Regiment [of chasseurs] deployed by the right, the others by the left. Just exposed, it flew at the enemy, but successively and in isolation, resulting in disjointed movements. They charged the enemy infantry one after another, as far as the edge of the sunken lane, where the first line was covered up to eye level. The other lines were also under cover on the reverse slope of the ridge which fell towards Mont Sainte Jean. This sunken lane made our soldiers describe attacking the English as in their entrenchments.

It appears that several masses stopped to reply to this fire, executed at point-blank range by troops under good cover; that the centre of the sunken lane, between the road to the right [the main road] and the crossroads to the left, which was shallower, was crossed; for the Prince Royal of Holland was wounded beyond it, whilst the lateral parts, more sunken, were able to resist. These four masses [Footnote: From the beginning of the engagement, two echelons, the 1st and 2nd Bns of the 3rd Chasseurs had closed to the point that they formed a single one] heroically sustained a terrible fire; of the four battalion commanders, three, Angelet and Cardinal (of the 3rd Chasseurs) and Agnes (of the 4th), fell dead along with a great number of officers and half the chasseurs. The masses, which found their ranks cruelly thinned, were charged by several fresh squadrons which came from a nearby valley. They retired in order and stopped down the slope.

One of the company commanders, the brave Minal (of the 3rd Chasseurs) who had already lost an arm, called again, '*En avant!*' and went with the rest of these brave battalions on the hidden infantry which recommenced its terrible fire and repulsed this desperate attack. There remained only 800 men in the two regiments [2,168 at the beginning of the campaign].

All agree that the regiments of grenadiers had remained several hundred paces behind and were not able to take part in this attack [though he seems to contradict the statement he made above]. One can also say that the cavalry of the Guard was at the foot of the ridge of La Haye Sainte, behind the brave regiments of foot chasseurs.

One is obliged to admit that the heroic attack of the chasseurs *was very badly directed* [his emphasis, and this probably means 'led' rather than sent in the wrong direction] and that if the faults had not been accumulated there, so much valour and devotion would not have remained without reward. First, they did not await the arrival of the grenadiers, then the masses were not deployed and the distances were not maintained during the crossing of the bottom of the valley. Finally, they did not await the completion of the deployment executed under enemy fire, to make simultaneous charges. All the attacks were isolated and disjointed. Finally, several masses stopped to fire, exposed to perfectly sheltered troops. So much precious blood was the cost of these faults, and although it seems improper to mention it, the truth demands it.

This particular combat, delivered on the highest point of the battlefield and in full view of both armies, decided the result of the day. Success for us would have forced the English to retire on all lines to Brussels; its loss had the saddest influence on our troops. Twice, the half-destroyed battalions of this invincible Guard descended the slope, hundreds of wounded were strewn the length of the main road from the position that was attacked, a profound silence replaced the terrible din. The morale of the rest of the army was shaken, it was ready to follow the élan of victory; it gave ground and unfortunately headed to the rear.

Napoleon, who was between La Haye Sainte and la Belle Alliance, in the middle of his troops and the fire which in the space of a few minutes struck several officers and generals that surrounded him, moved in front of this noble debris, addressed them with some words of consolation and ordered them to reform at the foot of the ridge of la Belle Alliance. The men who saw him at this moment and those who followed, remarked on his handsome and noble face, that in the middle of all this he did not lose his calm, that the traces of this profound emotion occasioned by the misfortunes of *la Patrie* and the army. His complexion was slightly increased in colour, his face animated. He went ahead towards La Haye Sainte, without doubt to hold back the cavalry that was placed there and which was preparing to follow the move of the infantry.

[d'Avout's commentary: There remained in the rear, in the folds of La Haye Sainte, three battalions of the Old Guard; 1/2 Grenadiers, 2/1 Chasseurs as well as the 2/3 Grenadiers that had been sent by the emperor to the left flank; they went into action in their turn.]

[*Memoirs*] From 7 to 8 o'clock in the evening, after the charge of the 3rd and 4th Chasseurs had been checked, General Cambronne, who was with the 2nd/1st Chasseurs, close to the road in front of la Belle Alliance, received the order from a general, who was said to have been Morand, to move forward on the left. Cambronne followed the crest of the ridge which separated the valleys of La Haye Sainte and Hougoumont; advanced on a line a little in the rear of a line drawn between these two habitations, and found there the *Sapeurs* of the Guard [Footnote: These were the *sapeurs* of Lieutenant Colonel Borrel-Vivier, who after having captured La Haye Sainte remained near la Belle-Alliance until the rout][7] with five guns. On the right, on the valley floor, he saw the four battalions that had been repulsed. Cambronne was formed in square. Having met the enemy, he had to suffer a terrible musketry and artillery fire which knocked down the first division. He replied with five or six volleys. Cambronne ordered the retreat and approached the main road. At this time, Napoleon was seen close to this square. Soon the English cavalry charged this square at about 8.30, but was not able to break it after numerous efforts and breaking it down with its artillery.

General Roguet set off a few moments after General Cambronne with the 2nd/3rd Grenadiers which was commanded by Belcourt and were placed on the left of the main road. This battalion had hardly more than 300 men. It advanced between la Belle Alliance and La Haye Sainte, with the main road to its right which was two or three *pieds* above ground level. During the march, General Roguet encountered the wounded Friant, returning on foot and Harlet [commander of the 4th Grenadiers], also wounded, supported by some of his grenadiers.

The emperor came close to this battalion and said to General Roguet that he was too close to Cambronne and it was necessary to spread out a bit. The general replied that it was too dangerous to execute this movement in square whilst so close to the enemy.

Effectively, there were no more troops in front of them and the English had re-occupied La Haye Sainte.

The emperor did not insist and immediately returned to la Belle Alliance. Soon after, General Roguet was heavily attacked by considerable forces, composed of both Prussians and English. His weak battalion was not able to put up much more resistance than that of Cambronne; he retired on la Belle Alliance. The emperor found the 2/1st Grenadiers, commanded by M. Combes, and continued with him on the road to Genappe. The other battalion, commanded by General Petit, followed the emperor in the same direction under his orders.

The 2nd/2nd Chasseurs, placed next to la Belle Alliance, remained there after the departure of Cambronne until nightfall, still having on its right some regiments of cuirassiers and one of chasseurs à cheval. This cavalry moved off, it is said, without orders and without being seriously charged. Commandant Monpez [*sic*] [2nd/2nd Chasseurs], struck by the crowd of men who were abandoning the battlefield and without cavalry support, started his retreat moving along the road without being seriously threatened. This battalion, soon reduced to about 30 men, had received the eagle of the Guard from Cambronne. Marching always in square, they could not maintain their order for long and ended up dispersing. Soon, all those that remained joined the bloody remains of the 1st Battalion that had evacuated Planchenoit.

D'Avout, and Pelet, put the failure of this final attack down to:

- *The formation used; compact and difficult to deploy.*
- *The intervals between the battalions were not maintained.*
- *The battalions deployed too late; whilst under fire and before attempting to attack with the bayonet.*
- *The attack was made in insufficient strength; they should have attacked simultaneously with all the available battalions, even leaving no reserve, so decisive was the moment. He claims that with another seven battalions the attack would have been decisive.*

He gives the losses of the 3rd and 4th Chasseurs for the 16th, 17th and 18th, as 1,141 men killed, wounded and prisoner, out of a total of 2,168; this being after all the separated men had rejoined. 'The total loss of the whole Guard was in the same proportion; half its effectives.'

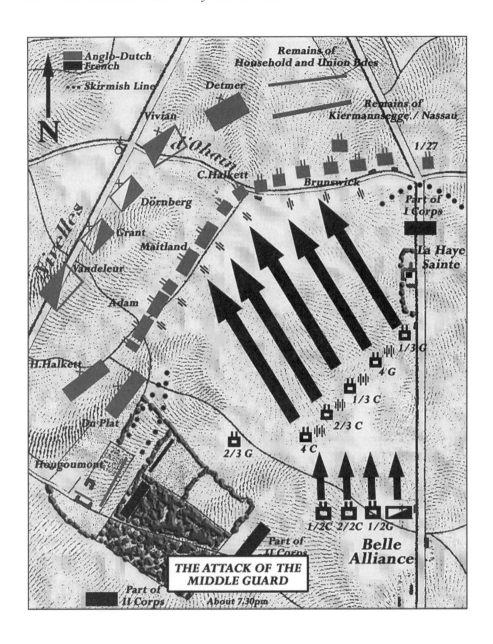

THE ATTACK OF THE
MIDDLE GUARD

About 7.30pm

Chef de Bataillon Jan-Coenraad Duuring

In: d'Avout, *L'infantrie de la garde à Waterloo*, in *Carnets de la Sabretache 1905* (Paris: Leroy, 1905), pp. 116–19.

During the Waterloo campaign Duuring commanded the 1st Battalion of the 1st Regiment of Chasseurs à Pied (Cambronne) of the Imperial Guard.

Duuring was born in Rotterdam in 1779. He began his military career in the Batavian army in 1796, serving in the campaigns of 1796–7. The following year he was transferred into the navy, serving until 1802 when he became lieutenant in the 22nd Infantry Battalion in the Dutch East Indies. On his return in 1806 he found himself incorporated into the army of his new king, Louis Bonaparte, as a captain in the Grenadiers of the Royal Guard. In 1810 the Kingdom of Holland was incorporated into France and the regiments of its army incorporated into the French army. He served with the Dutch Grenadier Guard Regiment which became the 2nd Regiment of the Grenadiers à Pied in the French Imperial Guard, but soon after the 3rd Regiment. He commanded the second battalion of this regiment and fought in Russia in 1812 (Borodino), but when it was virtually destroyed, he was sent to command the 2nd Battalion of the 2nd Grenadier Regiment. He fought in Saxony in 1813 and France in 1814. Having been turned down for service in the new Netherlands army in 1814 after Napoleon's abdication, he became a battalion commander of the Royal Chasseurs. After Waterloo he was sent back to the Netherlands and died in 1834.

As Duuring makes clear, his battalion remained at le Caillou to protect the headquarters established there and Napoleon's baggage and treasury. He therefore saw nothing of the battle or the final attack of the Guard, but does describe the Prussian encroachment into the rear of the French army and his attempts to halt the increasing flood of men to the rear.

17th June ... In the evening, I was again detached [from the regiment] to join the emperor at the farm which was to the right, about a quarter of a league from where the battle was to be fought the next day. The battalion bivouacked in the garden, without fires; the weather was terrible.

18th June. Around seven o'clock in the morning, the emperor gave me the order to remain at the farm [Caillou] with my battalion to guard his general headquarters, treasury etc. Several regiments of infantry and cavalry passed one after the other on the side of the line of battle, as well as the Old Guard: at the passage of the 2nd Battalion, I handed the eagle to General Cambronne.

The cannonade engaged on both sides. The battalion that I commanded remained at the farm. From time to time we saw some prisoners arrive. Close to two or three o'clock in the afternoon, I was informed that some soldiers were scattering, without their arms; this flight came principally from our right. I had the battalion take up their arms, detached a company to the right and one to the left, keeping two in the centre [battalions of the Guard had four companies, unlike those of the line that had six]. I mounted up with the headquarters *gendarmes* [military police], stopped those fleeing, formed them up and led them to the centre of the army. This flight ceased an hour later and everything was very quiet; we saw several English cavalry officers arrive as prisoners.

An hour later, several caissons and guns arrived from the battlefield, saying they had run out of ammunition; in truth, I found some empty, but others still had some. I had them park up to the right and left of the road behind the farm and told the emperor's *écuyer* to have the treasury harnessed up.

About five or six o'clock, I was informed by a post to my right that two columns could be seen leaving a wood, so I went to reconnoitre. Immediately I arrived I was convinced that they were enemy; each was of about 800 men. But the rear was still in the wood and it was very difficult to be sure of their exact strength.

I took my dispositions to receive this attack, putting two guns in battery loaded with caseshot and covered by a detachment of an officer and fifty men posted in a manner that they would be difficult to see, giving them the order not to open fire without my order. My adjutant-major came to inform me that many stragglers were arriving; I had two of my companies that I had kept back in the centre, bayonets crossed, on and either side of the main road with the order to let no one pass that was not wounded (I found amongst this number several officers, including a battalion commander who I forced to take command of an *ad hoc* battalion that I had assembled, with the threat of shooting him if he did not. I even found a *maréchal de camp* [brigadier] whose name I do not know, who I forced to take command of another column).

The officer that I had detached to cover the two guns, sent me word that the artillery officer that commanded them had decided to leave with his guns, saying that he was not under my command and that the enemy was approaching. I then begged some senior artillery officers to put other guns at my disposal, but without effect.

Seeing myself on the point of being attacked by a superior force unsupported by anybody else, I decided to form a battalion of about two hundred men that I had assembled, I put them in a position *en potence* a little behind and to my right to prevent me from being outflanked, I sent off the imperial treasure and equipages and then the guns without a single man as escort, and then attempted to repulse an attack that would have been very harmful to the army if the road behind us had been cut. I reassembled my battalion with its back to the farm, detached a hundred men as skirmishers into the wood and a hundred others as a reserve. At the same time, the general (the provost marshal of the army) had the *ad hoc* battalion of infantry deploy at short range at the *pas de charge*, and also to deploy into the wood. This combination had a happy outcome: we suffered few casualties and the Prussians were repulsed. I had, at the same time, sent my adjutant-major to inform the emperor what had happened and that I had held the position.

A little time later, we saw a complete rout arrive that we could not stop; infantry, cavalry, artillery; all were mixed together. Then, fearing that I would be charged by enemy cavalry, and to be able to make a move if necessary, I had the battalion re-assembled in column by division [a division in this context was two companies/*pelotons*] at a *peloton* distance; officers and soldiers of all regiments wanted to join our ranks, but I allowed no one to do so, for it would have been impossible to maintain order. Thereafter, I gave orders for men who were of the Old Guard to be put in the ranks so that at the end my divisions were around three hundred men each.

In this sad disorder and at the moment that there was skirmishing in our rear, we saw the emperor arrive accompanied by some chasseurs à cheval and generals, including Counts Drouot and Lobau. His Majesty came to me, asked me what I had done, my strength and deployment (I gave him all the detail) and personally ordered me to form in mass and follow him, saying, 'I am counting on you'.

I set the battalion off; it marched through the corn which was so high it reached above the men's heads. After an hour on the road, we encountered several Guard generals who were gathering members of the Guard together (where I passed on to you and General Roguet the orders that the emperor had given me), finding myself amongst the other corps and then ravines that were very difficult to cross, I lost many men.

Night advanced; I continued to march in the direction that I thought the emperor had intended. In the end, having no guides, I noticed that I had wandered far from the main road; I moved this way and encountered several detachments of the Guard, as well as the eagle of the Grenadiers that I instructed to remain with me. But soon, I was forced to move away from the road for the place where I wanted to go turned out to already be behind the enemy's advance guard. In the direction that I then took was found a house where there was some men; I enlisted their help myself and with much concern for us, they led us by a back road in the direction of Fleurus, that we reached at daybreak and which we bypassed with the necessary precautions. We saw to the left of the road, close to the town, the guns that had been captured from the enemy on the 16th.

Between five and six o'clock in the morning [of the 19th], we approached Charleroi where the local people advised us not to approach the town, saying that it was already occupied by the enemy (indicating to me to cross the river more to the left in the direction of Philippeville). I continued along the road from Charleroi which I passed through with about three hundred men including some grenadiers as well as the eagle. We found all the roads obstructed and to our left, in a small square, we saw several enemy guns taken during the 16th.

Captain Prax

In: d'Avout, *L'infantrie de la garde à Waterloo*, in *Carnets de la Sabretache 1905* (Paris: Leroy, 1905), pp. 119–21.

During the Waterloo campaign Prax was adjutant-major of the 3rd Regiment of Chasseurs à Pied (Poret de Morvan) of the Imperial Guard. This regiment took the heaviest casualties of all the Guard regiments having almost certainly faced the British Guards on the ridge. He writes that the attack was made in closed column.

A letter written to General Pelet dated Cholet, 23rd April 1835.

The strength of the two battalions of the 3rd Regiment of Chasseurs was 1,040 men on our departure from Paris. We left none on the road.

This regiment suffered no loss on the 16th; not having been engaged. The 3rd Grenadiers under command of General Poret had alone been sent on Ligny and suffered little loss, the impetuosity having quickly decided the affair. [Footnote: The 1st Chasseurs and 1st Grenadiers were also engaged at Ligny. The 2nd and 3rd Grenadiers went round the position of Ligny by the west, whilst the 1st Chasseurs and Grenadiers went by the east.] The 3rd Regiment of Chasseurs were not then with the rest of the Guard; they had been detached to go in observation of the extreme left of our line, the side from which it was said that the enemy were coming; it was actually the corps of General Drouet d'Erlon.

On the 17th, we left late from Fleurus and, towards 10pm, we established our bivouacs close to the farm occupied by the emperor, on the right of the *chausée* from Charleroy [sic] to Brussels.

The weather was horrible, the rain fell in torrents.

On the 18th, at 7am, we took up arms. It was said that the emperor would have need of his Guard this day. This warning was received with enthusiasm, with gratitude, and the chasseurs prepared their muskets to be ready for firing. However, we did not leave our bivouacs until towards 8am and, after having crossed the main road and marched parallel to it for an hour, we took position behind a height on which the emperor and his headquarters were located [Rosomme]. Several enemy balls fell around there, but soon, the army coming up into line, we were established on the plateau of the height that dominated the whole army. The emperor dismounted.

In the course of the day, the Guard was placed in mass behind la Belle Alliance and remained there until 5pm. The 3rd and 4th Chasseurs, 3rd and 4th Grenadiers, less a couple of battalions, were placed in columns in mass by battalion and led one by one to the left of La Haye Sainte. The slope which led to the ridge was neither steep nor of difficult access; we climbed it with shouldered arms. We were surprised to find it almost abandoned and covered in dead!

On our left was a numerous battery, unlimbered and abandoned by its crews. These were not far away and their hesitation to return to their guns could be clearly seen. However, we did not advance much further before noticing a formidable line and meeting a lively resistance. All our heads of column were put *hors de combat*. I cannot help thinking that if we had engaged the enemy first with some skirmishers which could have caused some disorder in his ranks and if we had marched behind them quickly and with the bayonet, our attack would have succeeded.

So we were repulsed, but the enemy did not commit the imprudence of pursuing us. So we left the high ground of the plateau between us. From this position we contained the English with skirmishers. It was then about 7 o'clock and already the centre of the army appeared in rout; mounted officers rode to the front of the columns that were fleeing to try and stop them, but confusion reigned everywhere and their efforts were useless. We found ourselves surrounded on all sides. Night came and we followed the torrent. Alas! Alas!

The Imperial Guard Cavalry

The decree of 8 April 1815 included the following direction for the Guard cavalry:

The cavalry was to consist of a regiment each of grenadiers à cheval, dragoons, chasseurs à cheval, cheveu-légers lanciers (light horse lancers) and a company of gendarmerie.

Each regiment of cavalry was to be of four squadrons, each squadron of two companies. In time of war the companies were to be brought up to 150 men including officers. A regiment at full strength in time of war was therefore 1,229 (four squadrons of 300 men each and a headquarters of twenty nine. A decree of 22 April raised the number of squadrons of the lancers from four to five; the first squadron was to be composed of the Poles who had joined

Napoleon in exile. On the 15 May the chasseurs à cheval were also increased to five squadrons.

To bring the Guard cavalry up to strength, each regiment of the line was to provide two officers, twenty non-commissioned officers and soldiers who were 'vigorous and distinguished for their courage and good conduct'. They were to have eight years' service.

Grenadiers were to be a minimum of 5 *pieds* 5 *pouces* tall.
Dragoons were to be a minimum of 5 *pieds* 4 *pouces* tall.
Chasseurs were to be a minimum of 5 *pieds* 3 *pouces* tall.
Lancers were to be a minimum of 5 *pieds* 2 *pouces* tall.

If any regiment was short of men the balance was to be drawn from the lancers. The lancers were certainly the poor relations of the Guard; they were all considered of the second class (only four years' service) and got lower pay than the senior regiments. In fact regimental strengths for the campaign lay between the strongest (the chasseurs à cheval) at about 1,200 and the weakest (the grenadiers à cheval) at just under 800.

Interestingly, Napoleon also ordered the raising of a Young Guard regiment of éclaireurs-lanciers (scout lancers), drawing its personnel from previous members of the Young Guard cavalry of 1813 and 1814. They were formed in Paris but were not complete in time for Waterloo. However, they took part in the skirmishing around Paris prior to the Allied entry which ended the war and were disbanded with the rest of the army south of the Loire.

The Guard cavalry had been lightly engaged at the battles of Quatre Bras (the light cavalry) and Ligny (the heavy cavalry) on 16 June, and had only suffered minor casualties. At Waterloo, they were deployed into the third line; Lefebvre-Desnouëtte's light cavalry behind Milhaud's 4th Cavalry Corps and Guyot's heavy cavalry behind Kellerman's 3rd Cavalry Corps. Although each consisted of only two regiments, and would therefore normally be classed as a brigade, their regiments were much stronger than those of cuirassiers or light cavalry and therefore their brigade strength exceeded that of all the other cavalry divisions; they are therefore generally referred to as divisions. For example, the chasseurs à cheval of the Guard numbered nearly 1,200 men at the beginning of the campaign, considerably more than any of the line cavalry brigades and in some cases well over twice as strong. Who ordered the commitment of the Guard cavalry to the great cavalry charges during the battle remains an unresolved controversy; the eyewitnesses that follow clearly disagree!

Lieutenant-General Baron Claude Etienne Guyot

Carnets de Campagnes (1792–1815) (Paris: Librairie Teissedre, 1999), pp. 385–6 and pp. 393–7.

During the Waterloo campaign, Guyot served as the commander of the Imperial Guard Heavy Cavalry Division, which consisted of the regiments of grenadiers and dragoons, and two batteries of Guard horse artillery (twelve guns).

    Claude Guyot was born in 1768 and enlisted in the Bretagne Chasseurs in 1791. His first service was in the Army of the Rhine and he was quickly promoted to maréchal des logis *(sergeant) and was commissioned in 1793. The following year he was posted to the Vendée where he spent three years fighting the insurgency. In 1799 he served with the Army of Germany in Bavaria and Württemberg, being promoted to captain, and then taking part in the Hohenlinden campaign where he distinguished himself in the pursuit after the battle. In 1802 the size of the Consular Guard was substantially increased and so started Guyot's long association with the Guard. He was posted into the Guard chasseurs à cheval in 1802 during the short period of peace at this time. He took part in the Austerlitz campaign as a* chef d'escadron *and was present at Ulm. He fought at Austerlitz in the dramatic cavalry action against the Russian Guard cavalry and took a leading part in this combat. At the end of 1805 he was promoted lieutenant colonel. Leaving Paris commanding Napoleon's escort, Guyot was left behind as the emperor rushed forward and thus Guyot missed all the major engagements of the Jena campaign! However, he went with Napoleon into Poland and fought at the bloody battle of Eylau. The regiment suffered heavily at this battle and with the colonel wounded, Guyot took command and was promoted colonel. Although present at Friedland, they remained in reserve throughout the battle. He then followed Napoleon into Spain and whilst taking part in the pursuit of Moore, was present at Benevente when the commander of the Guard chasseurs, General Lefebvre-Desnouëttes, was captured by the British. Guyot succeeded him to command and in 1809 marched the regiment back in time to take part in the battle of Wagram after which he was promoted to* général de brigade. *Early in 1811 he returned to Spain and was present at the battle of Fuentes d'Onoro, but despite having little opportunity to acquire further glory in the Peninsula he was promoted* général de division *at the end of that year. Although he took part in the Russian campaign he was forced to give up command of his regiment on Lefebvre-Desnouëtte's return, leaving him to command Napoleon's escort. He was present at the capture of Smolensk and the battle of Borodino, but the emperor's escort took no part in the fighting. In 1813 he fought with the re-built regiment at Lützen, where he was wounded, but this did not stop him serving again at Bautzen. After the armistice, and now* baron d'Empire, *he was captured with Vandamme at Kulm, but was soon exchanged. He fought again at Leipzig, but his regiment was mauled by Cossacks during the retreat. However, this did not stop him making a significant contribution to the battle of Hanau. At the end of 1813 he was transferred into the Guard Grenadiers à Cheval which he commanded into the 1814 campaign. He fought at Brienne, la Rothière, Montmirail and Vauchamps where his regiment played a part in each of these battles; but, blamed by Napoleon for the loss of some guns from the Guard artillery, the emperor relieved him of his command. However, loath to lose the services of one of his most experienced Guard cavalry commanders, Guyot was soon appointed commander of Napoleon's personal escort. He subsequently fought at Craonne, Reims and Arcis-sur-Aube. He retained command of the grenadiers after the First Restoration, but waited until Napoleon was in Paris before moving to join him. He commanded the division of heavy Guard cavalry through the 1815 campaign, fighting at both Ligny and Waterloo where he was wounded leading his men in the great cavalry charges. After the disbandment of his regiment he retired in 1816. He accepted the recall to service from Louis-Philippe in 1830, but soon retired again in 1833. He died in Paris in 1837.*

Napoleon accused Guyot of engaging his division in the great cavalry charges without orders and that because of this, he was left without a capable reserve once the attack of the Guard infantry had been repulsed. In his account, Napoleon ascribes the attack by British cavalry as responsible for the rout of the French in front of the Anglo-Dutch army and that he could have repulsed this if Guyot's division had been available. Guyot spent many years writing to deny the charge and trying to expose the truth. What follows are some examples of these efforts in which he describes his contribution to the battle.

Drawn from a letter to Lieutenant General Count Drouot, dated Cachant, 4 July 1820;

... from about two o'clock, I was put under the orders of Marshal Ney who had already directed Kellerman's cavalry and other troops against the enemy's line. I had no sooner arrived close to him than he also employed me there several times in the same way, each time without success despite all our efforts, because he had need at this point of a lot of artillery and infantry to defeat the same type of troops and the defence that the enemy opposed to us. I was dismounted in the second charge and was even left in the enemy lines from which, after having been rescued by my grenadiers, I was noticed on foot by the emperor, who, seeing me covered in mud and bruised, asked me if I was wounded. When I told him I wasn't, he said to me, 'Well! Go to your division, prepare it to return against the enemy and tell it that Marshal Grouchy is deploying 30,000 men this time'. I was quickly remounted and punctually executed everything that he ordered me to, but we always encountered the same problems; that is to say a line of fourteen guns (without their limbers) on the crest of the ridge and several masses of infantry at half range on the reverse slope where the gunners took refuge when, despite their fire of canister, I three times arrived at their guns from which I was forced away each time by their murderous fire.

In the last effort I received a musket ball in the chest and a heavy bruise from a shell on the left elbow.

I was no longer able to maintain the command of my division; I confided it to General Janin who was killed immediately after. This unfortunate event happened at the very moment that the emperor was advancing himself against the enemy with his infantry of the Guard.

Extract from the 'States of Service' of General Guyot drawn up by himself;

... From ten o'clock in the morning of the 18th, half our army was put in line at Mont-St-Jean in front of the English who had taken position close to Waterloo at the entry to the Soigne forest. The ground having been thoroughly soaked by the heavy rain of the last twenty four hours, our attack was postponed until two o'clock in the afternoon. It was lively and the movements which followed gave us every hope.

Towards 6pm I received the order to charge twenty guns placed in front of several English squares. I conducted three charges one after the other without a break which achieved no success because I had neither infantry nor artillery to support me; each time I lost many men and horses. I had my own horse killed by a shell splinter in its head during the second charge. For several minutes I was within the enemy lines; I received several sabre blows on the head which cut my hat in two places. But soon rescued by my division I got hold of a troop horse and as I prepared to execute a third charge, I received a musket ball to the chest and a shell splinter to the left elbow; the horse I had mounted was killed at the same time. I thus handed command to General Janin, Major of the regiment. He executed the third charge that I had prepared; he was killed immediately. My division then retired from the mêlée under the orders of a lieutenant colonel of dragoons. I immediately retired to the rear, exhausted and losing a lot of blood.

The emperor, seeing that the victory was going to escape him, personally moved at the head of the infantry of the Guard against the same squares that I had been unable to break. He obtained no more success, not least because more than 30,000 Prussians commanded by Bülow arrived from Wavre to save the English.

The battle was then lost for us and our army was put completely to rout; our loss was immense. We marched all night to arrive at Charleroi at dawn on the 19th. The Emperor retired himself (without giving any orders for a point of retreat) ...

Extract from a letter to General Pelet dated 27 April 1835;

At night time on the 17th June, this division left the main body of the army near Planchenoit to go to sleep at the village of Maransard [*sic*] where it was only able to remain there by maintaining a close lookout and repulsing several reconnaissances that the English left wing sent a number of times to this place during the night.

During this night the emperor established his general headquarters at the village of Planchenoit.

Towards 7am in the morning of the 18th, I received the order for me to move immediately with my division to general headquarters which was about two leagues away and where I arrived at 10.30 in the morning.

The army was immediately put into motion and about midday deployed on the ground that it occupied until the end of the day.

My division was placed in line with the height that the emperor personally occupied until towards about seven o'clock.

My right touched the road from Genappe to Waterloo and the left was in the direction below Braine-la-Leud. To my left front was Lieutenant General Duc de Valmy's division of heavy cavalry. [Kellerman. He actually commanded the 3rd Cavalry Corps, not a single division.]

The English army had its right beyond Braine-la-Leud, its centre in front of Waterloo and its left on Ohain.

At two o'clock the emperor had the army advance to attack the enemy along the whole line; the English responded vigorously with their artillery from the position they had established the day before. Their centre was strongly posted; it was on a low hill on the crest of which they had placed twenty guns which could cover the entire plain without changing position, which we were obliged to cross to reach them. This artillery was unlimbered, but several infantry squares were close enough on the reverse slope to be able to offer sufficient protection against mounted attack and receive the artillerymen that served them if a cavalry charge forced them to abandon their guns.

The enemy cavalry occupied the rear or intervals between the squares. In spite of this well-established defence, and despite a great part of these forces being sheltered, our army nevertheless made progress. It was in the hope of containing us that at 3pm a strong mass of English cavalry executed a general charge against our right flank which threw it into a little disorder. But it was immediately repulsed with advantage.

The action did not continue with any less determination on our part because the enemy's resistance weakened noticeably towards five o'clock in the evening; he probably made such a great effort because he awaited Prussian support. Towards six o'clock the emperor, wanting to force the centre of the enemy's line, ordered the Duc de Valmy to charge it; this division was forced back to my left. At that time I received the order to advance my division and to come under the command of Marshal Ney. He immediately had me execute a charge on several squadrons which masked the artillery until on my approach they retired behind the squares. This retrograde movement exposed me to artillery fire and the fire from the squares that protected it, and we suffered heavy losses. Our two divisions charged this line of artillery alternately, seizing it each time, but always being obliged to retire quickly because we only had sabres to oppose to the fire from the squares and to the volleys of canister that we received on our approach. The enemy cavalry profited each time from the disorder that the musketry and canister caused in our ranks to instantly pursue our scattered squadrons, but we did not allow him success for long, pushing him back quickly into his defence line. It was in the second charge that I was dismounted and obliged to retire on foot; I did not have time to escape, for I had not gone ten paces backwards when I was knocked down and ridden over by cavalry which sabred me as it passed by; however, it was not able to grab hold of me, for I was immediately freed by a third charge executed by my division. I retired through the mêlée that I encountered ... which went at the enemy. A troop horse was quickly procured for me, but I was hardly in the saddle when I received a ball in the chest and a shell splinter to the left elbow. I then handed command over to General Jamin, who in a new charge was shot dead. It was then close to 7.30pm. It was close to where the emperor had positioned himself during the first part of the battle that I learnt of a Prussian corps of 30,000 men commanded by General Bülow which, having been first seen at 4pm had finally deployed towards the village of Planchenoit and threatening general headquarters, threw alarm into our rear.

The infantry of the Guard were not strong enough at the point where the emperor had directed them; they were obliged to retire after enormous losses. The retrograde movement of these troops was the signal for a complete rout along our whole line towards 8pm; however, this rout did not last long; either some troops put up resistance or the enemy had employed too few troops in the pursuit. I had several hundred men of my division remaining close to me as the rearguard towards nine o'clock in the evening on the road to Genappe where we only arrived at midnight; it was in this area that I noticed for the first time the effects of a manifest treason; several artillery caissons had been attached by their wheels with chains and placed across the road; by the sides of these caissons were others that were empty, the shaft passed into the windows of the ground floor of the houses that bordered the road. The obstacle was so great that I was not able to pass through it, so I was forced to make a detour around this town across the fields to go further to find the road to Charleroi; it was behind this obstacle that a great part of the artillery that we had saved from the battlefield was abandoned. The two batteries attached to my division during the battle had been employed somewhere else throughout the day, and had lost only two or three men and six horses. It was abandoned at Genappe because it could not get through. We took ten guns and some caissons at Charleroi towards 7am on the 19th. These guns were led back to Paris. I led the retreat by Avesnes and Laon.

Captain Antoine-Fortuné de Brack

La Cavalerie de la Garde à Waterloo, published in *Carnet de la Sabretache 1901* (Paris: Leroy, 1901), p. 356 and pp. 361–71.

During the Waterloo campaign, de Brack served as a captain in the chevaux-légers-lanciers of the Imperial Guard which was commanded by General Édouard Colbert. The regiment was part of the Imperial Guard Light Cavalry Division (commanded by General Lefebvre-Desnouëttes) along with the Guard chasseurs à cheval and two batteries of Guard horse artillery (twelve guns).
  The son of a Royalist, de Brack was born in 1789 in Paris. In 1806 he entered the École Spéciale Militaire and was commissioned into the 7th Hussars under the then Colonel Eduoard Colbert. He went straight on campaign and fought at Heilsberg and Friedland. He was promoted to lieutenant in 1809 and became aide-de-camp to Colbert who had recently been promoted general. He went on to fight at Ratisbonne, Essling, Raab, Wagram, Smolensk, La Moskowa, Malojaroslawetz, Krasnoë and La Bérézina. He was present at Lützen before being promoted to captain in the Old Guard, giving him the rank of chef d'escadron *in the 2nd Chevaux-Légers-Lanciers. He fought at the head of his company at Dresden, Kulm, Leipzig and Hanau. On 5 January 1814 at Hoogstraten, near Antwerp, his horse was killed by a ball during a charge. He continued to serve in the Corps Royal des Lanciers de France under the first restoration, but, despite being decorated he quickly returned to Napoleon's side in 1815, commanding a company in the 2nd Lancers. He was put into retirement on half pay in November 1815. He returned to service in 1829 and became lieutenant colonel in the 13th Chasseurs and soon after was promoted to colonel of the 4th Hussars (1832). He became* maréchal de camp *in 1835, but, as inspector general he suffered what was apparently a stroke late in 1838 which paralysed his right side and forced him to retire in 1840. He died in 1850 at Évreux. He is perhaps best known for his instruction manual for the light cavalry;* Advance Posts of Light Cavalry.

At Waterloo I was part of the *lanciers de la Garde imperial*. It is true that Lieutenant-General Domon made me ask the emperor for command of the 9th Regiment of Chasseurs, whose Colonel, Dukermon [d'Avrange baron du Kermont] had, it was said, deserted to the enemy; but this request was made too late for it to have any result.

The four regiments of the Horse Guard formed a division under the orders of Marshal Ney, not having been separated during the whole day, remaining with our reins over our arms, close to the Nivelles road and executing no movement until the moment when our attack, at first so astonishing and vigorous, but then so powerfully repulsed by Ponsonby's English brigade, had moved forward the division of cuirassiers into the front line which until then had remained for several hours level with us.

Ponsonby's cavalry had committed three faults, common in inexperienced cavalry, mistakes which would without doubt be ours, if tomorrow, with inexperienced superior officers, if it presents itself on the battlefield:

1. That of not conducting a reconnaissance of the ground before the charge.
2. That of setting off from too far away.
3. That of not knowing when to stop and to rally in time.

In its impetuous course, it passed through our badly supported batteries, one of our young regiments, I think the 44th [45th] from which it took its eagle; but, because of the difficulties of the terrain, by the irresistible élan of its officers, arriving dispersed on the point where it found itself with a strong opponent, fresh, in order, well-commanded, it lost all the advantages it had acquired and, under the thrusts by the points of our cuirassiers' sabres and the lances of our 4th, commanded by Colonel Bro, scattered the ground with its dead.

Certain English newspapers of the time announced that General Ponsonby had paid for his temerity with his life, and that only twenty-five men of his brigade returned to report the news of this incredible disaster to the English army.

The eagle was re-taken and returned to our infantry by a *maréchal des logis* [sergeant] of the 4th Lancers.

This success electrolysed our cavalry, more impatient than ever to cross swords [with the enemy].

The division of the Horse Guard having received the order to advance, we marched towards the enemy, in the direction of the fortified farm called la Sainte-Alliance [*sic*], and separated from it by a slight elevation of ground, a gentle slope and a small plain rather close together.

The four regiments were on the same line, astride the main road; lancers to the right, then, to the left, the chasseurs, the dragoons and the grenadiers.

Now happened one of those unbelievable events, which, however, I can confirm of its authenticity, one of those freaks of war which overturn all calculations of reason, of prudence, and which form however, one of the chapters so frequent in our military history, freaks which occasionally deliver victories, when genius, in its promptitude, recognises them from the beginning and sanctions them by supporting them.

I have said that the cavalry of the Guard was on a single line and that an undulation of the ground separated them from the plain on which they were to fight man to man. This undulation was not continuous across our line of battle and only hid the first four squadrons of our regiment which, holding the right, was the alignment for the division.

General Curély had been a captain aide-de-camp with me to General Eduoard Colbert, our old colonel. We loved each other as brothers. Without his own command on this day, and acting within general headquarters whilst awaiting what would be confided to his courage, he saw the regiment from afar and came to see me. Embracing me and while chatting with him, we climbed to the top of the undulation several *toises* [a *toise* was about 2m] from the extreme right of the regiment.

Hardly had I reached this point, than I recognised the terrain which opened up to me. In January 1814, under the orders of General Maison, I had, at the head of a squadron and a battalion, occupied for several days the position of the junction of the two roads to cover the headquarters of the *armée du Nord*, which was then in Brussels.

Intoxicated by the recent success against Ponsonby, by the forward movements that I saw executed by the cuirassiers which were to our right, I shouted, 'The English are lost! The position on which they have been thrown back proves it clearly ... They can only retreat by a single narrow road between impracticable woodland. A broken stone on this road and all their army is ours! ... Either their general is an ignoramus, or he has lost his head! ... The English realise their position ... There you are ... look ... they have uncoupled their guns!' I did not know that the English batteries normally fought uncoupled.[8]

My loud words were heard; from the front of our regiment, several officers pushed forwards to join our group. The files of the right followed them; the movement spread along the squadrons to maintain their alignment, then in the chasseurs. This movement, which was only of a few paces to the right, became more pronounced to the left. The brigade of dragoons and grenadiers, who were imminently awaiting the order to charge, thought it had been given ...; it set off and we followed!

This is how the charge of the Guard cavalry happened, on the causes of which so many writers have made so many different comments.

From this moment, we took our alignment from the left, passing the road diagonally, so that all the Guard cavalry found itself to the left of this road; we crossed the plain, climbed the slope of the plateau on which the English army was deployed, and which we attacked together.

The deployment of this army, of the part that we could see was as follows:

To its right, Scots infantry, deployed in a wood which covered to the bottom of the slope; this infantry delivered a well-maintained and accurate fire; then squares of infantry of the line (in red) deployed *en échiquier*; then squares apparently of Hanoverian light infantry (in green), then the fortified farm. Between the squares, batteries whose gunners fired and then sought refuge under their guns; in the rear of this infantry were cavalry.

We were almost level with the farm [La Haye Sainte], between which, and us, our cuirassiers charged. We passed through the batteries which we could not carry off, turned and threatened the squares which opposed a very honourable resistance. Several of them were so well composed that they fired on us by ranks.

It was said that the dragoons and grenadiers to our left broke several of these squares; I did not see it, but I can confirm that our lancers did not have the same good fortune, and that our lances crossed ineffectually with the English bayonets. Several of our cavalrymen, to open the squares, threw their lances like the *djérid* [North African Arabs] into the front ranks.

The exhaustion of ammunition in the English front line, and the closed up nature of the squares which composed it, made the fire point-blank; but the harm that the artillery and the squares of the second line, and the absence of infantry and artillery to support and resume our attack, forced our retreat. We carried this out slowly, and we faced about again at the foot of the slope of the plateau, in such a manner that we could only see the English first line. It was then that Marshal Ney, *alone* [his italics], for not one of his headquarter officers accompanied him, came to our front, harangued us, calling out by their names the officers that he knew.

He looked upset and he shouted several times, 'Frenchmen, do not move! It is here that are the keys to our liberty!' I quote his exact words.

Five times we returned to the charge, but circumstances being the same, five times we returned to take position to the rear. There, a hundred and fifty paces from the enemy infantry, we were exposed to a most murderous fire and our men, struck at the same time from the front by balls, from the flank by bullets and by new projectiles (small shells) [he is probably referring to shrapnel shells], which exploded above their heads and plunged down, started to lose courage.

At last a battery of the Guard was sent over to support us; but instead of horse artillery it belonged to the Foot Artillery Reserve of 12-pounders. It had the utmost difficulty in moving forward through the mud and only took position behind us after endless delay. Its first shots were so badly aimed that they blew away a complete *peloton* of our own regiment.

Our retreat was ordered. We executed it at the walk and reformed to the rear of the battery that had rushed forwards. The chasseurs, the dragoons and the grenadiers went further back in their movement, and echeloned themselves a short distance to the rear and left of the lancers.

The English cavalry came through the intervals to follow us; but when they saw us face about again, they stopped, respecting above all our lancers, whose long arms intimidated them, at first at pistol range, then retiring to the rear of their infantry which had made no movement, leaving between us and this infantry some squadrons of light dragoons (blue pelisses, with white fur), which formed a line of skirmishers supported by the Scots on foot.

Then a voluntary truce, so to speak, was reached between the combatants due to the complete exhaustion of the troops. Half of our squadrons dismounted in half musket range. The Intendent-general, d'Aure, can testify to this fact for, with his usual bravery, he came to visit us during this particular episode. This suspension of arms lasted about three-quarters of an hour, during which we hoped that the emperor's genius would change the face of the battle, by organising a general attack with decisive support ... but nothing! Absolutely nothing!

It was then that from actors, we became spectators of an incomprehensible drama, and whose terrible absurdity was soon recognised and highly condemned, even by the simplest of our cavalrymen.

The small plain which we bordered on one side was, you could say, like a large circus, whose boxes were occupied by the English. In this bloody arena, descended successively the unfortunates devoted to death, and whose sacrifice was all the easier and prompt because the English, without danger to themselves, awaited them at point blank range.

At first, these were several battalions which came from our left and presented themselves in column in front of the English right and the Scots hidden in a wood.

When these were lying on the ground, it was the brigade of carabiniers which emerged on our right at a gentle trot, crossed the arena alone in column of pelotons, and rode along all the enemy batteries to attack the English right.

Then Wellington's musketry and batteries awoke together, to all strike at the same point, and, with the thunder of their blows, was mixed the triple *hourras* of the butchers. Within a few seconds the carabiniers had vanished, in death or flight.

To complete our desolation, news circulated in our ranks ... Our right is in rout ... Grouchy has sold out to the enemy ... [General] Bourmont, [and his aides de camp] Clouet, Dubarrail and many other officers have deserted ... a senior officer belonging to the infantry column which had attacked the Scots, struck by a piece of shrapnel, lost his shako in falling, from which escaped two hundred white cockades ... The English, in retiring from their first position, had left on the ground proclamations signed by Louis XVIII, which promised pardon, forgetting or conservation of ranks and jobs.

When there were no more victims to offer for the great sacrifice, when the fun of the circus was over, our attention turned to a new spectacle which worthily crowned this day. On the plateau to our right, formed black lines, which advanced preceded by their cannons, these were the Prussians! They had escaped Grouchy! ... Oh! Then how do you paint the consternation of the Guard cavalry! Ask the emperor! It had not seen him since the engagement started ... it did not see him again!

The order for retreat was given. This retreat was gloomy! It was a funeral procession! ... Our brigade of light cavalry, reduced to two and a half squadrons, commanded by Generals Lefebvre-Desnouëttes, Lallemand [Major of the Chasseurs], Colbert (wounded) [commander of the Lancers], retired slowly and it extended its line in order to form a curtain which, at our point, hid to some extent the rout of our army from the English.

We marched thus until we found ourselves to our left of the Old Foot Guard, who, like us, was the extreme rearguard. It was formed in square on the road and the southern slope of a fold in the ground, whose crest served it as a parapet against the English balls. It faced to the rear.

We stopped level with it and, like it, faced ahead. We were then composed of from one hundred to a hundred and fifty officers and cavaliers of the lancers and chasseurs, exhausted and full of grief, and we were about five hundred paces to the left of the rushing infantry, separated from it by low open ground with some undergrowth.

The sun had quite disappeared below the horizon; it was almost dark.

Our three generals came together in front [of our line] and some officers joined them – I was a member of this group.

A powerful assault column of the enemy was marching on the road and was heading for the Guard's square. As far as the darkness allowed me to make it out, this column was composed of infantry in battalions, flanked by a double column of artillery and by cavalry in divisions; it marched with order and confidence.

Its head had hardly appeared on the crest behind which the Guard were standing when the Guard opened fire. This fire was well enough co-ordinated, but was perhaps premature; and it seemed to me that it would have produced more effect if it had been delivered from closer to the crest and thus as a plunging fire.

This firing was answered by a rather poor volley from the enemy; then there was a mêlée which was concealed from me by the darkness and the distance. General Lefebvre-Desnoëttes cried out in the greatest excitement, 'that it was here that we must all die; that no Frenchman could survive such a horrible day! That we must seek death among this mass of English that faced us . . .' We tried to calm him down. A discussion began in which we all took a part and, strangely enough, the man who best maintained his *sang-froid* – who still saw for us a tomorrow to look forward to, who spoke of making a useful retreat all the way to Paris, was the one who would instantly lose his life if the Bourbons found him: General Lallemand. He ignored his own interests in order to consider the general situation, discussing matters coolly and with authority. That night I formed the highest opinion of the soundness of his character and his spirit.

I strongly supported General Lallemand, and suggested throwing ourselves into the closest fortress, Maubeuge, to rally there all the isolated men that we could find during the day, then, in a few days, to move on the enemy's rear and conduct a terrible partisan war which, if our ranks grew and there was early success, perhaps, by the anxiety that it would produce, operate a large and useful diversion.

This advice was supported by the majority, but it was agreed after considering everything, we would march on Quatre Bras, where we would doubtlessly get some news.

General Lefebvre-Desnoëttes repeated his desperate proposal; but we were just a handful of exhausted men, whose horses could barely carry us. A shell fell at our feet; several English squadrons were heading towards us; we carried out our retreat at the walk.

Thus it was that we were *the last* [his emphasis] to abandon the field. We followed paths running parallel to the road, and our isolation was such that we did not hear the slightest sound of war.

During this silent march we rallied the debris of all arms. We found Colonel Grobert [commander of the 5th Cuirassiers], of the cuirassiers, who we had been told had been killed.

After several hours we began to make out a muffled sound to our left. This sound grew louder, and soon we came out at Quatre Bras, where we found the most crowded, breathless and disordered retreat that I ever saw.

We lined up in line facing to the rear, our right being very close to the Charleroi road. Hardly was this movement complete than one of our officers said, 'There is the emperor!' Immediately, all our eyes turned towards the road and, in the middle of a mass of infantry, vehicles, cavalry and wounded, we indeed saw the emperor mounted, accompanied by two officers wearing riding coats just like him and followed by four or five gendarmes (it was, I believe, one o'clock in the morning).

Recognising troops still under discipline, the emperor came towards us.

Never has such a bright moon lit a more terrible night. The moonlight fell squarely on the emperor's face as he stood before our ranks. Never, even during the retreat from Moscow, had I seen a more troubled and unhappy expression on that majestic face.

'Who are you?' asked His Majesty.

'The Lancers of the Guard'.

'Ah yes! The Lancers of the Guard! And where is Piré?' [General Piré commanded the cavalry of II Corps, including the 5th and 6th Lancers of the Line]

'Sire, we know nothing of him'.

'How, and the 6th Lancers?'

'Sire, we do not know, he was not with us'.

'That's right ..., but Piré?'

'We have no idea', replied General Colbert.

'But who are you?'

'Sire, I am Colbert, and here are the Lancers of your Guard'.

'Ah, yes ... and the 6th Lancers? ... and Piré? Piré?'

(I report these words with religious accuracy.) A few phrases which I did not hear left his mouth, when, at the sound of a shot from back down the road, one of the generals with him dragged him away, and he disappeared from our sight.

Our grief knew no bounds!

Maréchal des Logis-Chef Jean Michel Chevalier

Souvenirs (Paris: Firmin-Didot, 1970), pp. 322–6.

During the Waterloo campaign Chevalier served as maréchal des logis-chef *(the senior sergeant or First Sergeant in American parlance) of the 4th Company of the regiment of chasseurs à cheval (General Lallemand) of the Light Cavalry Division of the Imperial Guard (Lefebvre-Desnouëttes).*

Chevalier was born in Versailles in 1780; it appears his family worked in the court. He joined the navy as a naval artilleryman in the Year VIII and actually sailed to Egypt. However, on his return, accused of being a deserter he joined the 9th Chasseurs à Cheval (presumably without a discharge from the navy!). In 1801 he marched to Italy to join his regiment. He was involved in the campaigns in the south of Italy against Naples and the insurgents, but comments most on the quality of the women and wine! During these campaigns he was promoted brigadier *in 1802 and fought at the battle of Morano (Campo Tenese) in 1806 which saw the defeat of the Neapolitan army by General Reynier, but also at Maida where he first met defeat at the hands of the British. In the same year he was nominated by his regiment to join the chasseurs à cheval of the Imperial Guard, which he finally did in 1808. Having returned to France to join his new regiment he remained based at Versailles until the campaign of 1809 against Austria. He spent much of this campaign as part of Napoleon's immediate escort and was present at Eckmühl and Ratisbonne and entered Vienna. He fought at both Aspern-Essling and Wagram and was promoted* brigadier *and then* fourrier *in 1810 and 1811. His next campaign was in Russia where he fought at Smolensk and Borodino. He entered Moscow and took part in the retreat, being present at Malo-Jaroslavetz and the crossing of the Beresina. At the end of this campaign he returned to Paris for the re-building of his regiment and returned to the fight in the campaign of 1813, being promoted* maréchal des logis-chef. *He fought at Lützen, Bautzen, Dresden, Leipzig and Hanau. He retreated into France with the rest of the army and fought at all the major engagements of the 1814 campaign. After Napoleon's abdication he remained part of the re-named Chasseurs of France which rejoiced in the emperor's return. After Waterloo and the disbandment of his regiment, he took a job with an architect in Soissons, but unpaid for six months, when he complained to the police his employer denounced him as a Bonapartist. He finally settled down in Paris, married and had a family, and filled his time socialising with his old comrades of the Guard. He died in 1865.*

    Chevalier's manuscript appears to have been written in 1835. His souvenirs give a fascinating glimpse into the lives of the light cavalry and particularly in the campaigns in which he took part. Unfortunately, the detail he gives becomes increasingly thin as his career progresses and his personal anecdotes reduce as he spends more time on a general history of the campaigns in which he took part. Therefore, much of his account of Waterloo is general history clearly based on what he has read rather than experienced. However, there is enough of his personal experiences for it to warrant inclusion, but it will be noted that much of it closely follows Napoleon's account whose 'themes' are repeated.

It was six o'clock in the evening [on the 17th]. The main road, which we were following, passed through the middle of a forest and led to Brussels, which was only four leagues away ... But, arriving at this point, a numerous and violent artillery saluted our appearance and marked a stop, a little brutal, but in war, one does not stand on ceremony. We were forced to spend the night in our present positions.

    Marshal Grouchy was to have arrived at Gembloux [Wavre?] before the Prussians, to prevent them from making their junction with Wellington, but, by a fatality or otherwise, the marshal was so slow in his march on this point that the Prussians arrived three hours before him and was able to open their communications with the English. Marshal Grouchy's army corps of 35,000 men which, certainly, would have ensured our victory, became useless due to the marshal's fault.

At dawn on 18 June, the emperor mounted and carried out a reconnaissance of the battlefield and, at eight o'clock, the whole army, despite a heavy rain the day before, advanced. The Imperial Guard, concentrated, formed a second line, our General Lefebvre-Desnouëttes with the light cavalry to the right, the Grenadiers à Cheval and the Dragoons to the left and the infantry in the centre. The emperor was in the centre at the farm of La Belle-Alliance, from where he was able to see everything, observe everything and command.

The enemy occupied an immense plateau in front of Mont-Saint-Jean with a formidable artillery. They had there more than 90,000 men and we did not have 60,000. At eleven o'clock, the battle commenced on all points; the enemy occupied a château [Hougoumont], the emperor sent a battery of howitzers there to set it on fire. Marshal Ney had moved to the right, on La Haye Sainte. After a vigorous resistance, the château had been burnt, he was master of La Haye Sainte and part of the wood. The battlefield on this side was covered with an immense quantity of English killed, nearly all of the Royal Guard.

At midday, eighty guns moved before us, vomiting canister and death and opening a bloody passage for our infantry which rushed there, broke and destroyed an English division and broke all, but a strong enemy cavalry executed a vigorous charge, threw back our infantry and took sixteen of our guns. Then Napoleon rushed there with his cavalry of the Guard and the cuirassiers. We charged, heads lowered; we knocked over the English cavalry in our turn, sabred all those that opposed our passage, re-took all our guns and took two colours and seven guns in addition, despite the terrible fire of artillery. The mêlée became terrible, it was a dreadful carnage, the ground was covered with dead or dying men and horses; it was the height of terror.

In this terrible fight, the emperor crossed the field of carnage in the middle of the balls and canister, the brave General Desvaux, commander of the Guard artillery, and with whom my brother was orderly during the Russian campaign, was killed close to the emperor and a great number of officers wounded. I should cite here a feat of arms perhaps unique in history: as the cavalry of the Guard advanced, we were moving forward; when we saw rushing towards us, a regiment of English cavalry, which came to charge us. It could not tell our strength because we were in *colonne serée par escadron*: 'Let them come', said our generals, 'but do not use the edge of your blade, use the point, make good thrusts with the point'. They arrived on our position in their red jackets, perched on their horses, drunk with their blades in their hands, slashing to right and left with their poor sabres ... we opened up a little ... they came in ... and, in less than ten minutes, there were no red jackets still on horseback. I believe this fine regiment was of the Royal Guard and was completely wiped out. We also destroyed a regiment of English dragoons and killed their general (Picton) [he probably means Ponsonby].

It was only 4pm, the victory appeared to have been won, the English army, sabred by the cavalry, fled in all directions in a terrible rout. Throwing themselves in disorder on the Brussels road, caissons, artillery, baggage, cavalry, infantry, wounded etc., all fled mixed together. Commanders, officers, soldiers, all fled, the English army appeared to be entirely lost. Wellington, dragged away, fled like the others and, without the obstructions that were on this road, we would probably never seen Wellington or the English again; but, unfortunately, the Prussians commanded by Bülow entered into the line of battle. These Prussians should have been engaged with Marshal Grouchy and they fell on us with 30,000 men. General Lobau, who only had 10,000 men and who were at this point, was forced to fall back and the Prussian balls fell into our ranks. Napoleon sent General Duhesme, two divisions of the Young Guard and twenty-five guns to seize La Haye and cut the communications between the English and the Prussians. Marshal Ney was at La Haye Sainte, he had received the formal order from the emperor to remain at the farm, but, from when he saw the enemy attack, he clumsily left his position to throw himself on the enemy; the Guard cavalry and the cuirassiers followed the movement and penetrated onto the plateau.

General Lefebvre-Desnouëttes, who commanded our regiment and the Polish Lancers, had us break and sabre the squares and capture several guns. In a moment, all was overthrown and we were masters of the plateau of Mont-Saint-Jean and the enemy fled in every direction in a complete rout. It was 6pm, we had triumphed over all obstacles and we sang out our victory ... but Napoleon did not see it this way! 'This is a premature movement which could cost us dear; it is an hour too early ... but it is necessary to support what has already been done.' The emperor sent Kellerman's cuirassiers to support us; they galloped forwards with shouts of '*Vive l'Empereur!*' The grenadiers and dragoons of the Guard, commanded by General Guyot, followed the movement at the gallop. The emperor noticed this and sent General Bertrand to recall them, but he was too late, they were already engaged. Napoleon found himself totally deprived of all his cavalry reserve which, more than once, had assured him of victory. However, English, Prussians, Dutch, cavalry, infantry and artillery, all fled, all was overthrown, sabred, broken, killed or taken ... the rout was complete on all points ... It was seven o'clock in the evening. Suddenly, we heard a lively cannonade on our right, without doubt it was Marshal Grouchy who was in contact with Blücher's Prussians ... To finish it, Napoleon ordered a general charge, the orders were given ... the enemy, facing being wiped out at all points, hurried his retreat and we were the victors ... but suddenly, the fugitives stopped, it was not Marshal Grouchy whose artillery was heard, he had not only seen the Prussians that he had charged and that he had stopped with thirty-five thousand men, he had all the means (history will perhaps one day know the truth of this enigma, until now unknown). But this cannonade was Blücher himself with more than 30,000 Prussians. He rallied the fugitives of Wellington and Bülow, who thinking themselves lost, rallied a few troops which returned to the line Thanks to the obstacles on the roads, the English and Prussians had not all been able to flee, they were brought back to the fight. It was 8pm, and, despite the darkness, it was necessary to continue the battle and we had no reserve ... Three battalions which were ahead of us fell back on us, the emperor hurried in front of them and asked,

'Why are you retreating?'

'Sire, we were ordered'.

'Who gave you this order?'

'We do not know'.

'Return to the advance'.

Napoleon himself reformed the Guard and put himself at the head of four battalions of the Old Guard, and moved in all haste on La Haye Sainte where Marshal Ney had been forced to retire, he left him these four battalions and ordered him to re-take the plateau of Mont-Saint-Jean by main force.

The brave soldiers, despite the resistance, re-took their first position. Marshal Ney had his horse killed underneath him, marching at the head of the grenadiers. General Friant, with eight other battalions of the Guard, threw themselves on the enemy. The general was wounded ... but these invincible battalions marched in closed columns under a hail of balls and canister and, followed by their artillery, unshakeable and like walls of iron, they marched always forwards, overthrowing all in their way. Everywhere the carnage is terrible, another instant and our victory is certain . . . and with 60,000 men we have beaten 120,000 ... All is going well ... But suddenly, a shout of alarm can be heard ... Blücher has seized La Haye Sainte ... this movement has cut our army in two, and the night is extremely dark ... It is then that the cowards, the traitors, the deserters and all the execrable brigands appear in the French army, profiting from this moment to spread error and disorder everywhere; then is shouted in the ranks, the shouts that until then have been unknown in the French army; 'Save yourselves! – All is lost! – Save us! – We are taken!' etc.

Some soldiers that are seized by fright retire ... the traitors and miserable villains re-double their clamour ... Finally, the ranks are broken. The cowards mix with the army and spread the terror, exciting flight.

The battalions of the Old Guard, strangers to fear and terror, form into battalion squares and block the whole battlefield, nothing is yet desperate, the fugitives could reassemble behind the old moustaches and hold there ... but the cowardly provocateurs are always there. Six regiments of cavalry, English and Prussian, flood the field and throw themselves on our rear to prevent our troops from rallying. The emperor launches on them his four service squadrons to stop them, but what can these two hundred cavalrymen do against more than 8,000? These squadrons are overthrown ... The brave Marshal Ney still holding against the enemy masses on the plateau of Mont-Saint-Jean, but the soldiers have exhausted all their cartridges, they are forced to retire. The plateau is occupied by a numerous artillery which immediately launches terror and death ... Our eight battalions of the Old Guard are swept away by the mass of fugitives and crushed by a great number of the enemy. However, these old warriors remain together in battalions of iron, invincible and unconquerable. The rout is terrible. Napoleon is forced to throw himself into a battalion square of the Old Guard, commanded by the intrepid and brave Cambronne, who was to be thrown from his horse by a howitzer shell and wounded in the head, he commands on foot.

Napoleon commands the fire himself, several officers are killed around him. They call on him to retire, but he, fearless and without misgiving seems to want to die in this square, surrounded by these braves. A shell falls near him, his horse shies in dread, but he holds it with a firm hand and forces it to go close to the shell. (In an exhibition of pictures in the main room of the Louvre in 1836, a fine picture, although not grand, shows this episode, and it is well done.)

Marshal Soult and several generals lead the emperor out of this square. Surrounded by a vast number of enemies, the brave and immortal Cambronne, summoned to surrender, makes this very French response and worthy of the most glorious days of Rome; 'The Guard dies ... It does not surrender!' Sublime words which pass to prosperity, like those of the French heroes ...

The emperor makes vain efforts to rally the army ... He is forced to give up ... The canister, the cavalry which floods everywhere, the darkness, the traitors, all increases the disorder ... it is complete. Commanders, officers, soldiers, all march mixed together and each looking out for himself, except the major part of the units of the Old Guard. There is no longer an army, disorder and rout are at their height.

However, Marshal Grouchy had heard our terrible cannonade, but generals Exelmans and Gérard were unable to persuade him to march towards us, he amused himself at the mustard. History will judge ...

The Imperial Guard Artillery

The decree of 8 April gave the following direction for the re-establishment of the Guard artillery.

There were to be

Six companies of foot artillery (Old Guard).
Four companies of horse artillery (Old Guard).
One company of specialist tradesmen (Old Guard).
One squadron of train (Old Guard).
One company of *sapeurs* (engineers) (Old Guard).

Each foot artillery company was to have a strength of 120 men, and the horse artillery, 100 men.

On 28 May a company of Young Guard artillery and a company of train were added to the Guard artillery establishment.

Each horse artillery company had six pieces (four guns and two howitzers) and the four companies were attached to the Horse Guard. Each foot company had eight pieces (six guns and two howitzers); two batteries were attached to the Foot Guard, and the remaining four companies were to form the reserve. The artillery attached to the Young Guard (four batteries) was drawn from the line, which also provided four foot and four horse batteries for the artillery reserve.

To be admitted into the Guard Artillery, a soldier was required to have eight years' service and be at least five *pieds* and five *pouces* tall. Each foot and horse artillery regiment was to provide two officers and thirty non-commissioned officers and soldiers for the Guard. All soldiers that had served in the Guard Artillery, but had been sent to the line in 1814, were to be sent back to the Guard.

Lieutenant Philippe-Gustave Le Doulcet de Pontécoulant

Souvenirs Militaires, Napoléon à Waterloo, ou Précis de la Campagne de 1815 (Paris: Libriarie Militaires, 1866), pp. 314–25.

During the Waterloo campaign, Pontécoulant served as a sous-lieutenant *in the horse artillery of the Imperial Guard (Duchand); he commanded the 3rd Section of the 3rd Company which was attached to the Grenadiers à Cheval. He was the son of a prominent French politician, beyond which we know little, other than he was born in 1795 and was thus twenty years old on the day of battle. He wrote his account on the Waterloo campaign fifty years after it had ended; he claimed it was never meant as an eyewitness account, but to rectify the many errors he claimed were present in the recently-published French accounts by historians such as Thiers, Quinet and Charras.*

Pontécoulant is an unrepentant admirer of Napoleon and his account closely follows Napoleon's memoirs, suggesting that he did not witness much of what he describes. However, in the book he tells a couple of anecdotes of his own personal experiences and it is these that we are most interested in. However, in order to put those into context, they have not been translated in isolation, but presented in the text that surrounds them in his book.

Marshal Ney, desperate to see the victory which was escaping him and recognising too late the fault which he had committed by engaging the cavalry before he could be sure of being able to support it, had again sought an effort from Napoleon. He had sent to him his aide-de-camp, Colonel Heymès, to inform him of his position and to ask for a few infantry battalions to support his cavalry and to replace the troops of I Corps, occupied with holding the positions that they had taken, but were overcome with exhaustion. It was at precisely this moment that Napoleon had been forced to commit his most precious reserves, the entire Young Guard and part of the Old Guard, to repulse a Prussian attack, which had already reached the first houses of Planchenoit in our rear; he only retained intact eight battalions of the Old or Middle Guard, that he kept carefully like a miser guards his treasure, to ward off any last eventualities. Thus he replied to Marshal Ney's aide-de-camp that for the moment he didn't have a single battalion available, and Colonel Heymès had to take this desperate response back to his marshal.

Napoleon however, not being prepared to abandon the ground that we had conquered, and which had cost us so dear, detached two batteries of the Guard horse artillery, which he ordered to advance as far forward as they could go. It was 5.30pm. They deployed to the left of the farm of La Haye Sainte, which the enemy no longer disputed with us, on the slopes of the Mont-Saint-Jean plateau that had been occupied for some time by our own cavalry, and soon swept the whole English line with balls and caseshot. The author of these lines found himself amongst the officers who commanded one of these batteries, and he can confirm that in the most celebrated battles of the empire, there were few examples of such a lively and well directed fire. The artillery of the Guard was composed of élite men in an élite unit. All our gunners seemed to be electrolysed by the danger of the crisis that we saw approaching without being able to prevent: each of our shots struck home and we were so close to the enemy that we distinctly heard the shouts of the English officers closing the thinning ranks of their battalions with loud swearing and blows with the flats of their swords, to close the gaps that we were causing. Unfortunately, having the support of neither infantry nor cavalry, we were not able to make any progress nor to achieve any decisive result, and for two hours our role was confined to a very murderous exchange of balls and shells with the enemy, whose fire was very lively, but which seemed determined to maintain a purely passive attitude, as we saw them make no attempt to advance and retake the offensive, which would have been very favourable for them as at this time all our resources in infantry and cavalry in this part were almost entirely exhausted. But the phlegmatic Wellington, doubtlessly anxious about the losses he had suffered during the day, had himself lost all inclination to recommence a desperate struggle against us; he contented himself with defending the positions that he still occupied foot by foot and patiently awaited the arrival of the Prussians or night, which were advancing, and which would save him. We could see them take all the precautions, normally neglected in the French army, to spare the lives of their soldiers by exposing them as little as possible to the fire of our guns. Part of his infantry were hidden behind the crest of the plateau; they sometimes lay down so they could not be seen by those at the foot of the valley and always ready to get up to be able to fire immediately a cavalry charge approached them. Others, deployed as skirmishers in front of their lines, hid in all the folds of the ground or behind all the obstacles that would give them cover, and, armed with long range muskets [rifles], killed our gunners at their pieces almost with impunity, because of the lack, at this time, of similar arms in our own infantry which gave them a marked inferiority ...

Two hours, as I have said above, having passed since the great cavalry charges of Milhaud's and Kellerman's cuirassiers, two hours which, better employed, would have given us victory. It was seven thirty ... [*gives the overall situation of the French army and says that the whole army was exhausted, demoralised and waiting for the order to retreat*].

Another half hour passed in this uncertainty. Still nothing had been decided; we could see the attitude of the English army visibly weakening and, full of confidence in the genius of our chief, we impatiently awaited his orders. It was eight o'clock, night was already starting to fall; it was becoming difficult to clearly distinguish things. It was now that Napoleon, freed from the obstinate pursuit of Bülow, resolved to strike the decisive blow against the English which would give him the long disputed victory. He ordered General Drouot, who fulfilled the functions of aide-major of the Guard, to recall the eight battalions of the Old Guard [Footnote: Only four of these battalions had been engaged against the Prussian attack, the four others had remained in observation], and the six foot batteries which had remained in position along the Charleroi *chausée*, and which had still not been committed. This élite force, supported by all that still remained of the corps of Count d'Erlon, was to march on the centre of the English line, whilst General Reille, on his side, with II Corps, was to attempt to take and turn his right flank with a vigorous attack.

He then describes in some detail the arrival of a second Prussian corps and the demoralisation of the French that this caused. Also the movement of the British cavalry from the left flank to the centre of Wellington's army.

Indeed, in his impatience, Napoleon did not stop for long in front of the farm of la Belle Alliance, where he had given the order to rally all the infantry of the Guard; he moved to the bottom of the valley in front of La Haye Sainte near the two batteries of horse artillery of the Guard which, placed on the slopes of the plateau, had not ceased their fire, and which again showered the English squares with balls, so that he could preside over the grand attack that he planned on the centre of the enemy army [Footnote: It was there that I saw Napoleon for the last time. He came and placed himself a few paces to the rear of the two batteries of which I was a part and where the enemy's caseshot decimated our gunners. He ordered me to fire on the English squares that we could distinctly see several hundred metres away; I aimed the guns myself, the captain [Mancel, who was wounded at the battle] held the swab; all the *premier* [senior] gunners had been killed by the enemy's balls. If this was not the last, it was one of the last cannon shots fired on this sad day. Napoleon's face was sombre and very pale; a weak twilight spread a sad light on everything.] The artillery salvoes succeeded each other slowly, as at a funeral; the battalions of the Old Guard climbed silently up the slopes of the plateau: everything seemed in unison in this gloomy picture, worthy of a brush of a grand master.

Chapter 6

The Medical Services

Introduction

Early in his reign, Napoleon had conducted a complete overhaul of his military medical services in an effort to make them better organised and more efficient. Some of his initiatives were innovative for the time and were further developed and improved by the famous Larrey. However, like many aspects of his army, constant campaigning had taken its toll and after the disastrous campaign in Russia, his medical services became increasingly under strain, lacking sufficient equipment and trained manpower for the campaigns of 1813 and 1814. During Napoleon's exile they had suffered from further neglect, and on the emperor's return, despite the best efforts of Larrey who had re-assumed his post as surgeon-in-chief of the Imperial Guard, there remained a shortage of equipment and properly qualified manpower. During the Waterloo campaign, the French army once more relied on the carts of the local people to evacuate the wounded. We know that field hospitals were established at both la Belle-Alliance, where Larrey worked, and le Caillou; many British accounts mention the number of dead and wounded left lying around the former as they advanced at the end of the battle. Larrey was captured by the Prussians and, thought to be Napoleon due the grey riding coat that he wore, was narrowly saved from summary execution thanks to a Prussian surgeon who recognised him. Brought before Blücher, he was released by the Prussian field marshal whose son's life he had saved in an earlier campaign.

Pharmacien Antoine-Laurent-Apollinaire Fée

Un témoignage inédit sur Waterloo: Souvenirs du pharmacien aide-major Fée,
reproduced in *Souvenirs Napoléonien* No. 251, March 1970, pp. 4–5.

During the Waterloo campaign Fée served as pharmacien aide-major *to Marcognet's 3rd Infantry Division, which was part of d'Erlon's I Army Corps.*

Feé was born in 1789 and was to become one of the best-known botanists of the nineteenth century. Although he only trained as a pharmacist clerk, he entered the army as pharmacien aide-major *in 1809 and served in Spain until 1813. He was*

taken into Marcognet's 3rd Infantry Division in the same rank for the Waterloo
campaign (there is no apparent reason for his break in service from 1813). He con-
tinued his career in medicine after the Second Restoration becoming a Doctor in
Medicine and then Professor of Natural History. He died in 1874.

His account of Waterloo is interesting in so much as he seems to have generally
neglected his medical responsibilities during the battle; his account centres on his
observations of Napoleon and ignores any attempts he might have been expected to
make to find his ambulance from which he was separated at the very beginning of the
battle! It was only towards the end of the day that he joined Larrey's hospital and
carried out his duties as a doctor.

[On the 17th] A sudden thunderstorm that ended in a deluge of rain, held up
our pursuit. The enemy fled before us, abandoning several caissons; we took
some prisoners and there was no one amongst us that was not persuaded that
we would arrive in Brussels the next day. The weather became terrible; the
rain was pouring down and the wind blew violently. The army which was in
bivouac without fires, suffered much, but we were victorious and no one dared
to complain about their misery.

18th June. I passed the night under a caisson, with my feet up on some
stones, body bent, soaked and shivering with cold. The weather remained
poor until morning; it lifted towards nine o'clock. The action started at ten.
The enemy army crowned the heights called Mont-Saint-Jean; his right was
on the village of Hougoumont; his left on that of Waterloo; our line deployed
in the plain; the divisions took their order of battle, several artillery shots were
exchanged and the battle became general.

The divisional field hospital of I Corps had not been given a destination.
No wounded came, so at this moment [early in the battle] we had no service
to render. To better see the situation of the troops I mounted, with several of
my comrades, a small thatched roof leaning against the wall of la Belle Alliance. Our caissons were two paces from us and we were awaiting orders.
Whilst we were examining the prelude to this great battle with much interest,
the roof collapsed beneath our feet and we rolled over each other. We fell and
found ourselves in the courtyard. Happily we were stunned but unhurt.
Having regained our senses, we tried to find the ambulance but we were badly
disorientated and could no longer see it; we were very annoyed.

From this moment, I found myself a simple spectator of this great drama.
Already the armies were in contact and the guns rumbled as if to imitate the
sound made by loaded carts ponderously rolling over a bridge of bronze. From
time to time, shells rose in the air alone dominating this formidable thunder.
To my left, several villages were on fire and I could distinctly see cavalry

charges, division against division, without the clashing of arms or the detonation of pistols reaching my ear. However, horses without riders detached themselves from the squadrons and, free of their masters, galloped randomly in the plain, struck by some projectile. It was the same for the infantry, whose fire was only a dull sound covered by the cannon. One could have thought it was some harmless war, but seeing the wounded leave the ranks, alone or supported by their comrades, and leaving the lines to go to get their wounded attended to, one realised without difficulty the gravity of these terrible manoeuvres.

I occupied a height that permitted me to see clearly. However, close by, towards my left there was another, higher and further forward, which seemed to be more favourable for observation. A group of spectators had already stopped there and I resolved to join them. I boldly advanced without anyone stopping me. Imagine my astonishment when arriving there I saw the emperor surrounded by generals and aides-de-camp who went to carry orders to the various corps. Amongst them I recognised Marshal Soult.

The emperor was standing a little in front of his staff, a small table before him with a spread map on it, kept open by two large stones; such was the picture or sculpture showing him to us, with the small hat and grey riding coat, under which one could see a uniform of a senior officer in simple green cloth. He held a large telescope in his right hand that he used often. Several of his officers had rolls of paper under their arms, without doubt maps and plans.

All that was happening at this moment so pre-occupied the attention of the people that composed this group, that nobody noticed that I should not have been there. Although at this moment the grandeur of the action powerfully sought my attention, it could not draw it away from the man who controlled these masses; they caused or received death. The emperor's face was perfectly calm, such an extraordinary calm contrasted starkly with the general emotion and I did not grow weary of observing it. At every moment, officers of the headquarters arrived on their horses at the gallop, describing the execution of orders they had transmitted, then departing again at top speed on a new mission. I distinctly heard the emperor say to one of his generals, 'It is going well; the enemy manoeuvres poorly'.

However, the battle continued with an indescribable fury and the ear was seized by only an indefinable noise, composed of a thousand mixed-up sounds mixed into a single unique one. It was about two o'clock when the emperor, in a tone of voice that was more weak than strong, said these few words, 'Have the Guard march'. It was in reserve at some distance and a few instants passed before it marched past at the foot of the mound on which Napoleon posed like a statue on its pedestal. All these fine regiments passed in succession under my eyes, each band playing the republican tune, '*Veillons au Salut de l'Empire*', composed in other times and for other armies. To describe the enthusiasm of the soldiers, the violence of the shouts of '*Vive l'Empereur!*' uttered in full voice, portrayed the martial ardour which shone on these male faces, all this is impossible. Each colonel and each superior officer saluted the emperor with his sword; immediately he moved his hand to his hat and saluted in his turn as if he was at some parade on the Carrousel or the Champs de Mars; that was the *morituri te salutant* ['those who are about to die salute you']. I could not watch these brave men without pitying them as most marched to their death, and indeed their renowned bravery made it a duty for them to prove they were the best soldiers in the army; and it is known that on this sad day it was not courage they were lacking. The march past complete, a short time afterwards I guessed that the guard had begun its fire due to the intensity of the noise. An hour and a half passed, the emperor asked for a horse, mounted, as well as his officers, descended the mound to move forwards, leaving the paved road to his right; I followed him.

He moved at the walk, as well as his escort, often stopping to examine the line and to receive orderly officers. He was so close to the line of battle that not only cannon balls, but also bullets whistled past our ears. A French artillery caisson exploded a short distance away and wounded an officer in the emperor's entourage. It was then that a *gendarme d'élite* brought in a Prussian officer as a prisoner. I noticed his shortness and undistinguished face [!!]. The cavalryman, to make him arrive more quickly, lifted him off the ground for five or six paces and, with a strong arm, pushed him forward. The emperor had him questioned. Already towards our extreme right a new fusillade had broken out; the officer prisoner was sure it was caused by the corps of Prussians of General Beucher [*sic*: Blücher]. The emperor, not wanting to hear any more, re-started his march after having said very distinctly, 'Have this officer eat and take care of him'. Human and remarkable words at such a moment. Continuing to advance was a waste of time for me and exposed me to inevitable loss. I was unarmed and tired of the uselessness of my role; it was dangerous without a reason to be brave. I thus turned back, but slowly, feeling some shame at sparing my life when so many brave men were giving their own. After having marched for a quarter of an hour, I entered a spacious barn where Larrey's ambulance was established and remained there until the end of the battle.

This ambulance, primarily for the Imperial Guard, was overcrowded with wounded of all arms and the surgeons, although numerous, were insufficient to dress them. What could be said of the heroic words that I heard leave the mouths of the dying! What we read in the Greek and Roman histories cannot compare to the sublime phrases which then struck my ears. Many wounded refused care, judging it useless, contenting themselves with asking us in a dying voice if we were victorious. A mutilated officer held in his arms the sword of an English officer and died, like Bayard, putting his lips to the grip of the weapon that he had captured during the fight. Some, in dying, seemed happy to have given their life for the emperor, whilst others accused him of the harshness of their death. Words of regret to be dying prematurely, words of goodbye to absent families could sometimes be heard and these were no less touching. The lightly wounded men, as soon as they were bandaged, left the ambulance to avoid the overcrowding and left the battlefield. Soon, only the most serious wounded remained which could only be treated with the knife and the saw.

There was nothing more for me to do. I thus left the ambulance, hardly able to stand; weakened by a lack of food for almost twenty-four hours. When I was in the open air, I saw I was surrounded by a multitude, officers, soldiers, cavalrymen and infantrymen, marching in silence and without order. Luckily, the darkness partly hid the painful and humiliating spectacle from my sad view. The air was clear and I suffered from cold, having only a very light small coat and nankin [a type of cotton cloth] breeches. In the middle of this disaster a happy circumstance came to my aid. I marched alongside an infantry soldier mounted on a horse which I later learnt had belonged to an English lancer. The soldier was not wounded and he was still armed. I proposed to buy his mount from him, but he replied that he was looking after it for his captain. Whilst praising him for his resolution, I tried to make him understand that in the middle of this fracas it would be impossible to fulfil his good intentions and I added that the first wounded officer would use his authority to seize his horse. After having reflected, he accepted my reasoning and asked me how much I would give him to give up his prize. 'All that I have', I told him and I gave him my purse, which he found very light, which it indeed was. He opened it, and took sixty francs in gold, and although he could have taken all the money and even the purse, he contented himself with the gold, returned the rest to me and I acquired a magnificent beast of great size with a porte-manteau and a cavalryman's full set of campaign equipment: sack of corn, haversack with a piece of beef and a quarter of ration bread; both disappeared and I satisfied my hunger.

One can easily understand how this acquisition eased my situation. When it was dark I looked in the porte-manteau in which I found an almost new pair of trousers of iron grey material with a broad red stripe; I put them on without being delicate; it seemed that they were made for me. I felt an immediate shelter from the cold of the night and more content with the future.

The cannon could be heard until very late. A league from Waterloo, a cordon of gendarmes of the Guard was attempting to rally the debris of the army. Orderly officers shouted, 'Stop! Why do you flee? The emperor has re-taken his positions; the enemy is beaten'. The cannonade that seemed to get closer and closer contradicted these words and the retreat continued.

Chirurgien Louis-Vivant Lagneau

Journal d'un Chirurgien de la Grande Armée, 1803–1815 (Paris: Émile-Paul Frères, 1913), pp. 299–303.

During the Waterloo campaign Lagneau served as chirurgien-major *to the 3rd Regiment of Grenadiers à Pied of the Old Guard. This regiment was commanded by General Poret de Morvan and with the other regiments of foot grenadiers of the guard were under the orders of General Friant.*

Lagneau was born to a bourgeois family in 1781 and studied medicine from the end of 1799, becoming a doctor in June 1803. Taken by the conscription of that year, he became surgeon 3rd Class in the armée des Côtes. *In 1804 he was attached to the 9th* de ligne *and followed the regiment to Italy. In 1806 he was promoted to* chirurgien aide-major *to the 12th Dragoons and attended to them on the campaign of Poland where they fought at the bloody battles of Eylau and Friedland. He then went with them into Spain and having been present at the battle of Talavera in 1809, immediately afterwards he was promoted* chirurgien-major *in the 2nd Regiment of Conscrits-Grenadiers of the Guard. He then passed to the Fusilier-Grenadiers of the Guard for the campaign in Germany of that year before returning to Spain from 1810 to 1811, being present at the battle of Fuentes d'Onoro. He took part in the invasion of Russia and was present at Smolensk, Borodino, Krasnoié and the crossing of the Beresina. In 1813 he was made surgeon to the 4th Regiment of Tirailleurs of the Guard and served at the battles of Bautzen, Wurtchen, Dresden, Leipzig and Hanau. He took part in the 1814 campaign, being wounded at La Fère-Champenoise. At the end of that year he was put on the inactive list. In April 1815 he was nominated* chirurgien-major *of the 3rd Regiment of Grenadiers à Pied of the Old Guard and was present at Waterloo. After the disbandment of the army he was again put on the inactive list, but continued to study medicine. He became well known in medical circles across Europe and was commended for his service during the cholera epidemic in Paris of 1832. He continued his services to medicine until his death in 1868 aged 87 years, as an elected member of the Academy of Medicine.*

Lagneau kept a record of his day-to-day movements and some impressions of his campaigns throughout his career starting in 1804. He re-copied them and completed them in 1847 although they were not published until 1913.

Lagneau speaks little of the battle, which he was unlikely have been a witness to, but still writes blaming Grouchy for the loss of the battle.

18th June 1815. Battle of Waterloo, or of Mont-Saint-Jean, four leagues from Brussels. We fought with several advantages throughout the day, but to date from three or four o'clock in the evening, the enemy, after taking us in the flank, on our right, came, these were the Prussians who we thought were far away at the bridge of Vavre [*sic*: Wavre]) on our rear and threatened our line of retreat.

In the evening we were obliged to withdraw, which was not done without disorder.

The emperor, behind whom I was only ten paces away, between his head-quarters and the farm of la Belle-Alliance, from where I had been chased along with my wounded, by the Prussian skirmishers that came out of a small wood on our right, had his attention fixed for a moment on this point, where he was awaiting to see the arrival of Marshal Grouchy, to whom orders had been sent; but they had not arrived with the marshal.

The emperor counted well on him, for he often looked at his watch and had sent to General Duhesme who was on the right wing and who asked for support, that he should hold firm and that Grouchy would not hold back from coming to his aid.

I was with Larrey, the Surgeon-in-Chief of the Guard and the army; there was also Zinc[1] with an ambulance. He had been forced, like us, to abandon the party and had approached, like me, the emperor's group.

There was also our colleague Champion[2] who, with Zinc had established the Guard's ambulance close to mine, in a barn under the orders of Larrey.

Napoleon thought the battle was won at the time when we were forced to abandon our ambulance, because he thought the Prussians, who were firing at la Belle-Alliance, were themselves attacked in the rear by Grouchy. It was then about 2.30 or 3pm. Unfortunately, it was the Prussians and the Prussians alone, commanded by General Bülow.

Grouchy had not received three messages that had been sent to him by the emperor. The aides-de-camp were captured by the enemy and he, Grouchy, who had had at the beginning of the battle and perhaps from the day before, the order to hold back the Prussians at the Vavre [Wavre] bridge, so the English could be finished with, before they could join them, that he could suffice, with his 25 to 30,000 excellent troops to observe the bridge where the Prussians would leave a single division whilst with the rest of their army Bülow headed for our battlefield.

More experienced men of war, Gérard amongst others, who were part of Grouchy's troops, had all pressed the marshal, when they heard the fearful cannonade which was taking place on our side, to make a movement towards us, leaving a single division before the Vavre bridge, saying that it was the rule to move to where the engagement was the most lively, whatever the orders that were received to the contrary. Marshal Grouchy resisted, thinking that he was obliged to remain there, following the orders that he had received. [Footnote: This obstinacy is lost to us. I have heard, during the Restoration, Marshal Gérard explain this affair, stating how he regretted that his advice and his insistence had no success with Marshal Grouchy.]

I often saw Marshal Gérard (for he had been made marshal since) at the house of Senator the Count of Pontécoulant, where I often heard this brave general return to this sad subject.

General Pajol, who commanded the fine cavalry of Grouchy's corps, was also very vocal about Marshal Grouchy. Later, and in the same salon, I several times heard the son of Marshal Grouchy (colonel of a cavalry regiment and later a general) try to excuse the conduct of his father, but he convinced no one and there were there men of talent, between others General Exelmans, who has since become a marshal himself.

This conduct, or this absence of Grouchy lost us this battle, which had started in a brilliant manner to the point that we had heard the emperor say, towards two o'clock, that it had been won.

The sad truth was that the Prussians, not hounded by Grouchy as Napoleon thought, crushed Duhesme and the Young Guard corps which he commanded on our right wing and then came in on our rear, on the Charleroi road, to cut off our retreat. Happily, at first they only had some pelotons of cavalry. The retrograde movement became pronounced; I was lucky enough, with some wounded who were able to walk and some fit men who were not able to re-join the fighting, to get away thanks to my excellent horse. During this retreat, I had as a companion in misfortune, Captain (*chef de bataillon*) Friant [Jean-François Friant], of the Old Guard. He was the son of General Friant of the Guard.

We marched all night in the middle of retreating columns and isolated men and we crossed [the Sambre] at Charleroi, where everything was in disorder, the streets blocked by coal carts and military baggage.

Appendix

The French Army at Waterloo Order of Battle

Commander-in-Chief
The Emperor Napoleon I

Commander of the Right Wing Marshal Ney, Prince of Moskwa
Chief of Staff Marshal Soult, Duke of Dalmatia
Chief Staff Officer Lieutenant General Count Bailly de Monthyon
Commander of Artillery Lieutenant General Ruty
Commander of Engineers Lieutenant General Baron Rogniat

IMPERIAL GUARD (Lieutenant General Count Drouot)

INFANTRY OF THE GUARD
Old Guard
   1st and 2nd Regiments Grenadiers (4 bns)
   1st and 2nd Regiments Chasseurs (4 bns)

Middle Guard[1]
   3rd and 4th Regiments Grenadiers (3 bns)
   3rd and 4th Regiments Chasseurs (4 bns)

Young Guard (Lieutenant General Count Duhesme)
   1st and 2nd Regiments Tirailleurs (4 bns)
   1st and 2nd Regiments Voltigeurs (4 bns)

CAVALRY OF THE GUARD
Light Cavalry (Lieutenant General Count de Lefebvre-Desnoëttes)
   Guard Lancers
   Guard Chasseurs à Cheval

Heavy Cavalry (Lieutenant General Count Guyot)
   Grenadiers à Cheval
   The Empress Dragoons
   Gendarmerie d'Élite

ARTILLERY OF THE GUARD (Lieutenant General Baron Desvaux
de St Maurice)
13 Foot Batteries
3 Horse Batteries
Engineers of the Guard (1 coy)
Sailors of the Guard (1 coy)

I CORPS (Lieutenant General Drouet d'Erlon)

1st Division (*Maréchal de Camp* Baron Quiot du Passage)
1st Brigade (Colonel Charlet) 54th and 55th Line (4 bns)
2nd Brigade (*Maréchal de Camp* Bourgeois) 28th and 105th Line (4 bns)

2nd Division (Lieutenant General Baron Donzelot)
1st Brigade (*Maréchal de Camp* Schmitz) 13th Light and 17th Line
(5 bns)
2nd Brigade (*Maréchal de Camp* Baron Aulard) 19th and 51st Line
(4 bns)

3rd Division (Lieutenant General Baron Marcognet)
1st Brigade (*Maréchal de Camp* Nogues) 21st and 46th Line (4 bns)
2nd Brigade (*Maréchal de Camp* Grenier) 25th and 45th Line (4 bns)

4th Division (Lieutenant General Count Durutte)
1st Brigade (*Maréchal de Camp* Pégot) 8th and 29th Line (4 bns)
2nd Brigade (*Maréchal de Camp* Brue) 85th and 95th Line (4 bns)

1st Cavalry Division (Lieutenant General Baron Jacquinot)
1st Brigade (*Maréchal de Camp* Baron Bruno) 7th Hussars and
3rd Chasseurs à Cheval
2nd Brigade (*Maréchal de Camp* Gobrecht) 3rd and 4th Lancers

I Corps Artillery (Colonel Desalle) 5 Foot Batteries and 1 Horse Battery

II CORPS (Lieutenant General Count Reille)

5th Division (Lieutenant General Baron Bachelu)
1st Brigade (*Maréchal de Camp* Baron Husson) 2nd Light and 61st Line
(6 bns)
2nd Brigade (*Maréchal de Camp* Baron Campi) 72nd and 108th Line
(5 bns)

6th Division (Lieutenant General Prince Jérôme Bonaparte)
1st Brigade (*Maréchal de Camp* Baron Bauduin) 1st Light and 3rd Line
(5 bns)
2nd Brigade (*Maréchal de Camp* Baron Soye) 1st and 2nd Line (6 bns)

9th Division (Lieutenant General Count Foy)
1st Brigade (*Maréchal de Camp* Baron Gauthier) 92nd and 93rd Line
2nd Brigade (*Maréchal de Camp* Baron Jamin) 100th Line and 4th Light
(6 bns)

2nd Cavalry Division (Lieutenant General Baron Piré)
1st Brigade (*Maréchal de Camp* Baron Huber) 1st and 6th Chasseurs à
Cheval
2nd Brigade (*Maréchal de Camp* Baron Wathier) 5th and 6th Lancers

II Corps Artillery (Colonel Pelletier) 5 Foot Batteries and 1 Horse Battery

VI CORPS (Lieutenant General Mouton, Count de Lobau)

19th Division (Lieutenant General Baron Simmer)
1st Brigade (*Maréchal de Camp* Baron de Bellair) 5th and 11th Line (5 bns)
2nd Brigade (*Maréchal de Camp* Thévenet) 27th and 84th Line (4 bns)

20th Division (Lieutenant General Baron Jeanin)
1st Brigade (*Maréchal de Camp* Bony) 5th and 10th Line (4 bns)
2nd Brigade (*Maréchal de Camp* Count Tromelin) 107th Line (2 bns)

3rd Cavalry Division (Attached from III Corps) (Lieutenant General
Baron Domon)
1st Brigade (*Maréchal de Camp* Baron Dommanget) 4th and 9th Chasseurs
à Cheval
2nd Brigade (Colonel de Grouchy) 12th Chasseurs à Cheval
1 Horse Battery

5th Cavalry Division (Attached from 1st Cavalry Corps) (Lieutenant
General Baron Subervie)
1st Brigade (*Maréchal de Camp* Count Colbert) 1st and 2nd Lancers
2nd Brigade (*Maréchal de Camp* Merlin) 11th Chasseurs à Cheval
1 Horse Battery

VI Corps Artillery (Colonel Noury) 4 Foot Batteries

III CAVALRY CORPS (Lieutenant General Kellerman, Count Valmy)

11th Cavalry Division (Lieutenant General Baron l'Héritier)
　　1st Brigade (*Maréchal de Camp* Baron Picquet) 2nd and 7th Dragoons
　　2nd Brigade (*Maréchal de Camp* Guiton) 8th and 11th Cuirassiers
　　1 Horse Battery

12th Cavalry Division (Lieutenant General Baron Roussel d'Hurbal)
　　1st Brigade (*Maréchal de Camp* Baron Blancard) 1st and 2nd Carabiniers
　　2nd Brigade (*Maréchal de Camp* Donop) 2nd and 3rd Cuirassiers
　　1 Horse Battery

IV CAVALRY CORPS (Lieutenant General Count Milhaud)

13th Cavalry Division (Lieutenant General Watier)
　　1st Brigade (*Maréchal de Camp* Baron Dubois) 1st and 4th Cuirassiers
　　2nd Brigade (*Maréchal de Camp* Baron Travers) 7th and 12th Cuirassiers
　　1 Horse Battery

14th Cavalry Division (Lieutenant General Baron Delort)
　　1st Brigade (*Maréchal de Camp* Baron Farine) 5th and 10th Cuirassiers
　　2nd Brigade (*Maréchal de Camp* Baron Vial) 6th and 9th Cuirassiers
　　1 Horse Battery

Notes

Introduction
1. De Gaulle

Chapter 4: The Artillery
1. This presumably refers to the Union Brigade, but this would not have been visible to the French lines.

Chapter 5: The Imperial Guard
1. Most of the following detail is taken from Couderc de Saint-Chamant, *Napoléon, ses Dernières Armées* (Paris: Ernest Flammarion, undated).
2. The service squadrons were drawn from each of the Guard cavalry regiments to serve as Napoleon's bodyguard. In fact they were not actually a squadron in strength, but a company (about 100 men) from each regiment.
3. There is some disagreement with Petit's statement regarding the number of battalions in the 4th Chasseurs. Whilst it is accepted that the 4th Grenadiers had insufficient numbers to fill a second battalion, and therefore entered the campaign with a single one, this was not true of the chasseurs who did have two battalions before the battle of Ligny. Some historians [probably following d'Avout; see Pelet's account (next)] claim that the two battalions amalgamated into one after that battle due to the casualties suffered. Pelet himself speaks of a single battalion of the 4th Chasseurs at Waterloo (see his account below). However, even with these subtracted, 800 men remained, sufficient for two viable battalions. There is currently no convincing evidence one way or another and thus some histories describe two battalions in the 4th Chasseurs and others just a single one.
4. There is still uncertainty as to whether it was the 1st or 2nd Battalion that deployed there; Petit says the 2nd and is supported by Christiani (see below) who commanded the 2nd Grenadiers, who also says it was the 2nd Battalion. However, d'Avout is not the only one to claim it was the 1st. The confusion seems to revolve around which battalion was commanded by *Chef de Bataillon* Golzio, who is credited with commanding different battalions in different published orders of battle.
5. Pelet seems to be including the two battalions that had been deployed to Planchenoit, the 1st Battalion of the 1st Chasseurs which were at le Caillou and the two battalions of the 1st Grenadiers which remained near the junction of the Brussels and Planchenoit roads, all of which did not take part in the attack on the Allied ridge. This explains d'Avout's following note.
6. The foot regiments of the Guard only carried two eagles; one for the grenadiers and one for the chasseurs. They did not have an eagle for each regiment as in the line regiments.
7. D'Avout claims he owns a letter confirming this dated 8 May 1835.
8. Here he is referring to the French use of a *prolonge*, a long rope that was used to manoeuvre the gun without having to limber it up first. The *prolonge* remained attached to the gun and limber whilst the gun was in action. By not using a *prolonge*, the British did not have to waste time detaching it before the limber moved to the rear.

Chapter 6: The Medical Services

1. Pierre-Joseph Zinck, surgeon major to the ambulances of the Guard.
2. Jean-Pierre-Joseph-Eloi Champion, surgeon to the ambulance of the Guard. At Waterloo, he was wounded in the presence of Larrey by three lance thrusts and a sabre blow to the right forearm.

Appendix

1. Whilst it is true that the 3rd and 4th Grenadiers and Chasseurs were officially part of the Old Guard, nearly all French accounts, and even many British, refer to them as Middle Guard, as this is clearly how they were perceived in the French army and, it appears, even in the Guard itself. Indeed, one British officer claims that having asked a wounded French soldier to which unit he belonged, he replied that he was in the Middle Guard.